WHY IS THE CHURCH KILLING CHRIST A SECOND TIME?

RANDOLPH WRIGHT

Library of Congress Control Number: 2020918885

ISBN: 978-0-578-77919-5 (eBook)
ISBN: 978-0-578-77920-1 (Paperback)

Printed in The United States of America

This book is dedicated in memory of Ann Johnson.
Most people do not get to see their guardian angel.
I thank God I did.
A friend who became my relative and my best friend.

TABLE OF CONTENTS

INTRODUCTION

This book is about the end time prophecies and how our world is heading towards the final conclusion. It is only fitting that the COVID-19 Pandemic has given this book the appropriate atmosphere to reveal the message of the apocalypse.

It is where the Christian Church stand and which road it will take when issues of importance needs moral and spiritual guidance that will determine it's relevance in the world. What happen to the Church when biblical prophecy is happening all around us and the religious leaders remain silent? What if the church was given a second chance at redemption? This book paves the way for religious leaders of our time to step up to the plate and restore the Christian Church the way God intended it to be over two thousand years ago.

Since my first book, titled "Mikhail Gorbachev is Gog and Magog, the Biblical Antichrist," I have evolved and come to realize that the person I identified as the Antichrist is only part of the story. As you read through this book you will undoubtedly see that there will be two beast sent by the devil, one will have a mark on his forehead, the other will have a mark on his hand. One will be the "man of sin," the other will be the biblical Antichrist.

How does anyone distinguish between magic or a miracle? Is it really determine by the eye of the beholder? In this book I reveal how I ask God a question and he answered in a profound way that the reader of this book may ask himself, is it magic or a miracle? The answer may show us all how to have an intimate relationship with Jesus.

A climate of darkness has entered our world and has surrounded a dark figure who projects an atmosphere of evil and destruction. Everything around him turns to decay. The bible prophesied that this individual would appear at the end of the world but you must read the holy scriptures on how to identify him. This book describe certain elements of his character that will lead you without any doubt of who he is.

This book would not be complete without the thoughts of Nostradamus on what he was able to see concerning our world. He describes certain things about our time that we cannot deny. He even describes the plight of the Christian Church during this historical time period and have a surprise for me that I can't ignore.

Come walk with me as we explore our world through the eyes of God. What we see as everyday occurrences could be biblical related. How do we distinguish the difference? Is the COVID-19 pandemic an act of God? Or was it man made in a lab?

This book shed light on what is done in darkness by using the power of God who is able to see dark secrets that is held by men who did not factor in the all knowing father of justice, Jesus Christ. With that thought in mind, there may be a hundred conspiracy theories floating around in the world, but only one TRUTH. If I were able to show you something concrete, then maybe you would believe.

We are presently living in the book of Revelation and prophecies are being fulfilled. It just matters who will take notice.

CHAPTER 1

GET GOD'S HOUSE IN ORDER

If the second coming of Christ was imminent, would the Christian Church be ready? I am writing this book to let the Church know that it must get its house in order. The Church has inherited a culture of blindness that has eroded its integrity.

The silence from the Church has been so deafening that one must wonder if our religious leaders have become cowards from the ongoing assault on the Church's ability to utilize its most basic weapon in defending itself. That weapon is the Holy Scriptures which is here for us to litigate what is right from wrong.

Today, religious leaders have become complacent with ceremonial and traditional settings that have become the norm that seems to satisfy the Christian experience. But is this the way God wants us to behave?

In the following chapters, I will point out to you some scriptures that the church has ignored. These omissions or blindness of scriptures has led to killing Christ a second time because these prophecies are so important to Christ's second coming.

This one prophecy from the bible that I'm about to describe is the most important prophecy of our time that has been ignored by religious leaders of the Christian faith. Pastors all over the country do not even talk or teach its meaning anymore to eager listeners. This particular prophecy is the key to Christ's second coming, and without its fulfillment of the Church's ability to identify the "man of sin," Christ will not return to this earth, therefore, killing him a second time. This prophecy alone is the key to Christ second coming. 2 Thessalonians 2:3-4, "Let no man deceive you by any means, for that day (the day Jesus Christ comes back to this earth) shall not come except there come a falling away first and that man of sin be revealed. The one who opposes and exalts himself as God..."

Throughout the Christian experience we have always read or been taught by ministers certain incidences of Christ's crucifixion. We always hear the ministers tell us that Christ was chosen to die on the cross instead of the thief and murderer whose name was Barabbas. But before He was taken for execution, He was taken to stand trial and stand before religious leaders of his day.

This one act is the most crucial part of the story that should have been told more forcefully because the religious leaders of today must play an important role in the return of our Lord and Savior Jesus Christ. Not that the horror of seeing the savior of the world being crucified wasn't important to know and how he returned from death after three days. It's just as important to know how the religious leaders responded to Jesus 2000 years ago and why they could not recognize him, and if presented with the same task, would the religious leaders of today fail the test too?

The Trial of Jesus Christ at the Sanhedrin

It is the Church's responsibility to reveal the man of sin in today's world. Over 2000 years ago, the Church or religious leaders could not recognize Christ as the well prophesied messiah. The Church or religious leaders at that time was considered a congregation, not a building. Is the Church of God a building or people? A building cannot make decisions. It was the religious leaders who condemned Christ to death. Today, we find ourselves in the same predicament. It would be the religious leaders of our time that must identify that "man of sin" who is so crucial to the second coming of Christ.

We must first review the facts that the Church or religious leaders during the time of Christ actually condemned Jesus. After Jesus Christ was arrested He was taken to the High Priest whose name is Caiaphas a member of the Sanhedrin. The Sanhedrin was the supreme council and highest religious legal authority of the ancient Jewish world. It is well documented that Jesus Christ was not taken after his arrest directly to Pontius Pilate for dispensation.

He was taken directly to what we may call today the Church or the highest religious authority in which was the Sanhedrin. The Sanhedrin trial of Jesus Christ is the greatest trial ever performed in world history. Jesus was charged with threatening to destroy the Jewish Temple, sorcery, violating the Sabbath law by healing people on that day, by claiming to exorcise demonic possession, and claiming to be the Son of God or the Messiah.

The High Priest and his fellow religious leaders were well educated and were familiar with biblical prophecy. They knew about the prophecy proclaiming a messiah would come. But they did not see Jesus Christ as the Son of God. They did not see the divinity in Him. They only saw His human frailties.

Prophecies look different on paper when compared to live historical events. When the Pharisees, who were religious leaders, saw Jesus and studied his teachings, it did not have the impact of spirituality like it should have. Even Christ's name of "Immanuel," which means in Hebrew "God is with us," did not register to the Pharisees, scribes, and Sadducees that this man was the prophesied messiah.

Nicodemus, another religious leader, knew that Jesus was from God. He said to Jesus, "Rabbi, we know that thou art a teacher come from God" (John 3:2). Still, the religious leaders or Church at that time did not recognize Jesus as the prophesied Messiah.

After the trial was conducted by the Sanhedrin they took Jesus to Pontius Pilate, the governor of Roman Judaea where his fate was sealed on the cross.

The biblical text gives us four different accounts of the trial of Jesus Christ by religious leaders that includes the High Priest. Matthew 26:57-67. "And they that laid hold on Jesus led him away to Caiaphas the High Priest, where the scribes and the elders were assembled." Mark 14:53-65. "And they led Jesus away to the High Priest; and with him were assembled all the chief priests and the elders and the scribes." Luke 22:54-71. "Then took they him, and led him, and brought him into the High Priest's house." John 18:13-28. "Then the band and the captain and officers of the Jews took Jesus, and bound him. And led him away to Annas first; for he was father-in-law to Caiaphas, which was the High Priest that same year."

The Jewish religious leaders, or Pharisees, stumbled in identifying Christ. For two thousand years they endured the blame for condemning Christ to death. But because of their stumbling, that act brought to us (the Gentiles) away to reap the benefit of salvation. In Romans 11:11-12, the patriarch Paul said, "I say then, have they stumbled that they should fall? Certainly not, but through their fall, to provoke them to jealousy, salvation has come to the Gentiles. Now if their fall is riches for the world, and their failure riches for the gentiles, how much more their fullness." The moment has arrived for the Christian Church (Gentiles) to step up to the plate and fulfill its destiny. The Jews and gentiles are involved in a great mystery.

Why did God intentionally blind the Jewish religious leaders so they could not identify Jesus Christ? God blinded the Jewish religious leaders so that the Gentile Christians could have away of receiving salvation. This spiritual blindness will last until Jesus returns to redeem the Gentile Christian Church. The biblical scriptures reveals this fact in Romans 11:25 "For I do not desire, brethren that you should be ignorant of this mystery, lest you should be wise in your own opinion, that blindness in part has happened to Israel until the fullness of the Gentiles has come in."

The Gentile Christian Church has a tremendous duty to perform that was set in stone by the will of God. God placed a stumbling stone so that the Jews would not recognize Christ. Take a look at this scripture in Romans 9:32-33 “Wherefore? Because they sought it not by faith, but as it were by the works of the law. For they stumbled at that stumblingstone; as it is written, Behold I lay in Zion a stumbling stone and rock of offense....”

God blinded the Jewish religious leaders intentionally. Romans 11:7-10 “God has given them a spirit of stupor, eyes that they should not see, and ears that they should not hear, to this day. Let their tables become a snare and a trap, a stumbling block and recompense to them. Let their eyes be darkened, so that they do not see, and bow down their back always.” An invisible veil was placed on the eyes of the Jewish Religious leaders so they could not recognize Jesus. As Gentile Christians progressed in their belief in Christ, they became a powerful force in spreading the word of God throughout the world.

This decree was sanctioned by God over two thousand years ago for the intention of gaining Gentiles (Christians) salvation and provoking Jews to jealousy so that they would be able to finally see Jesus Christ as messiah. The Gentile Christians must make amends for the atrocities they perpetrated against the Jews throughout the ages.

Today the table has turned in the favor of the Christian Church. It has a profound duty to come full circle and identify that man of sin. The Gentile Christian Church must fulfill biblical prophecy and redeem the Jewish Religious leaders for stumbling because they could not identify Jesus.

This profound guilt was place on the Jewish Religious leaders throughout the ages until the Gentile Christian Church realize their duty. It is what the Christian Church must do that will unlock the door for the return of our Lord and Savior Jesus Christ back to this earth that will define Christianity for this new age of enlightenment.

The Trial of Mikhail Gorbachev, The "Man of Sin"

Mikhail Gorbachev was the former President of the Soviet Union now called Russia from 1985 to 1991. He drew national attention when he visited America in 1986 and from there he rose in popularity like a superstar. He was and still is admired by nations all over the world for his charismatic charm and sweeping changes. He was responsible for dismantling the Berlin Wall and ending the cold war with America. He was awarded the Nobel Peace Prize for accomplishing this miracle.

No other leader could compare to Gorbachev when it comes to bringing hope to the world. Just his mere presence made women scream and men envy. His presence overshadowed any American President of that time. It is how he chose to use his power in the political realm that got my attention. How he used a mixture of religion and politics that got the Seven Day Adventist Church to write an article about him concerning their feeling that Gorbachev maybe biblical related was a testament for me to investigate.

The Christian Church has yet to bring Mikhail Gorbachev to trial. It is because they have a blind eye to the evidence that point to him as the man of sin so I was compelled to write this book.

Will the Christian Church make the same mistake as the Jewish religious leaders did over two thousand years ago when they failed to identify Jesus Christ as Messiah? It is the paralleling of the two stories that is so mind boggling. Isn't silence from the church in this trial a vote? The Christian Church is being presented an opportunity to redeem itself for the stumbling of religious leaders over 2000 years ago who could not identify Christ. Now the ball is in the court of the Church. The religious leaders of today has come full circle.

Jesus Christ will not return to this earth until this prophecy is fulfilled. 2 Thessalonians 2:3-4 "Let no man deceive you by any means; for that day shall not come, except there come a falling away first, and that man of sin is revealed, the son of perdition; who opposes and exalteth himself above all that is called God, or that is worshipped; so that he as God sitteth in the temple of God, showing himself that he is God."

In the second chapter of this book I explain my interpretation of this prophecy that pertains to Mikhail Gorbachev's legacy. The man of sin must be identified by the Church in order for the restrainer to be removed so that Jesus Christ will return to this earth.

Evidence is crucial to any trial held by any court in any universe. The evidence I compiled concerning Gorbachev must be examine by the highest officials in the Churches hierarchy. In the following chapter I outlined crucial evidence that the Church must examine.

After reviewing the evidence, the Church will be left with many questions. One of the crucial questions will be this, why would an atheist want to imitate the crucifixion of Jesus Christ by performing his own mock crucifixion exalting himself as God? Doesn't this statement fulfill the prophecy in 2 Thessalonians 2:3-4?

The trial of Mikhail Gorbachev by the Church would give religious leaders of today a chance to use all their theological skills in determining a verdict. It is a chance to make amends for the debacle that was perpetrated against Jesus Christ over two thousand years ago. God has given us this one chance to uplift his holy name in away that will open the door to his return that has been closed for two thousand years. The Christian church has the only key to unlock the door. Over two thousand years ago, the High Priest and fellow religious leaders could not identify Jesus as Messiah. Today the Christian Churches hierarchy is given a chance to identify the man of sin from the pages of the bible. It is the flip side of history of what God is asking humanity to do. Can we identify the man of sin? Can we identify Satan? It is the basic principle of good versus evil.

This book charges Mikhail Gorbachev with proclaiming that he is the other Christ and exalting himself as God. He even performs his mock crucifixion to demonstrate that he is in the "likeness of the most High". Isaiah 14:14. Only Satan confessed that he want to be in the likeness of God. He even went further and said to the world, "For some people I am like God, for others I am like Satan, the Prince of Darkness, historians will have the advantage of time to evaluate me." This statement by Gorbachev reveals to us his enormous ego. He did not want to be compared to any average human being. He specifically informs the world that he wants to be compared to the most important figures in biblical theology. God describes this type of person in Ezekiel 28:1 "Because thine heart is lifted up, and thou has said, I am a god, I sit in the seat of God, in the midst of the seas; yet thou art a man, and not God, though thou set thine heart as the heart of God."

The trial of Mikhail Gorbachev is an opportunity for Gentile Christians to reap the benefit of salvation. Although the Jewish religious leaders could not identify Christ, how would religious leaders of today respond if given the same task? Well here is our opportunity right in front of us. Can the Christian Church identify the man of sin now that he has manifested in our world?

Let us have Gorbachev trial right now in front of our churches hierarchy. We must put our feet in the shoes of the High Priest Caiaphas when he ask Jesus, 'are you the son of God?' Matthew 26:63 "I adjure thee by the living God, that thou tell us whether thou be the Christ, the son of God?" Our religious leaders must ask Gorbachev, what did he mean when he said, "For some people I am like God and for others he is like Satan, the prince of darkness." We cannot afford to just dismiss his comments as just a figment of our imagination.

The religious leaders must ask Gorbachev why did he walked in the footsteps of Jesus Christ when he compared what happened to him in his election campaign when he said, "the election campaign reminded him of Jesus on the way to Golgotha when people spat at him." Why would an atheist want to imitate the crucifixion of Christ? What did he meant when he said he is that "OTHER CHRIST"?

These are the reasons and there are many more why Mikhail Gorbachev must stand in front of today's churches' hierarchy and answer these important questions in the religious world. Even Gorbachev said that "historians will have the advantage of time to evaluate me."

The Christian Church hierarchy must identify that "man of sin" from the biblical scriptures. The world's fate is depending on this most important spiritual act. Gorbachev must be convicted. I rest my case in the hands of the Church.

Silence

This book is not intended to offend the Christian Church but only to uplift it to a greater height and awareness and to prepare the way to restore its credibility. In order for the Christian Church to continue to be a viable creation of God, it must accept responsibility for past wrongdoings and mistakes perpetrated by its ministers and bishops as well as parishioners.

My mission is to be like John the Baptist and prepare the way for the second coming of Christ. I must repeat my warning to the Church. Get our house in order before the day of the Lord is upon us!

The Church has no power because it has been rendered useless. It must take a stronger role in today's challenging society. It must be visible and not hide behind a building. From politics, wars, and gun violence, to abortion, LGBTQ, homosexuality, and child abuse by priests and ministers, the Church must become an active entity in solving everyday problems, or the Church will become non in void, therefore killing Christ a second time.

The separation of Church and state is being used as a weapon to destroy the Church. The Christian Church should have equal power as the state. If the Church does not have an active role in daily politics, it will be viewed by people as having no binding power or credibility. The Church will become an empty nest where parishioners will lose faith.

A good example of equal power at work is our American government where our President and Congress share equal power. Neither entity is above or has more power than the other. The Church must adopt this type of policy where church members have a voice in decision making that have moral and ethical issues.

Another example of the plight the Christian Church is in, just look at the debate between whether gay marriages should be recognized as unethical and immoral union according to the scriptures. I will not give my point of view in this chapter but will discuss it in later chapters of this book. Moral and ethical issues are mounting as the Christian Church remains silent as if our religious leaders are reluctant to get involved. This complacency by our religious leaders is killing Christ a second time.

A John the Baptist Type

Isaiah 40:3, 9-10, "The voice of him that crieth in the wilderness, Prepare ye the way of the Lord."

This book is also about myself who may play an important role in discovering my mission to unlock the key to that great mystery: 2 Thess. 2:3-4. Who is that man of sin?

Like John the Baptist, who announced the coming of Christ over 2000 years ago, I personally pointed out and named a world figure as that man of sin 2000 years later. In doing this great task, the restrainer that kept Christ from coming to this earth a second time has been removed therefore preparing the way for Christ to return.

I wrote letters and sent a copy of my book titled "Mikhail Gorbachev is Gog and Magog" identifying the "man of sin" to many churches of my devoted mission of discovering who I thought was the "man of sin" with evidence to prove it. What is so mind-boggling to me as I studied the scriptures concerning the prophecy 2 Thess. 2:3-4, I realized that God works in duality. Over 2000 years ago, in Rev. 1:11, John was told by an angel of God to "write down what you see and put it in a book and send it to the seven churches." Today, 2000 years later, I've done the same thing without realizing that God had placed His will in my mind.

While studying the scriptures, I also realized that there may be a place in the bible specifically planned out for me written thousands of years ago to have me step into the role of a person with a message to give to the churches.

To my surprise and astonishment, I found what I was looking for in Malachi 3:1. It states, "Behold, I will send my messenger, and he shall prepare the way be fore me." Am I that messenger Jesus Christ sends before he returns to his church? In the following chapter of this book is a letter I sent to all the major churches here in America and to the Pope in Rome revealing that man of sin.

The Gospel and the Good News that was preached by Jesus over 2000 years ago has touched millions of people all over the world with the inventions of TV and radio. Now we have the internet which has reached more people in an instant. So the Good News and Gospel have been preached to the whole world just as the prophecy stated by Jesus before he returns to Earth. Matthew 24:14, "And this gospel of the kingdom shall be preached in all the world for a witness unto all nations; and then shall the end come." So why is this last end time message from THE MESSENGER so important if the Gospel has already been preached throughout the world? The answer is, if this last end time message to the church is not proclaimed by his messenger, Jesus Christ will come and destroy the world because the Church has not learned anything in 2000 years. Malachi 4:5-6, "Behold, I will send you Elijah the prophet before the coming of the great and dreadful day of the Lord. And he shall turn the heart of the fathers to the children, and the heart of the children to their fathers, lest I come and smite the earth with a curse."

Jesus Christ will not return to this earth until this prophecy is fulfilled. 2 Thessalonians 2:3-4, "Let no man deceive you by any means, for that day (the day Jesus Christ comes back to this earth) shall not come except there come a falling away first and the man of sin be revealed. The one who opposes and exalts himself as God." Christ is restrained from returning to earth until his messenger prepares the way, removes the obstacles, and restores the Christian Church.

Democracy in Crisis

This book reveals step by step how top news events of today and the past are biblically related and are intricately tied together culminating in an end time scenario that will shock the world into believing the word of God.

From the mouth of a prominent politician who stated that the battle for the soul of democracy is upon us brings the biblical scriptures to life and reminds us that we are in a war like no other since the beginning of time.

What happens in our elections will stand as a beacon for other democracies to follow. Whether it be for good or evil will be determined by the eye of the beholder.

The destabilization of democracy in America didn't begin when Russia interfered with our elections. It began with Mikhail Gorbachev. Russia decided long ago to stage multiple attacks on American democracy. It had to be implemented in different stages as we witnessed in the elections in 2016. But the assault on American belief systems started with Mikhail Gorbachev's charismatic, enigmatic, and magnetic appeal in 1986. He captured the heart and soul of most Americans. It was stated at the time that if he had run for president of the United States, he would win.

You may ask how a former atheist president of Russia can have any effect or influence on the Christian church in today's world. What if the coup d'état in 1991 in Russia was staged by their leaders to disguise a more sinful plan. A master plan that would gain the Russians total domination of the world. A master plan that would dethrone the belief in an unseen God. A plan that involves acting out the biblical prophecy concerning the Antichrist or man of sin. What if the Russians' plan is to test the waters, the biblical waters? It would be the most diabolical plot in history.

Russia is an atheist government that relishes on its communist past. This is what Joseph Stalin said. "We have deposed the czars of the earth and we shall now dethrone the lord of heaven." Satan's master plan is to remove Jehovah God as master of the universe. His objective is to dethrone God as ruler over earth. His plan is to destroy our faith in Jesus Christ. Doesn't this belief of Satan mirror or imitate the atheistic belief of Russia?

On October 4th 1957, Russia became the first country to put a rocket ship into outer space. The rocket ship was named "Sputnik." This great accomplishment advanced their idea of denouncing the existence of Jehovah God. While in space, American listening devices overheard a transmission from the Russian orbiting spacecraft. What was heard is how they view the universe. They said, "our rocket has bypassed the moon. It is nearing the sun. We have not discovered God. We have turned out lights in heaven that no man will be able to put on again. We are breaking the yolk of the gospel, the opiate of the masses. Let us go forth and Jesus Christ shall be relegated to mythology."

The Christian Church must examine the legacy of Mikhail Gorbachev. Just examine his statements carefully. You may find his identity in his mindset. He said, "we need a new paradigm or development in which the environment will be a priority...World civilization as we know it will soon end...We have very little time and we must act...We have to change our mindset, the way humankind views the world." He went even further when he creates his own bible to take the place of the original bible when he said, "My hope is that this charter will be a kind of Ten Commandments, a Sermon on the Mount that provides a guide for human behavior toward the environment in the next century and beyond."

Only Satan realizes that we are approaching the end time and that he has just a short time left. So he must convince the world civilization to abandon our lord and savior Jesus Christ, and he (Satan) wants us to see the world through his eyes.

It is how the Russian government used Gorbachev as a weapon of misinformation targeting the Christian Church that must be recognized. Gorbachev deliberately left evidence behind so that the Christian world could take notice. What was he hoping to gain?

If the Christian Church continues to ignore him as they still do today, then he would have proven his point. Christianity does not have any backbone. The continued silence from the

Christian Church has proven Gorbachev and the Russian leaders right. Therefore, the Christian Church is killing Christ a second time.

There is a time in the history of the world when the Church must seize the moment and recognize when to rise to the occasion. This is that moment. The Christian Church has a duty and responsibility to Christ. It must prepare the way for the second coming of Christ.

The forces that Russia unleashed on American belief systems strike at the heart of democracy. The attack focused on the basic principles that America was founded on. Phrases like "one nation under God, indivisible with liberty and justice for all," and "in God we trust" serve as a beacon of light for new democracies that are forming as well as the old. The Christian Church must uphold these principles. If Christianity falls, democracy falls as well.

Russia strikes at the soul of Christian faith, and our belief system. That is why identifying Mikhail Gorbachev as that "man of sin" is so crucial to the Christian Church's integrity.

The letter I wrote and sent to all Christian churches is a reminder to uphold the mission that Jesus Christ began long ago. That mission is to become the body of Christ and to overcome Satan. Jesus message to the Church, "He that overcometh, and keepeth my words unto the end, to him will I give power over the nations; and he shall rule them with a rod of iron..." (Revelations 2:26-27).

The letter I sent is about how over thirty years ago Russia began its master plan to undermine the pillar of democracy and to destroy the Christian Church by using the oldest weapon the Christian Church fears the most, Satan.

An Unexpected Miracle

Very seldom do we hear of miracles being performed by God. But there are miracles being perform by our Lord and Savior Jesus Christ every day. Some are rare occurrences, and others are hard to believe.

Just the other day, a lady by the age of 40 needed a kidney to survive after waiting for a donor for one year. Her prayers were answered when a teacher was willing to donate one of her kidneys in a desperate attempt to save the lady's life. As anyone can see this is a miracle sent from God. Prayers were answered. A happy lady was able to go home and live a normal life, thanks to the organ donor and the intervention of Jesus Christ.

There are many stories like this one that takes place all across the world, but the miracle that happened to me was unexpected and exhilarating.

We should never underestimate the power of prayer. Jesus Christ teaches that we must pray to God everyday.

We should not wait until times of trouble to seek God. Pray to Him even when times are good to show gratitude.

In this book is a story of a miracle that happened to me that has changed my life forever. I must say that I am blessed to have seen the glory of God appear to me in a dramatic fashion. I hope by sharing this miracle to others will strengthen their belief in Jesus Christ and believe that God still work miracles in one's life.

Although there are many different types of miracles that are performed by Jesus, my experienced was different and awe inspiring. I will discuss this miracle in chapter 8.

I worked in a hospital for many years and while there, the patients and I became very close. I loved them as much as they loved me. Patients would come by to see me from all walks of life including their relatives. While working on many occasions, I would get a message in my head that one of the patients died. When I say message I mean thought. His face would appear in my head saying, goodbye. I immediately enter his name in the computer to confirm what I just thought of. To my amazement that particular veteran died the night before.

We must be wired to Christ in a unique way. I could not tell you how it works but God hears our prayer. We must learn how to dial into God utilizing all our senses. In other words, turn off the man-made radio and turn on the radio receiver that's already built into your head. Then you will be able to receive the blessings of Jesus Christ.

Sunday Morning

Wife: Honey, you need to attend Church with me today. I've been attending Church by myself for years now, and you have not made any attempt to join me.

Husband: I don't need God or church. All they do at Church is take my money. Plus, I don't believe in God.

This scenario is played out among family members all over the world. Christians who are in a relationship with a spouse who do not believe in God struggle with family members participating in the belief in Jesus Christ. So when these issues erupt, what tools can be used to convince a relative or even a friend to join them in becoming a Christian?

Many relationships are destroyed because they didn't consult the doctor's prescription, the Holy Bible. God left all Christians a book that is the tool to be utilized in time of need. In this scenario one of the spouses is not willing to participate in the Christian experience. The remedy is plain and simple so says the Holy Scriptures. 1 Corinthians 7:12-14. "If any brother hath a wife that believeth not, and she be pleased to dwell with him, let him not put her away. And the woman which hath a husband that believeth not, and if he be pleased to dwell with her, let her not leave him. For the unbelieving husband is sanctified by the wife, and the unbelieving wife is sanctified by the husband: else were your children unclean; but now are they holy. But if the unbelieving depart, let him depart."

So, when a husband or wife does not want to attend Church with you on Sunday morning, go by yourself. That person is saved because of your faith in Jesus Christ. Even your children will reap the benefit of your devotion to the Lord Jesus Christ. If he or she do not want to participate in a Christian relationship then let that person go if they desire to leave.

Put Prayer Back in School

Over the past 30 years, I've noticed an increase in school shootings after the removal of prayer in school. This argument of the removal of prayer in school has been debated among school teachers, parents, law enforcement and civic leaders. As the death toll mounts due to children killing children, one of the most important institutions that could be a powerful influence on the subject remained silent.

We must put prayer back into school. Prayer cannot do it alone. We must put God back into school. If we don't rely on the teaching of Jesus we are going to experience a hard lesson. Since prayer has been taken out of school Satan has filled in the void.

The Christian Church can be a powerful tool to stop the violence among youths if they would get involve. Matter of fact if the Church would get involve in the war against violence, change would come in the form of a white dove. Jesus Christ is the answer to all types of violence in the world.

The church can get involved by giving all youth at the age of 7 a pocket size duplication of the Ten Commandments. Make it mandatory that they learn what it says by heart. Just like its done with the Boys Scout motto. The words clean, brave, trustworthy are some of the words in the Boys Scout Motto. Why can't the church use the same method in order to build character in our youth? The church must get involve in our daily lives or remain silent which will allow the elements of Satan to grow into what we see today in the violent killings of youth by youth.

Satan is making a loud noise in the violence among our youth because the Christian Church is reluctant to get involved. Just look at the horror stories of mass killings around the world. The massacre at Christ Church in New Zealand was perpetrated by the followers of Satan. It didn't stop there. It continued in countries all over the world. The evil's of Satan is spreading across the globe without being stopped by our religious leaders.

Why would a kid obtain a gun and go to his school and take the life of another? As a gunman walked through the school hallways looking for his next victim, he spotted a girl and asked her, "do you believe in God?" All the mass killings are biblical related and the Christian Church must get involve.

There have been many books, newspapers and magazines written about horrific deeds perpetrated by Satanic cults. Why is Satan so appealing to our youth?

The reason is that youths of today are more incline to rebel against traditional values, as the founder of the Church of Satan explains why, "Instead of commanding members to repress their natural urges, we teach that they should follow them. This includes physical lust, the desire for revenge, and the drive for material possession."

Satanic worship is spreading throughout the mainstream of today's culture. It is able to touch the lives of well to do upper class people. Teenagers who come from good homes are targeted as well as any type of background. Why does the youth find devil worshiping so appealing? The youth has learned that if you worship Satan, he will give material gain. That is why the youth has found Satan so appealing.

Teenagers are drawn so deeply in satanic worship they are willing to take their own lives as well as others. For some teenagers what began as a fad, they become overwhelmed by Satanism then cross the line of reality. Our world is a violent society and teenagers see this as the correct way to behave. Teenagers are being lured because of the mystery of Satanism. They go to the library and obtain books on Satanism, and then when the situations arise they don't hesitate to use what they have learned.

A fist fight breaks out between two students in the school cafeteria. After the fight is broken up, one of the youth holds up a clinch fist with his index and little finger sticking out. Unknowingly to the other kids, he just displayed the devil's hand signal. The report of satanic worship among teenagers gets worst. We read in the newspapers and watch the news on TV about kids killing their parents and other members of their families due to the power of satanic worship. We can never forget the grisly murders committed by youths hooked on Satanism.

There is a startling connection between drugs, some segment of music, and violence that are the symptoms of Satanism. An article in Wake Magazine explains this disturbing situation this way, Carl A. Raschke, director of the University of Denver Institute of Humanities said, "It is no accident that drugs, heavy metal music, brutality, and wanton violence have all become the grizzly ensigns that wave above the human desolation as we move toward the third decade of the age of Satan."

The glorification of drugs, violence, hate, rebellion, sex and the abuse of women is being portrayed in the lyrics of some segments of music. This type of music has influenced our youth to become followers of Satan. Reality becomes distorted and the power of suggestive imagery takes control. The age of Satan is upon us.

Ministers Falsely Claimed Called by God

Some of our ministers become preachers for prestige to satisfy their ego. They feel that they were called by God because they are superior to others. Some are drawn to the pulpit for financial gain and have a thirst for luxury.

Some of the ministers got to have that fancy car while parishioners struggle day to day just to make ends meet.

Some proclaim they have the know how to make their followers rich and lure them to church with a promise of material wealth. By following this method, followers forget about the real meaning why they are attending church and that is the word of God.

Some ministers commit adultery and have multiple wives in the name of Jesus. Some created their own religion and have 50 wives and many children who succumb to the false teachings and brainwashing by the bible carrying witch doctor.

Cults all over the country are on the rise with their own version of what God is. Some worship idols, snakes and UFO's.

Some ministers commit immoral acts against children that has corrupted the Christian Church and has lessened it's credibility in the world. All of these things are helping to kill Jesus Christ a second time.

If ministers do not teach crucial scripture that relates to the end time prophecies then the church is not living up to its mission. Today ministers do not teach that the Kingdom of God is coming. The church must examine other point of views in regard to deciphering scriptures. Some scripture could have double meaning that could only be validated by God.

Two Beasts Sent by the Devil

Revelation 13 describes two beast sent by the devil appearing at the end time. In this book, I identified "the man of sin," but I did not give a name for the second beast. I only used his characteristics so that you will be able to see him as the biblical Antichrist without calling his name and then you will be able to identify who he is yourself. This persona is in our world today and is fulfilling biblical prophecy. How can anyone be certain that the people we choose are the right one? Although there are many different interpretations of scripture, we must rely on the teaching of Jesus. God is the only one that can give us confirmation. But our faith is the only tool to guide us in the right direction.

I cannot leave no stone unturned. We must continue to investigate all scenarios that could be biblical related. We must examine everything through the lens of God. Fear is not an option.

If the church is not willing to search for that "man of sin" from the bible, then who will stand up for Christ? Today's ministers do not teach the most crucial scripture in the bible that is related to the second coming of Christ. How will the followers of Jesus learn about this unless the ministers follow the lessons of the apostles and teach relative information pertaining to that "man of sin" who is to appear at the end time?

God is giving us a lesson in the principle of good and evil. If we can identify that "man of sin" from the bible then we have just identified Satan. It is the basic principles of good and evil that the bible describes in Genesis. This is why it's so important for the church to get involve and identify that "man of sin."

The end time scenario is upon us and all the crucial players have been assembled in our world. It is in the political arena where we should pay close attention because the bible identifies two of the most crucial players that will fast track the second coming of our Lord and Savior Jesus Christ return to earth.

The bible speaks of a two headed beast in which one of the beast head is wounded to death. Revelation 13:3. "And I saw one of his heads as it were wounded to death; And his deadly wound was healed."

The irony of these two beast that is described in Revelation 13 is that their fate is sealed in the political arena where both survival depends on people's choice.

Over 2000 years ago, Jesus fate was left in the hands of His own people who could not recognize him. The man of sin's fate was left in the hands of his people who dealt him a deadly blow. The Antichrist fate will be left in the hands of his people also but they will elect him as the CHOSEN ONE. Today the Christian Church is left with a choice. It must choose to remain silent and inactive or stand up for Jesus and identify that "man of sin."

Divinity

If Jesus was stripped of His powers to do miracles, could we recognize him as God? We must first examine what make a human divine? How would we view Jesus if only His words were His powers and not the miracles He performed. The Pharisees, scribes, and Sadducees could not identify Jesus as God because when anyone would see him, He appeared like any other man. He felt pain when one of the religious leaders slapped him. He felt pain when the Roman soldiers used a whip with razor sharp edges impaled in his flesh that tore the skin off his body. He felt pain when nails were hammered into his hands and feet.

Why couldn't the religious leaders see the divinity in Jesus without seeing those miracles? Maybe that is the lessen God have been trying to teach to us for two thousand years. Maybe that is the reason why man cannot perform miracles like Paul did long ago. God's word is more powerful than his miracles. We humans would pay more attention to his miracles than his words. Although when Jesus raised Lazarus from the dead, it is a very great testament to who Jesus is. God knew that we humans would pay more attention to miracles and not much to His words. A great example of this is how Moses dealt with the Israelites when God displayed His awesome power before their eyes.

After Moses led the people of Israel out of Egypt and into the Promise Land, he made a fascinating statement concerning perception. In spite of the miracles and wonders that were performed by God, the people of Israel still could not see or understand.

Deuteronomy 29:2-4 "You have see all that the Lord did before your eyes in the land of Egypt unto Pharaoh and to all his servants, and to all his land; the great trials which your eyes have seen, the signs, and those great wonders. Yet the Lord has not given you a heart to perceive and eyes to see and ears to hear to this very day."

Today a spiritual blindness has taken over the minds and hearts of our world. As it was during the time of Moses, people of today listened to Mikhail Gorbachev used words that pertain to biblical prophecy, performed miracles in today's standard, quoted verses from the bible, and imitated Jesus Christ and still people were blind to biblical prophecy.

It's all about how we perceive an event while it's happening right in front of our eyes. We must take in what we see while utilizing all our senses. We must be able to see deeper than the eyes can see. We must open up our hearts and minds, and then we will be able to see the truth.

Jesus Christ left us his words of wisdom throughout the New Testament that will give us guidance if we elect to just read it. His words alone has power that will move and motivate us to live according to his design and instill in us to uplift his holy name, and to become Christ like. A good example of how the word of God has power without a show of miracles is when the religious leaders confronted Jesus and ask him who he is, his answer caused an unexpected reaction that displayed his divinity without the touch of Jesus hand. Mark 14:61 shows us his divine power when it states, "the High Priest ask Jesus; art thou the Christ, the son of the blessed? And Jesus said "I am", at which point the High Priest tore his own robe in anger and accused Jesus of blasphemy. Jesus words alone moved the High Priest to react in an abnormal way without using a miracle. That effect of Jesus caused the High Priest to break Mosaic Law (Leviticus 21:10).

When Mikhail Gorbachev was on the world stage, he performed a remarkable miracle. He was responsible for bringing down the Berlin Wall. His miracles was unlike what Jesus performed. Would that be the only way our religious leaders of today will take notice of Gorbachev if he walked on water like Jesus did? Religious leaders of today must be able to look deeper than the mesmerizing things of magic. Yes, although miracles do happen, only the Lord Jesus Christ can perform them. Things that are happening all around us could be biblical related if only we look a little deeper.

How can anyone on earth prove the validity of what I am writing about? Only an act of divinity can prove the truth of a certain matter. In this book I've named the biblical "man of sin" and have identified the biblical Antichrist. The definition of the word divine is #1, "of God or a god, #2, by or from God. #3,to or for God, #4 find out or foretell by inspiration, by magic, or by guessing or prediction." Obviously I am not God but numbers three and four in this definition of divine is where I fit in. I was inspired by God to write this book and foretell the return of Christ and reveal a dark secret that will change the world and to uplift the name of Jesus.

The cross or crucifix made from the sun's rays that is displayed on the cover of this book is God's personal stamp of approval, sealed by His hand, a bonafide miracle.

CHAPTER 2

A LETTER TO ALL CHRISTIAN CHURCHES OF THE 21st CENTURY

IDENTIFYING THE "MAN OF SIN"

What if the redemption of the Church rest solely on identifying the "man of sin"? What if the "man of sin" that is described in the scriptures has come and gone? If these statements are true, then the Church or religious leaders has missed the greatest chance at redeeming itself since stumbling in identifying Jesus Christ over 2,000 years ago. That is why I am bringing my argument to the Churches. We cannot afford to let this chance at convicting someone who in my view has the credentials like it is outlined in the scriptures.

Although there are many different views and opinions related to biblical prophecies concerning the "man of sin" when one looks deeper into the legacy of Mikhail Gorbachev, it becomes apparent that the prophecies are being fulfilled. Take for example, the prophecies contained in Revelation 13:3, "and I saw one of his heads as it were wounded to death," "A wound by the sword and did live." Biblical scholars hold many differing view points regarding the interpretation of these prophecies. However, when viewed from the perspective of the life and career of Gorbachev, the parallel begin to unfold.

As biblical scholars ponder over which interpretation of prophecies are logical or not, including my own, there's one prophecy by the Apostle Paul that cannot be ignored. After reviewing the legacy of Mikhail Gorbachev, a question arises that the Church must answer. And that question is… Why would an atheist who opposes God want to imitate the crucifixion of Jesus Christ and exalt himself as God? The answer to that ground breaking question is written in scriptures by Apostle Paul. 2 Thessalonians 2:3-4, "Let no man deceive you by any means, for that day (the day Jesus Christ come back to this earth) shall not come except there come a falling away first and that man of sin be revealed. The one who opposes and exalts himself as God." My book titled "Mikhail Gorbachev is Gog and Magog, the Biblical Antichrist" reveals how he deliberately accomplished and fulfilled this prophecy. The scriptures plainly give the man of sin's credentials that cannot be denied or ignored. That is what Gorbachev did. He is an atheist who performed his own crucifixion in order to imitate Jesus Christ and proclaim himself equal to or to become like God fulfilling that prophecy.

My fellow brothers and sisters in Christ, today the Church is in grave danger of losing its credibility as a functioning body of Christ. Something very important to biblical theology happened before our very eyes on a world wide scale and the church remained silent. A political figure that once was called the king of all politicians worked his magic and mesmerized the whole world.

Some of you may say that I'm still living in the 80's when this political figure had power. Even Gorbachev admitted to the world that time is just a measuring tool to be utilized in an effort to measure his life. Gorbachev said, "HISTORY IS A CAPRICIOUS LADY, FOR SOME PEOPLE I AM LIKE GOD, FOR OTHERS I AM LIKE SATAN OR THE PRINCE OF DARKNESS. HISTORIANS WILL HAVE THE ADVANTAGE OF TIME TO EVALUATE ME." That is exactly what I am doing.

I stand here today to plead my case. The church must evaluate Gorbachev's life and legacy. It does not matter how much time has elapsed, as long as we do it. The implication of his statements is too enormous to just ignore them.

As we look back in history, the pulpit became the battleground where arguments were fought and won. Pioneers like John Witherspoon who argued that church and state, politics and religion, should be linked and Martin Luther King who champion the civil rights movements. Clergymen who carried the belief in God in their debates won arguments that shaped the history of America. Without those brave ministers, our independence from Britain may not have happened. The Declaration of Independence would not have been written.

In the year 1776, John Witherspoon brought his argument on religion and politics to the pulpit where he argued that politics and religion should mix. He said, "If your cause is just, you may look with confidence to the Lord and retreat him to plead it as his own. You are all my witnesses, that this is the first time of my introducing any political subject into the pull pit."

In likeness of our forefathers, I am bringing a political figure to the pulpit. This political figure is no ordinary politician who kept religious ideas away from politics. Instead, Gorbachev was considered by his peers as the "King of all politicians" because he was able to straddle the fence between the belief in atheism and Christianity.

My fellow comrades in Christ, what I am presenting to you represent the final battle between Atheism and Christianity. My argument to convict Mikhail Gorbachev as that "man of sin" written about in the biblical scriptures by Apostle Paul (in 2 Thessalonians 2:3-4) represents all arguments that involve religion and politics, church and state, and even good versus evil.

The very argument to separate religion from politics is at the core of whether we should convict a political figure whom by the way is a confessed atheist who characterized a biblical figure from the bible itself. It is in this debate that we shall realize our civic duty as Christians to do the right thing and convict Mikhail Gorbachev as that "man of sin".

Over 2000 years ago, Jesus Christ had trouble convincing the church or religious leaders that he was the one talked about in the scriptures. Although, we know today he came to actually fulfill the prophecies. The riding of a donkey entering Jerusalem, the healing of the blind, and to even die for the sins of the world were all foretold beforehand. So why couldn't the church or religious leaders at that time recognize that he was the son of God and that he was the very one talked about in the scriptures?

During Gorbachev's time in political office, many people in the West believed that he was the Antichrist or "man of sin". By the same token, there were just as many who said he was not the Antichrist. The Bible captures both of these sentiments in the prophecy contained in Revelation 17:8, "when they behold the beast that was, and is not, and yet is." During the time of Jesus Christ, there were many people who recognized him as the son of God. Again, there were just as many who said he is not the Christ and as such put him to death. Today the Church finds itself in the same predicament. Is God giving the Church or religious leaders a second chance to redeem itself?

What's important to the Church or any court of law is FACTS. My argument is based on facts. It is a factual account of the life and legacy of Mikhail Gorbachev. In order to confirm biblical prophecy, you must have a bible in one hand and a newspaper in the other. You must compare historical facts to biblical facts.

After observing Gorbachev's many statements during his political career, I found a deliberate effort by him to leave a road map of statements that coincided with his life directed at the Christian community. The road map of statements involved a deliberate effort by him to imitate the crucifixion of Christ, right down to a conspiracy and betrayal in the likeness of Judas Iscariot infamous conspiracy. He even goes further and created his own mock crucifixion where he gives a statement during his re-election campaign in reference to the campaign trail reminding him of Jesus on the road to Golgotha when people spat at him.

Why would Gorbachev or anybody in their right mind who is an atheist want to create his own crucifixion in the likeness of Jesus Christ? Why would Gorbachev idolize Saint Francis of Assisi who was known in the world of Catholicism as the "OTHER CHRIST or IMITATION OF CHRIST?" The following is a factual account of Gorbachev's Mock crucifixion that shows how he exalts himself as God fulfilling the prophecy contained in 2 Thess. 3-4.

The Mock Crucifixion

From Judas Iscariot betrayal of Jesus to his arrest by soldiers to the crucifixion, Gorbachev patterned his life and legacy after Christ. When the soldiers arrested Gorbachev in 1991 in Russia due to a coup d'état, he made a statement in the likeness of Jesus Christ statement upon being arrested. Jesus said, "Friend do what you came for," Mark. 14:10-11. In likeness, Gorbachev said, "Do what you think is needed, damn you."

Gorbachev's mock crucifixion was carefully scripted in real live action. He wanted the world to know exactly what he was experiencing during his presidential campaign for re-election in 1996. He said to the voters, "I WILL FIGHT TO THE BITTER END AND WILL NOT WITHDRAW MY CANDIDACY. EVEN IF I AM CRUCIFIED. EVEN IF YOU ARE THE ONES WHO WILL CRUCIFY ME. SOME OF YOU ARE SO OVER EXCITED YOUR HANDS ARE TREMBLING. THIS REMINDS ME OF JESUS CHRIST ON THE WAY TO GOLGOTHA WHEN PEOPLE SPAT AT HIM."

Gorbachev carefully chose words that have special meaning to the Christian Church. Words like crucify would surely get our attention. He even goes further when he assures us that what he experienced is in the likeness of the crucifixion of Christ on his campaign trail.

It's a historical fact, the election result was brutal. Gorbachev received a humiliating defeat by the hands of his people. He only received one percent of the vote. Drowned in the agony of defeat Gorbachev states that, "he felt like he was dying." He stated that he felt like someone took a gun and shot him after being spat on, kicked and cursed throughout the campaign trail. His human emotions were dragged into the bottomless pit.

Although Gorbachev's mock crucifixion was pale in comparison to Christ, in a sense it had the same deadly outcome. Sometimes defeat can be viewed as dying when looking at what it does to a person's soul. The election result destroyed Gorbachev's political ambition and from that point on he was politically dead. The book of Revelation describes it this way, "AND I SAW ONE OF HIS HEADS AS IT WERE WOUNDED TO DEATH." Rev. 13:3. "A WOUND BY THE SWORD, AND DID LIVE." Rev. 13:14. "AND HIS DEADLY WOUND WAS HEALED, AND ALL THE WORLD WONDERED AFTER THE BEAST." Rev. 13:3.

Not the kind of death that takes a person to an actual grave, but the kind of death that will take you from the worlds mind and eyes. Not a gun shot or sword that can inflict a deadly wound, but the kind of wound that tears a man's heart and soul into pieces. The kind of wound that will break a man's spirit. "PRIDE GOES BEFORE DESTRUCTION, AND A HAUGHTY SPIRIT BEFORE A FALL." Proverbs 16:18.

Biblical scholars have interpreted these prophecies with many different meanings. Sometimes we must look deeper and not the first obvious meaning is always the right answer. Take for example the prophecy contained in Rev. 13:3. "AND I SAW ONE OF HIS HEADS AS IT WAS WOUNDED TO DEATH." How can any human being be wounded to death and still be alive? Unless it's the way Gorbachev is wounded in the elections and died a political death. Some biblical scholars believe that the "man of sin" or Antichrist would be wounded to death and miraculously come back to life. The Bible writers used a philosophical interpretation. For instance, "THE TONGUE IS SHARPER THAN THE SWORD, IT CUTS LIKE

A KNIFE." This statement satisfies the prophecy contained in Rev. 13:14. "A WOUND BY THE SWORD, AND DID LIVE." A wound by the tongue can be just as deadly as someone taking a knife or sword and inflict a deadly wound. A person's words can be as sharp as a double edged sword and inflict great harm on its victim.

Even Gorbachev used the word "CRUCIFIED" to describe the Russian people anxiety to deliver a deadly blow to his bid for re-election. After receiving a humiliating loss in the 1996 election in Russia, Gorbachev descends into the "bottomless pit"(a state of humiliation) only to be found in the ashes of the political grave. A defeat that rendered him politically dead forever. His spirit and soul was crushed by the loss of the highest office in the land. Revelation 17:8 states, "The beast (the man of sin) that thou sawest was, and is not, and shall ascend out of the bottomless pit, and go into perdition; and they that dwell on the earth shall wonder." Note: The Bible writers used the word "PERDITION" which means someone experiencing a great LOSS. It doesn't mean loss of his life, but a loss of one's soul. He doesn't literally die and go to Hell like most biblical scholars believe, but his state of mind and wounded heart takes him there. Gorbachev experienced a great loss in the election in 1996 in which is the exact definition of the word "PERDITION". He is politically dead to the world and yet he is still alive. Rev. 13:14 "A WOUND BY THE SWORD, AND DID LIVE." Many people still WONDER is Gorbachev that Biblical Antichrist or "man of sin"? Rev. 17:8 "and they that dwell on the earth shall wonder." Why would a confessed atheist who opposes God want to imitate the crucifixion of Christ and exalt himself as God? This is the question the Church must answer very carefully because it is the exact characteristic and identification of the "man of sin" or Antichrist written about by the patriot Paul in 2 Thessalonians 2:3-4.

Gorbachev does not believe in God therefore why is he making references to the story of Jesus Christ? Obviously, he is on a mission directed at the Christian community. He has been challenging the Christian community to pay attention to his legacy. From the moment of his meteoric rise to power, he has been speaking out loud and the Church continued to ignore him.

In 1996, Gorbachev continued to give the world clues to his identity. He continued to compare himself and his legacy to the time of Christ and made references to Jesus crucifixion and what happened to him as similar. On the 1996 ABC television show host Charles Gibson interviewed Gorbachev concerning the elections confirming his campaign to imitate Jesus Christ and fulfill the prophecies. This is what was said on national TV:

> CHARLES GIBSON: "It is an interesting paradox to so many Americans, you are so honored throughout the world for fundamental changes but I don't have to recite the election results to you, in the last election you got a very small, tiny percent of the vote. Why is Gorbachev seen so differently outside Russia and inside Russia?"
>
> GORBACHEV: "Well, let's recall another example. Jesus Christ was pelted with stones. He was blamed and condemned, and then he was put with a bandit and they were taken for execution. And when it was said that one of them could be spared, the people said the bandit should be spared and Christ was crucified."

Mikhail Gorbachev methodically plots his life as the "OTHER CHRIST". He systematically re-enact every aspects of the crucifixion of Christ according to the biblical event recorded in the Bible. Although, he was not nailed to the cross like Jesus, Gorbachev reminds us that what he experienced in the elections was deadly. It was a modern day crucifixion. Gorbachev wants us to know that he has fulfilled certain aspect of the life of Christ therefore completing his imitation of him. He even admits that the story of Judas has been accomplished in his legacy:

> CHARLES GIBSON: "Gorbachev's frank, though hardly contrite, about the failures of judgment that led him

to promote to senior positions the very men who would plot to overthrow him in 1991." Gorbachev's reply was, "How do you explain Judas-right there next to Jesus Christ?" He asked, "How do you explain that? And Christ did not recognize him for what he was. You could say that's a metaphor."

This statement by Gorbachev is an admission by him that the coup d'état in 1991 in Russia was part of a conspiracy to imitate a segment in the life of Jesus Christ. Only Satan confessed that he wants to be in the "LIKENESS OF THE MOST HIGH" Isaiah 14:14.

Gorbachev's statements pertaining to Christ were not some random conversation intended to uplift his or enhance someone's belief, but a deliberate attempt to imitate Jesus Christ's crucifixion and somehow make it his own thereby EXALTING HIMSELF AS EQUAL TO OR TO BECOME LIKE GOD. Step by step, he fashioned what he experienced in a real life setting as what Jesus Christ endured during his time. Gorbachev systematically relived the passion of Christ. In doing so, he has fulfilled biblical prophecy in my view. This is the core of my argument. An atheist who fulfills Biblical prophecy and then exalts himself as God is that "MAN OF SIN" Paul talked about in the scriptures. It is how he exalts himself as God is the question.

Saint Francis of Assisi

Saint Francis of Assisi was a great humanitarian who set an example for those of us to follow him with love for our Lord and Savior Jesus Christ. For his unique ability to bring people in to his Order in the religious world of Catholicism, biographers coined him the "Other Christ" or the "imitation of Christ." It was how he showed compassion for the poor that got him noticed by his peers. On the other hand, Gorbachev who is a confessed atheist and oppose God, idolized St. Francis of Assisi, he said. "St. Francis is for me, the OTHER CHRIST.

His story fascinates me and has played a fundamental role in my life."

Gorbachev idolization of Saint Francis is not because he showed compassion for the poor, but because he was fascinated with the term the "OTHER CHRIST." Gorbachev did not display a love for our Lord and savior Jesus Christ, but the term "OTHER CHRIST" played a fundamental role in his life, and that is the role of the Biblical Antichrist or the "man of sin." Why is that terminology so important to Gorbachev? He wants to be known as the "OTHER CHRIST." When Gorbachev looked at the life of Saint Francis legacy, it reminded him of his life. Although, there can only be one Christ and that is Jesus Christ of Nazareth, Gorbachev feels that if another human being can be considered as the Christ, so can he. In my view he has earned the title of the "MAN OF SIN" or ANTICHRIST. For the record, if there is any dispute concerning Gorbachev's religious belief, just examine his own admission, he said, in his own words; "Over the last few days some media have been disseminating fantasies-I can't use any other word about my secret Catholicism, citing my visit to the Sacro Convento friary, where the remains of St. Francis of Assisi lie. To sum it up and avoid any misunderstandings, let me say that I have been and remain an atheist."

Gog and Magog

Revelation 13 describes two beast sent by the devil appearing at the end time. One will be the "man of sin" and the other the Antichrist.

Let's examine the other prophecies related to the "MAN OF SIN" or ANTICHRIST, that fit with the life and legacy of Mikhail Gorbachev. Can the name Mikhail Gorbachev be found in the Bible? Ezekiel 38:1-2 "And the Lord came unto me, saying, Son of man, set thy face against Gog, the land of MAGOG, the chief prince of Meshech and Tubal, and prophecy against him." It is accepted by most Biblical scholars that the name Gog and Magog is the name of Satan at the end time that fights Jesus in the battle of good versus evil. When one looks closer at the name MAGOG it closely resembles the name Mikhail Gorbachev. Did the Bible writers used an ancient method of anagramming to disguise MAGOG's identity until the end time? When biblical scholars study the name GOG and MAGOG both names are synonymous of each other. God separates the name for a purpose, to show two distinct names but joined them together to disguise their identity. God did this so that we who live during the end times will be able to see two names and that is Mikhail Gorbachev. The bible writers are emphasizing a first and last name but joined them together to form one name, and that name is MAGOG. But the second beast also is joined with the first. We must remember this beast has two heads and one of his heads were wounded to death and that is Mikhail Gorbachev. The name of the second beast will be revealed in chapter 3.

The Bible gives us a physical description of the "MAN OF SIN." (Rev. 13:2) "And the beast I saw was like unto a leopard." The spots on Gorbachev's forehead are there for the whole world to see. During the time Mikhail Gorbachev was president of the former Soviet Union now Russia, the people feared that those days were the end times, they asked Gorbachev to put makeup over his forehead to cover a birthmark because people refer to it as the "MARK OF THE BEAST." This statement is a testimony of how Gorbachev was perceived by people in his home town as well as the whole world at the same moment in time.

Revelation 13:2 "And his feet were as feet of a bear." Mikhail Gorbachev's hometown is Russia in which its national symbol is a bear. During the cold war between America and the old Soviet Union former president Ronald Reagan called Russia "an evil empire" the beast of the east.

Revelation 13:2 "And his mouth as the mouth of a lion." While Mikhail Gorbachev was president of the old Soviet Union now Russia, he gave many speeches that astounded listeners. With his charm and charisma, and a voice of a lion, he shouted and the Berlin Wall crumbled before the world's eye.

Revelation 13:18 "Here is wisdom. Let him that hath understanding count the number of the beast, for it is the number of a man; and his numbers is Six Hundred threescore and six."

How do you measure a man? Is it by the things he does and says? The great philosopher Plato describes the measurement of a man this way, "You measure a man by the way he chooses to use his power." While Mikhail Gorbachev was president of the old Soviet Union, he was considered as one of the most powerful leaders in the world, even today he still hold that stardom. Not unlike other world leaders Gorbachev chose to use his power to imitate the crucifixion of Jesus Christ by performing his own Mock crucifixion in order to be considered as equal to God or to become like God therefore fulfilling the prophecy by Paul, 2 Thessalonians 2:3-4.

"When someone shows themselves who they are we must believe it."

Revelation 13:18 is God prophetic timetable that dramatizes the death and resurrection of the "man of sin" or Antichrist. This prophetic timetable explains his death and ultimate resurrection beginning with the time of his political death to his rise from the ashes of the political grave. The "man of sin" life is dramatized in numbers that reveals to us the length of time that he is dead to the world and rise again. That number is 18 years, the sum total of 666.

Do not look for the "man of sin" or Antichrist numbers to be written on his forehead or on top of his head like the movies portray him. But the bible assures us that numbers 666 is related to the "man of sin "or antichrist. The numbers are an identification assigned specifically for him. So how do we attach those numbers to Mikhail Gorbachev? You must look at Gorbachev's timeline from the date he was politically assassinated to the date he was resurrected compiling a total of 18 years. Keep in mind the Bible states that the "man of sin" or Antichrist would be "wounded to death and did live." He is taken away from the world's eye. We must count the years beginning with Gorbachev's politically death (1991) to the year 2009 the day of his resurrection. In 2009 Gorbachev announced his political return when he resurrected his own political party in the Russian elections exactly 18 years later. Is that a coincidence? But that doesn't necessarily fulfill the prophecy contained in Rev. 13:18.

Unwittingly, my book "Mikhail Gorbachev is Gog and Magog, the Biblical Antichrist" was first copyrighted in 2009 and published in 2010 exactly 18 years from the day Gorbachev was politically assassinated, resurrecting him as the "man of sin" or Antichrist.

When studying the holy bible, it infuses you with the capability to decipher the scriptures. The biblical scriptures open up doors to another universe. A universe although not seen with the naked eye, but never the less dwells amongst us. It is a place where the past, present and future team up together to reveal it's secrets. All the answers to mankind problems are readily available to solve with just a finger tip away.

So why would Gorbachev ignore a wonderful gift from God (the Holy Scriptures) and create his own bible for the world? His bible called "The Earth Charter" was created to set rules as a beacon to guide humanity. In Gorbachev's own words, he said. "My hope is that this charter will be a kind of Ten Commandments, a Sermon on the Mount that provides a guide for human behavior toward the environment in the next century and beyond."

How much more evidence does the church need to rule out coincidence? I have presented a considerable amount of evidence before you. What will the church do about this? Remain silent? Gorbachev is challenging the Christian church on a world wide scale. He and his fellow countrymen has devised an elaborate scheme to undermine the Christian Church and destroy the pillars of democracy. We must keep in mind the Russians aspirations of ruling the world in which is the same diabolical plot as Satan.

When we look at what's happening in America today that involves Russia meddling in our elections, it is a testament of how far they will go to disable the leader of the free world including our faith in Jesus Christ. In my book, "Mikhail Gorbachev is Gog and Magog, the Biblical Antichrist," I predicted a return of Russia to the world stage. In fact, I also predicted that they would have a master plan called Operation 666 that will shock the world. Go to page 104 of my book called Mikhail Gorbachev is Gog and Magog and you will see the astounding prediction. I called it Operation 666. The Russians called their operative G.U.C.I.F.E.R which is the operative that hacked into America's election process. The building where Russian agents and U.S. officials held a meeting was numbered 666. Oh, by the way, the numbers 666 and L.U.C.I.F.E.R are Satan's identification.

As Russia walks amongst the pillar of democracy, no one will notice that they are a snake in the grass. Russia is able to slither its way through the cracks in the walls of democracy. Just like a snake in the grass, they are able to camouflage themselves so no one can detect their true identity. "A nation can survive its fools, and even the ambitions, but it cannot survive treason from within. An enemy at the gates is less formidable, for he is known and he carries his banners openly, but the traitor moves among those within the gate freely, his sly whispers rustling through all the alleys, heard in the very halls of government itself. For the traitor appears not traitor, he speaks in the ascents familiar to his victims, and he wears their face and their garments and he appears to the baseness that lies deep in the hearts of all men……." (Cicero, 42 B.C.)

We, who are called Christians have arrived at the moment of truth. It is time for us to utilize all the Sunday morning worship and teaching of Jesus Christ. My instinct is telling me to pick up the banner of Christ and hold it up high so that the whole world can see you. Today is not the time to just sit back and ignore one of the most important time periods of our history.

Personally, I am shouting out a call to take action. AWAKE from the sleep that was placed upon you by the cunning of Satan. Stand up! In the world of Catholicism. Stand up! In the world of Jehovah Witness. Stand up! Baptist, Methodist and Protestant, and to all the Christian Churches who follow our Lord and Savior Jesus Christ and take back our world from the snares of the evil one. We must unite in the spirit of Jesus and remove this world from a place of evil and corruption to a place of a new heaven and new earth.

When the issues between church and state way heavy on the balancing scale and no one seems to agree, rely on the scriptures of the mind of God where we all can agree that the answer to all problems has been tested with time.

Christianity is being attacked from many places of society. From atheism to other religions are all partaking in the war against an unseen God. On top of all of this, today we have a world leader from our past who is a confessed atheist who performed a mock crucifixion and exalted himself as God.

Gorbachev deliberately left evidence behind so that the Christian Church would take notice. If the Christian Churches continue to ignore him, then he would have proven his point. Christians do not have any backbone. Gorbachev realizes that the stakes are high, and is counting on the Christian Church reluctance to take action and remain silent. He felt strongly that no one from the Christian community would come forward and reveal his dark secret. Gorbachev is conceited enough to proclaim that he is that "OTHER CHRIST."

In closing, my fellow comrades in Christ, this is our final hour to solve that great mystery that was spoken of by the Apostle Paul that he wrote to the Church of his time. We have arrived at that moment in the future when the "Fullness of the Gentiles has come in." Romans 11:25.

The Biblical scriptures are beckoning us to not make the same mistake as the Church or religious leaders did over 2000 years ago when they failed to identify Jesus Christ. My fellow comrades in Christ, we have come full circle. We must convict Mikhail Gorbachev if you agree that the facts are found to be true. To paraphrase a famous lawyer name Johnny Cochran, if the facts fit, you must convict. We must remember that the return of Jesus Christ to this earth hinges on the Church being able to identify and reveal the "man of sin."

If the Christian Church has the willingness to consider my argument and condemn Mikhail Gorbachev as that "man of sin" from the bible, a great miracle will happen. That ageless battle between Atheism versus Christianity will come to an end. All atheism will be destroyed. The Christian Church will be victorious. The brightness of his coming will be at hand. Jesus Christ is truly the light of the world would be confirmed without a doubt. The Christian Church will have redeemed itself.

I am urging the Churches hierarchy to please consider my argument. The integrity of the Church is at stake. If we as a Christian body believe in truth, justice, and have a great desire to uplift Jesus Christ's name, then we must have a healthy debate and shine light on the life and legacy of Mikhail Gorbachev. The Apostle Paul is beckoning us to remember his teachings and uplift the Church where it has never been before. We must have the courage to seize this moment and reveal the "man of sin" in his time.

CHAPTER 3

"THE COMING OF THE LAWLESS ONE"

"And the ten horns which thou sawest are ten kings, which have receive no kingdom as yet; but receive power as kings one hour with the (Antichrist) beast. These have one mind, and shall give their power and strength unto the beast." Revelation 17:12-13.1

Do you ever get the feeling that something has changed? We all go to bed at night thinking that the world is one way, then wake up the next day with a feeling of what's happening around us can't be real. Have you noticed that something has changed in the way we look at things? Whether it is in politics, religion, or family situations, something has changed dramatically.

From gun violence to homosexuality, tornadoes, earthquakes, diseases, famine, and wars, and the COVID-19 pandemic, things seems to be spinning out of control. Moral issues are right in front of us and we can't make sound decisions. Kids killing kids continue as part of the norm. "Wake up." We are not in Kansas anymore. If you want to know where hell is, it's right in front of us. We are living in it. Things are like this because we are killing Christ a second time. Now we know what sin looks like.

The holy scriptures describe two beast coming out of the earth in Revelation 13. In chapter 2 of this book I've identified Mikhail Gorbachev as the first beast (Gog). When describing the second beast I will not give a name for the moment. His name will appear in your mind when looking at his characteristic. In Ezekiel 38:1-2 describe this dynamic duo that will appear at the end time whom the bible calls Gog and Magog.

In politics, the Democrats and Republicans push the challenges of the day to the far right or far left. Who changed the order of things this way? The world was never set up to behave that way. It has always been good vs. evil. The world has gotten away from the laws of God.

Why can't people in law enforcement or politicians give a straight answer? Why is truth not truth anymore? Who is distorting the truth? The answer can be found in 2 Thessalonians 2:9-12.

"The coming of the lawless one is by the activity of Satan with all power and false signs and wonders, and with all wicked deception for those who are perishing, because they refused to love the truth and so be saved. Therefore God sends them a strong delusion, so that they may believe what is false, in order that all may be condemned who did not believe the truth but had pleasure in unrighteousness."

I hear on the news the attributes and characteristics of Satan being spoken everyday by politicians and their lawyers. There is one who sits in the highest office of the land who has told over 20 thousand lies since becoming our leader. Some of the characteristics of Satan is that he is the father of lies and a hater of the truth. He does not respect the law. He is a slanderer and an accuser and has an enormous ego.

It is important here to not be partisan and sound like I am for one party system or the other. I want you to see this person for the man that he is, naked of any title but only the description of him as it is laid out for us from the bible.

Every morning our leader attends a meeting with his staff just to hear them one by one tell how much they adore him and confess their loyalty to him. He brags to the media that he has the biggest crowds, the biggest mansion, and the biggest amount of money. During his election campaign, he told his audience, “If I go out and shoot someone, you will still vote for me.”

Ezekiel 26 describes the ancient king of Tyre who had a great ego and his heart was lifted up because of his riches foretells a prototype of a person to come in our day. The biblical scriptures call him by name that identifies its meaning in today’s world. The Holy Scriptures calls him MAGOG. In today’s world we call him a DEMAGOGUE. Its meaning: “A popular leader who stirs up the people by appealing to their emotions and prejudices. The chief aim of most demagogues is to get money, power, etc., for themselves alone.”

The ancient city of Tyre was a great commercial city, a metropolis that rivaled other cities of its time. It was the New York, Paris, and Tokyo of the biblical world. Their ancient city was admired by merchants and shippers and reminds us of America being the light of the world to many people. But the bible writers want us to pay attention to the King of Tyre, not the city’s beauty. It is how the scriptures describe this individual that draws attention to our leader here in America that is so mind-boggling.

In order to identify Satan we must magnify his characteristics. His human name is not needed when you can clearly see his attributes. “A spirit of darkness has descended on the White House.” This quote was stated by the White House Chaplin in 2019 who prayed to God for deliverance. What did he see that we can’t? CNN religion editor’s article entitled “House chaplain prays to cast ‘spirits of darkness’ from Congress,” states, “You know things are bad in Congress when the chaplain’s morning prayer on the House floor sounds like an exorcism. On Thursday, the Reverend Patrick Conroy said during his prayer that it had been a ‘difficult and contentious week in which darker spirits seem to have been at play in the people's house." The White House chaplain prayer went even further when he said, "In Your most holy name, I now cast out all spirits of darkness from this chamber, spirits not from You. May your wisdom and patience descend upon all so that any spirit of darkness might have no place in our midst."

What did the White House chaplain see that spooked him to pray to expel demonic activity out of the Congress? Reverend Patrick Conroy was so shaken he said to CNN, "I was on the House floor on Tuesday, and to me, it felt different than other days. It felt like there was something going on beyond just political disagreement. The energy of the House was very off. No one was relishing what was happening."

The Reverend Conroy was so disturbed by what he witnessed he had to mention the dark side of the supernatural has infiltrated the White House. This is the moment that religious leaders must go to the biblical scriptures to confirm if its prophecy unfolding right before our eyes.

Reverend Conroy said, "the idea for the prayer came to him after Tuesday's contentious House vote to condemn a racist remark made by the leader of the free world telling four Democrat congresswomen to "go back" to their home countries. Three were born in the United States, the fourth is a naturalized citizen"

The King of Tyre during ancient time was considered to be an Antichrist by Ezekiel who laid out the groundwork for future prophets to interpret. When deciphering scripture we must remember the principle of duality that God has put in motion. Events that happened long ago can be repeated. So when we identify today's Antichrist we must look at how the scriptures describe him in the past. Ezekiel 28: 2-5, "Son of man, say unto the prince of Tyrus, Thus saith the Lord God; Because thine heart is lifted up, and thou hast said, I am a God, I sit in the seat of God, in the midst of the seas; yet thou art a man, and not God, though thou set thine heart as the heart of God: Behold, thou art wiser than Daniel; there is no secret that they can hide from thee: With thy wisdom and with thine understanding thou hast gotten thee riches, and hast gotten gold and silver into thy treasures: By thy great wisdom and by thy traffick hast thou increased thy riches, and thine heart is lifted up because of thy riches"

The persona that occupies the greatest office in the land has shown us without a doubt that he has a great ego and his heart is lifted up because of his riches and he feels that he is the greatest human being on earth. It is no doubt this time period we are presently living in is abnormal. Many people have expressed the same sentiment with biblical connection in mind. It is what's in his heart that implicates who he is. This scripture points to him like no other. "Hast thou increased thy riches, and thine heart is lifted up because of thy riches." He wears his riches on his shoulders like he is God. "And through his policy also he shall cause craft to prosper in his hand; and he shall magnify himself in his heart." Daniel 8: 23-25.

Our leader who has bragged about our economy is viewed by many as being an economic wizard and is the envy of other countries. He is a billionaire who lavishes in his success and believes no one can beat him at his game. He has a big ego that need to be fed on a daily basis from his party members.

The bible explains the Antichrist likes sinister schemes and is able to exploit people's negative views of the world to his advantage. Daniel 8:23, "And in the latter time of their kingdom, when the transgressors are come to the full, a king of fierce countenance, and understanding dark sentences, shall stand up."

This leader of the free world brings with him an aura of darkness. Instead of bringing light to the world he brings unholiness. When he stood in front of Saint Johns Episcopal Church holding a bible a message was sent reverberating throughout the Christian faith. The battle for good versus evil is at hand.

Our leader has been called a demagogue many times by prominent leaders, newscasters, military advisers, and theologians. His characteristics have revealed to us a frightening conclusion. Are we witnessing the coming of the lawless one, the biblical Antichrist?

Our leader is not a respecter of the law, in fact, he has mocked our justice system and has lessened its credibility. The word transgressor means "a person who violates a rule or oversteps a boundary". Dan. 8:23 "And in the latter time of their kingdom, when the *transgressors* are come to the full, a king of fierce countenance, and understanding dark sentences, shall stand up." Doesn't that definition describe our leader of the free world? The biblical scriptures is alerting us to take notice of this crucial moment in world history. The patriot Paul wrote a letter to the Thessalonians so that the people of today would wake up and see this individual for who he is. In Thessalonians 2:9-12 points to this time period when people who have power do not believe in TRUTH. They would rather believe a lie for their own political gain. When the leader of the free world take an oath to serve and protect the laws of the land then take a blind eye to truth and justice and would rather love what is false and find "pleasure in unrighteousness" he is the biblical "LAWLESS ONE."

When his party members (ten horns or devils) gave up their moral aptitude, and hundreds of years of integrity, honesty and pride, and watched in silence as their person of choice erode their justice system in order to keep themselves in power, they would do anything, even Satan's bidding in order to keep him in power. They have succeeded in giving "their power and strength unto the beast," the great pretender, the adversary, "THE CHOSEN ONE, THE BIBLICAL ANTICHRIST." Revelation 17:12-13. "And the ten horns which thou sawest are ten kings, which have receive no kingdom as yet; but receive power as kings one hour with the beast. These have one mind, and shall give their power and strength unto the beast."

It was 10 Republican senators who voted to acquit the leader of the free world in his impeachment trial just as the biblical prophecy outlined, "And the 10 horns which thou sawest are ten kings..........." Revelation 17:12-13. They all knew that the leader of the free world's actions were wrong and inappropriate but yet they remained silent in order to GIVE THEIR POWER AND STRENGTH TO HIM. SO THAT THEY ALL REMAIN IN POWER. Senator Lamar Alexander said, "When elected officials inappropriately interfere with such investigations, it undermines the principle of equal justice under the law." Senator Mitt Romney said, "Corrupting an election to keep oneself in office is perhaps the most abusive and destructive violation of one's oath of office I can imagine." Al though their were 52 Republican senators who voted against the impeachment of the president, ten out of those Republican senators admitted that they believed the leader of the free world was guilty but remained silent. This statement was taken from an excerpt from the well known journalist Bob Woodward interviews in his book "Rage" fulfilling the biblical prophecy. "In total, 10 Republican senators who voted to acquit said in statements and interviews Trump's actions were wrong, improper or inappropriate." Bob Woodward explained the reason the 10 Republican senators voted to acquit because they had to make a "political survival decision" giving their power and strength to Trump so that they all could remain in POWER.

The "King Maker"

Although the biblical scripture (Rev. 17:12-13) describes for us 10 kings who have no kingdom, our American government is not ruled by kings or queens. That is why most theologians will fail to see the prophecy unfold. But when you listen to how the media and state representatives call former President Trump a "king maker" that term brings Rev. 17:12-13 to life. The term "king maker" points to the country and individual where Rev. 17:12-13 unfolds or plays out.

The American president who is popular and has great influence becomes a "king maker" when he chooses a candidate, then his followers vote for his choice over others. According to CNN Smerconish, "anyone who kisses his ring," or spends time with him "receive power as kings one hour with the beast" and confesses their loyalty has a greater chance at winning an election or staying in power.

In what universe or country have multiple kings with no kingdom? How can a person be crowned king without presiding over a country? This scenario can only happen in a system like our American democracy where congressmen and senators hold power. Their title and position that they hold is as powerful as the President, or kings, but they do not preside over any country or kingdom, yet. "And the ten horns which thou sawest are ten kings, which have received no kingdom as yet."

Congressmen and senators cannot hold on to power without the American president remaining in office. In order to keep themselves in power they must rally behind their choice for president "giving their power and strength" which makes him a king maker who endow all that endorses him as powerful as kings fulfilling the biblical prophecy. Is it a coincidence that the President's private limousine is called "The Beast"?

Rev. 17:12-13 "And the ten horns which thou sawest are ten kings, which have received no kingdom as yet; but receive power as kings one hour with the beast. These have one mind, and shall give their power and strength unto the beast."

Dan. 8:23 "And in the latter time of their kingdom, when the transgressors are come to the full, a king of fierce countenance, and understanding dark sentences, shall stand up."

2 Thessalonians 2:9-12 "The coming of the lawless one is by the activity of Satan with all power and false signs and wonders, and with all wicked deception for those who are perishing, because they refused to love the truth and so be saved. Therefore God sends them a strong delusion, so that they may believe what is false, in order that all may be condemned who did not believe the truth but had pleasure in unrighteousness."

The leader of the free world's Party members has been losing the popular votes as noted for the past 20 years so they rally behind dark and evil forces in order to defeat the normal function of democracy to hold on to POWER. To what extent or how far they will go to keep power in their hands is the question? Even if Satan himself was their leader they would uphold his disgraceful behavior and look the other way even if it means destroying the fabric of democracy.

The Battle for the Soul of Democracy

Our leader of the free world has been compared to Hitler and Mussolini. He has been called a racist, a fascist, and a bigot. He avoids promoting good deeds and thrives on magnifying hatred, division, and white supremacy. He only wants white people from rich countries to migrate to America. He calls countries that occupy people of color "shit-hole countries."

Countries that embrace democracy have reached a crucial point in world history. We must begin to see the nature of the beast. His characteristics are on display for the whole world to see. First, the beast showed the world one of his heads. When Mikhail Gorbachev brought down the Berlin Wall, those people who believe in freedom and democracy and have love for our Lord and savior Jesus Christ thought for that historical moment the world was headed in the right direction.

The wall that divided millions of people became a relic of souvenirs. Although this wall was made of stone, it represented all types of walls that divided humanity from the beginning of time. The walls of hatred, racism, separatism, communism, nationalism, and neo-Nazism are all the same type of walls. The miracles Gorbachev performed in 1989 envelop all races of people to this very day.

According to the biblical scriptures, there would be two beasts sent by the Devil. Their names are Gog and Magog. In my opinion, Gog has already appeared in the persona of Mikhail Gorbachev as I indicated in my letter to all Christian Churches.

In observing how the biblical writers describe their biblical characters, a name is identified when a distinct meaning or interpretation is given. Take for example the name Abraham, its meaning, "father of a multitude," or Baal, its meaning "the first king of hell," to us it's Satan. Is it a mere coincidence that the persona in question's family name is "Christ"? Do the research for yourself. (Wikipedia)

According to Thorndike and Barnhart dictionary the definition of the word trump is "any playing card of a suit that for the time ranks higher than the other suits. It is a trick card. It is to be better than and beat the other suits." The word trump has a double meaning, and that is "TO DECEIVE, TO TRICK." Satan is called the great PRETENDER, THE GREAT DECEIVER.

The characteristics of the persona in question fit the definition of the word that is described in the dictionary. This person feels that he is higher than any man. He considers himself better than anyone and can beat anyone in any game or anything. He feels that he has a trick up his sleeves that will give him the edge or advantage. He feels that he is "The Chosen One."

Deep within this person's soul he has come to realize that he is higher than man, for there is no man on earth that can be compared to him. So he must choose God. On national TV this persona said, he is "The Chosen One." His name is the exact word from the dictionary and he acts accordingly.

The characteristic of Satan is identical to the persona in question. Satan has a great ego and his greatest wish is to "be like the most high." Isaiah 14:13-14. His heart is magnified and he feels that he is larger than life.

It is important to identify the second beast whose name is Magog without calling a particular person's name. Using elements of his character should be enough to get our attention. The persona in question has been called a demagogue numerous times so the biblical scriptures name of Magog comes to life. The irony of Gog and Magog is that Mikhail Gorbachev is responsible for bringing down the Berlin Wall while the leader of Democracy builds a wall to keep people of color out. Now, do I have your attention?

We know that Armageddon begins in the Hills of Megiddo in Israel, but America is ground zero where the battle for the soul of democracy begins. If this mixing bowl of people with different ethnic backgrounds cannot survive, it will not prevail in other democracies. The whole world is watching how our leader of democracy tear down the basic freedoms for which it stands for. The statue of liberty stands for the welcoming of people from different ethnic backgrounds. It is a place where people can partake in the wonderful experiment of American greatness and be a part of the light of the world and adhere to the principles it was founded upon. "In God we trust."

This battle is also a spiritual war with Russia being the puppet master. They are the forces of evil that threaten to envelop the whole world. President Ronald Reagan made it clear in his statement defining Russia saying, "they preach the supremacy of the state, declare its omnipotence over individual man, and predict its eventual domination of all peoples of the earth – they are the focus of evil in the modern world."

There is a definite pattern by Russian aggression directed toward the pillar of democracy. From Gorbachev's ability to infiltrate the Christian belief system by imitating the passion of Christ and cyber warfare used to interfere in the American election process and rolling back the INF treaty that was began by Gorbachev and Reagan, these are just some of the tools used by Russia to destabilize the leader of the Western world.

Christianity with its broad influence in the world is an important target for Russia because of the country's atheistic point of view. But God has a way to bring these issues to the forefront. Is what we see in today's current events biblically related? Is it a coincidence that all of these crucial events are happening at the same moment in history?

Russia is attacking the heart of democracy which is the belief in Christianity. There is always a survey or poll given to people asking them how they feel about a certain politician, but they never poll people about how they feel about the state of the world. Most people I ask about world affairs gave me a gloomy picture of doom and gloom. There is something they see just around the horizon. A dark cloud is fast approaching. Some people feel that Jesus Christ is coming soon. Still others say that Armageddon is approaching. Others say a great war is coming between Russian/Iran vs. America/Israel that leads to World War III, and they feel that America is joining Russia.

Just the other day, I saw a bumper sticker on someone's car that displayed the hammer and sickle, the emblem of Russia. What? The emblem of Russia! What the hell is going on? Are people right in their prognosis of the world? In my book,

"Mikhail Gorbachev is Gog and Magog," on page 25, I asked the question, "What if the coup d'état in 1991 in Russia was staged by their leaders to disguise a more sinful plan? A master plan that would gain the Russian's total domination of the world. A master plan that would dethrone the belief in an unseen God. A plan that involves acting out the biblical prophecy concerning the Antichrist. What if the Russia's plan is to test the waters, the biblical waters? It would be the most diabolical plot in world history.

Russia is an atheistic government that relishes on its communist past. This is what Joseph Stalin said, 'We have deposed the czars of the earth and we shall now dethrone the lord of heaven.' Have the Russian's abandoned this belief or have they incorporated this belief into a master plan?" There is a definite and obvious plan by Russia to continue their goal to destabilize democracy and dethrone the belief in God. They have now infiltrated the halls of the U.S. government.

So, people are right in their assumption about Russia. Many Americans have been psychologically influenced by Russia's ongoing attack on our election process. From the media's continuous coverage of the Mueller Report to our leaders having affiliation with Russia and some people even going as far as renaming the U.S. to the United States of Russia, all this reveals the psychological effect it has on America and possibly the whole world.

Over 20 years ago, I wrote in my book "Mikhail Gorbachev is Gog and Magog" how Gorbachev seems to be on a designed time table put in motion by the leaders of the old Soviet empire. A secret mission to unleash psychological warfare against the Christian community. This is how Gorbachev describes a secret war against the Christian World. He said, "We have no right even to forget that psychological warfare is a struggle for winning people's minds." (Taken from "Soviet Disinformation Chief: a Master at Using Words as Cold War Weapons," New York Tribune, 7-27-87)

In Revelation 13 it describe two beast sent by the devil. One will come from the political arena and the other from the deep pit of the earth. One will come from Russia and the other from America. What is the possibility of both superpowers joining? Is the biblical scriptures referring to both superpowers as Gog and Magog?

Let us examine the leaders of the two superpowers to see if there are any similarities in what they are projecting to the world. Although Gorbachev is no longer the leader of Russia, the leader of the free world is similar to him in many ways. In 1986 the leader of the old Soviet Union now known as Russia visited America with anticipation of great changes in the world. Mikhail Gorbachev was accepted by the leaders of America with the laying of the red carpet. Gorbachev already attained superstar status before he even put his foot on American soil. As most Americans stood in awe of his magnetic present a strange thing happened that gave his arrival a spooky atmosphere.

In Washington DC the numbers game was being held at the same moment of the arrival of Mikhail Gorbachev. As the numbers 666 was revealed on local TV as the winning numbers for the day residents of the city became frightened and alarmed. I personally remembered people asking the question is Gorbachev the biblical Antichrist?

Today the leader of the free world was embroiled in scandal and at this writing has already been impeached. It all began with Russia interfering in America's election process where Russian agents and American politicians met in building 666 in secret.

Both leaders have a connection to Russia and has the same question asked by people concerning their identity. The question most people asked back in 1989 was Gorbachev the biblical Antichrist? During Gorbachev's election campaign he stated that "for some people he is like God, for others he is like Satan." In contrast the leader of the free world on national TV looked up at the sky and said,"he is the Chosen One." Why are both of the leaders indulging in biblical prophecy and have a messiah complex?

Not only does the two superpower leaders make biblical reference those politicians who is loyal to them express biblical reference in a diabolical way as well. During the impeachment hearing in America one of the opposing team members loyal to the leader of the free world displayed the sign of the devil on national TV. On a prominent late night talk show the host made reference to this person alerting his audience that these days are not ordinary times.

The TV camera got a shot of the member forming his fingers and hand that is recognized by the followers of Satan. This hand gesture echo's the time of Gorbachev when his own people ask him to put makeup over his forehead in order to hide his birthmark because people refer to it as the "Mark of the Beast."

In 1996 Mikhail Gorbachev entered the re-election campaign for the presidency of Russia. A hand gesture became the topic of discussion during the campaign trail. One of Gorbachev's opponents made this startling revelation concerning the election campaign. Excerpt from the Washington Post, "Gennady Zyuganov the Communist Party presidential candidate likes to tell crowds he has read the bible twice. Today he deployed fire and brimstone against his reformist opponents and suggest eerily that their intentions are strictly satanic. Let's remember the predictions of the apocalypse," he told his partisans in a Moscow sports arena, evidently paraphrasing the bible, "Two beast sent by the devil are coming out of the abyss. The first one has a mark on his forehead. The second has a mark on his hand."

Mikhail Gorbachev who is no longer the president of Russia frightened many people during his tenure as the leader of the old Soviet Union now known as Russia with a distinct blood stain mark on his forehead. Today the leader of the free world's representative makes a hand gesture of Satan in support of an American president in 2019 to show solidarity. Even the leader himself makes hand gestures to his eager followers.

After the leader of the free world was impeached his loyal representative said that he compared the leader of the free world to Jesus Christ referring to the trial which led to Pontius Pilate condemning Jesus to death. The representative said that Jesus was dealt a better hand than what happened to the leader of the free world.

In 1986 Gorbachev made the same sentiment about his defeat in the election campaign on national TV:

> CHARLES GIBSON: "It is an interesting paradox to so many Americans – you are so honored throughout the world for fundamental changes but I don't have to recite the election results to you, in the last election you got a very small, tiny percent of the vote. Why is Gorbachev seen so differently outside Russia and inside Russia?"
>
> GORBACHEV: "Well, let's recall another example. Jesus Christ was pelted with stones. He was blamed and condemned, and then he was put with a bandit and they were taken for execution. And when it was said that one of them could be spared, the people said the bandit should be spared and Christ was crucified."

Why are the two superpower leaders comparing themselves to Jesus Christ? Are they the two beast that is outlined in Revelation 13? Gorbachev felt that his defeat in the elections of 1996 in Russia was like a crucifixion. The Leader of the free world stated that his impeachment was like he was being crucified. Should we as Christians ignore these obvious displays of blasphemy? Why has the Christian Church remained silent?

A Coup D'état

Both Gorbachev and Trump's tenures as president ended in a coup. The similarities in their desire to imitate Christ led them to fulfill biblical prophecy just as I outlined in Chapter 2 when Gorbachev ended his presidency when a mob-like crowd stormed Moscow Square in the former Soviet Union.

This scenario was repeated with Trump when a mob-like crowd of hundreds stormed the United States Capitol in an effort to stop the certification of the Electoral College vote so that he could remain in power. Although the reason for the coup in both incidences are different, both Trump and Gorbachev's aspirations to stay in power ended in humiliation.

Both Gorbachev and Trump were wounded to death politically when they both lost power. Revelations 13:3 "and I saw one of his heads as if it were wounded to death; and his deadly wound was healed..." We must expect a return of Trump in the near future based on the biblical prophecy.

The Two Beasts

Revelation 13 describes two Beast coming at the end time. I've already identified one of the beast as Mikhail Gorbachev the former Russian president. The second beast is being put on trial using only his characteristics not his name. It is because I want the reader to see him in a certain light.

Let's begin with the word blasphemy as it is stated in Revelation 13. Did the Leader of the free world committed blasphemy when he looked up at the sky and said he is "the chosen one" comparing himself to Jesus Christ? Only Satan wants to be like the most high. Isaiah 14:14. "I will be like the most high."

A representative of the Leader of the free world explained to the media that our Leader was treated worst than Jesus Christ in his impeachment trial referring to Pontius Pilate condemning Jesus to death. This statement by the representative of the Leader is identical to what Mikhail Gorbachev did when he performed a mock crucifixion in the likeness of Jesus Christ.

The Leader of the free world has told over twenty thousand lies. His lies come so natural to him. It's in his DNA. John 8:44; "you belong to your father, the devil, and you want to carry out your father's desires. He was a murderer from the beginning, not holding to the truth, for there is no truth in him. When he lies, he speaks his native language, for he is a liar and the father of lies."

The Leader of the free world said that he could go on 5th avenue and shoot some one and you will still vote for him. Christianity Today Newspaper called our Leader of democracy a grossly immoral character. The attributes of Satan is as follow: No respecter of the law, hater of the truth, slanderer and accuser, and lies repeatedly, and is unethical. All of these have been attributed to our Leader of the free world. If Hitler was alive today and murdered millions would you vote for him if he could give you what you want? Christians around the world has abandoned the teachings of Christ and has adopted self gratification as a way to solve everyday problems.

Jesus Christ had a choice between submitting to the offerings of Satan. Satan had the power to give Jesus all the things he ever desired. It's all about choice. We must be careful when we select our leaders. Our Leader of the free world has not gone out and shot someone but that does not exonerate him from the crime. His statement concerning gun violence carries a lot of weight when we look at current events of murder and mayhem across the world.

Why does Christians do not look at someone's character before choosing a candidate? How can someone vote for a person who is a liar and hater of the truth? What happened to right and wrong and good versus evil? These are the teaching of Jesus that still carries a lot of weight. Some Christians has thrown away these moral characteristics for what you can do for me.

Those who claim to be followers of Christ must examine their moral compass when choosing a particular candidate. How can someone choose an individual who has proven to be immoral and unethical?

As the world struggles with bringing the word of God with it in the 21st century, world events mirror the biblical battle for the soul of humanity.

We who proclaim to be Christians cannot afford to let secular belief influence our thinking when it's time to choose right from wrong. Be careful what you ask for when making that final choice. You may end up voting for Satan himself.

God has shined his light on the leader of the free world and the reflection is not pretty. Is America still the light of the world? All of us will have to make a choice in defining what type of world we want to live in. Will we adhere to the principles that Jesus taught or will we choose a world of hate, lies, and xenophobia.

Today Christian Evangelicals are choosing a person whose moral character has proven to be unethical. They are willing to overlook his demeaning statue and how he degrades women and people of color. Christian Evangelicals has come to believe that character doesn't matter as long as they get what they want. Right and wrong and good vs evil is not a factor when choosing a particular candidate.

Bad things happen when we ignore the character of a person. As Jesus Christ walked through the streets of Galilee preaching the gospel his character was on display. When some of the people saw him they could see the honesty in what he was testifying about. Even the blind man was able to detect without his eyesight the character of Jesus and was healed because he believed.

It is the people who ignored Jesus character whom I want to concentrate my thoughts on why they did not recognize his divinity. They are the one's who voted to condemn Jesus to death. The Pharisees, Scribes and Seduccees who were the religious leaders of the time of Jesus Christ could not see that he was God. Even the residents of Galilee voted to condemn Jesus to death and save a murderer and a thief called Barabbas.

The religious leaders during the time of Jesus did not recognize his character because they were blinded by their religious belief. Sometimes there are many trees standing before you but you can't see the forest for the trees. Sometime some religions stand in the way of good common sense.

God uses this scenario in our world today to teach us the basic principles of Good versus Evil. When we choose our public leaders we must consider his character first. You would not choose a policeman if you knew he have a history of bad characteristics. People of all professions must be carefully scrutinized before selecting a candidate. They all must believe in Jesus Christ and adhere to his teachings.

We must come to the realization that God works in duality. What happened thousands of years ago can be repeated in today's world. What if God is asking us to repeat what happened to Jesus over 2 thousand years ago by making a choice but this time we must identify Satan instead of Jesus. Can we identify Satan with just his characteristic if he appeared in our world?

In the future we will be faced with the challenge of selecting a candidate. Should we overlook the candidate characteristic and choose him because he offers us a promise of gold? Even if his moral compass is off, it won't be a problem as long as we get what we want. Even if he told 20,000 lies and is a slanderer and hater of the truth who has no respect for the law, a demagogue and the great deceiver. Even if all of these are the characteristic of Satan it doesn't matter to them. Or should it?

The author Bernard Levi who wrote the book entitled "Madness in the Age of the Virus," states that the "leader of the free world has taken civilization back to the world before Christopher Columbus." In my opinion the leader of the free world has taken us farther back than that. He has taken us back to the beginning of time when Satan rebelled against his creator. He is taking us back to the time when the adversary rely on lies to achieve a common goal. He has taken us back to a time when hatred of your fellow man is the way of a superiority complex. He has taken us back to a time when a Wall like the BERLIN WALL was built to keep out people from pursuing a better life. He has taken us back to a time of bigotry, racism, xenophobia, demagoguery, and fascism reminiscent of WWI and WWII when the world went MAD. He has taken us back to a final choice of heaven or hell or Jesus or Satan.

Image of the Beast
The Golden Trump Statue, A Golden Idol

It is important to end this chapter with a visual account of the plight Christians are facing who proclaim a belief in God but disobey His commandments. We as Christians must examine the holy scriptures and see how followers of the Antichrist make an image of him to worship instead of Jesus.

When a golden Trump statue was displayed at the Conservative Political Action Conference (CPAC) in Orlando, Florida, Revelation 13 came to life right before the world's eye. The irony of this event was loud and clear as Christians worshiped a golden idol, a golden statue of the leader of the free world. The followers of the leader of the free world have become so possessed by his mere presence that a golden statue of him represents a cult. They are willing to follow him even though he has no respect for the law.

Over two thousand years ago a golden calf was created by Moses' brother Aaron who was influenced by followers to build an idol, a graven image to worship instead of God. This action was an insult to God. Leviticus 26:1. "Do not make idols or set up an image or a sacred stone for yourselves, and do not place a carved stone in your land to bow down before it. I am the Lord your God."

CHAPTER 4

"THE DAY THE EARTH STOOD STILL"

THE TRIBULATION PERIOD

In the movie "The Day the Earth Stood Still" depicts an invasion of extraterrestrials from outer space landing on earth. These aliens had the power to stop the world from existing by halting everyone and everything that move. The Aliens had to prove to the earthlings that they must obey their commands or suffer consequences. Cars, trains, and airplanes froze in place at the aliens command. Even people were frozen in place and could not move until the set time decreed by the Aliens. This scenario could only happen in a movie, right?

The pandemic of 2020 showed scenes like it was a doomsday movie displaying pictures of empty streets and abandon cars. Stores and shopping malls became a ghost town of lifeless mannequins. Panic buying by people caused store shelves to become empty of products due to fear of end of days. Government officials decreed that people should stay home and do not mingle with others due to the deadly virus. Even curfews were put in place to curve socialization.

Everyday life was frozen to protect oneself from the virus. This type of alien invasion cause many people all over the world to retreat into their homes and imprison themselves from the monster that lurked all around us.

Due to the deadly virus the economical system of the world was on the verge of collapsing that threaten to bring the whole world to a standstill. The world was frozen not because of an Alien invasion from outer space but it was frozen by a virus. No science fiction movie could ever have portrayed fear like the corona virus pandemic of 2020. Even wars around the world did not bring fear to our doorstep, but the virus brought it home and has forever shaken our peace.

As a nation we have been warned before this frightening event came upon us. The biblical scriptures warned us if we don't obey God's commandments there would be dire consequences. During the time of Moses there were plagues sent by God to convince Pharaoh to let his people go. Pharaoh resisted his commands and God sent devastating plagues upon his city. Today in our world the scriptures tells us to follow God's commandments but our nation has failed to listen and has ignored God's laws. We must take heed of God's warning, he said, Leviticus 26:3 -5. "If ye walk in my statues, and keep my commandments, and do them; then I will give you rain in due season, and the land shall yield her increase, and the trees of the fields shall yield their fruit. And your threshing shall reach into the vintage, and the vintage shall reach into the sowing time; and ye shall eat your bread to the full, and dwell in your land safely."

Our nation was founded on the principles of "In God We Trust" but has forgotten why our country prospered throughout the years. God protected us through two world wars because of its idea of enlightenment. God smiled on our nation when we uplifted every man, women and child of every color to come and be apart of the light of the world. Our nation has forgotten that there would be consequences if we turn away from God. We must listen to what our Lord and Savior Jesus Christ warning, he said in Leviticus 26:14-21. "But if ye will not hearken unto me, and will not do all these commandments; and if ye shall despise my statues, or if your soul abhor my judgments, so that ye will not do all my commandments, but that ye break my covenant: I also will do this unto you; I will even appoint over you terror, consumption, and the burning ague, that shall consume the eyes, and cause sorrow of heart; and ye shall sow your seed in vain, for your enemies shall eat it. And I will set my face against you, and ye shall be slain before your enemies; they that hate you shall reign over you; and ye shall flee when none pursueth you. And if ye will not yet for all this hearken unto me, then I will punish you seven times more for your sins. And I will break the pride of your power; and I will make your heaven as iron, and your earth as brass. And your strength shall be spent in vain; for your land shall not yield her increase, neither shall the trees of the land yield her fruits. And if ye walk contrary unto me, and will not hearken unto me; I will bring seven times more PLAGUES upon you according to your sins."

The Corona virus is just the beginning of plagues that will come upon this world and will not let up until the return of Jesus Christ. As history reveals, plagues will come in different forms as long as we turn a blind eye to the commandments of God. Another disease that has plagued the world is gun violence. This type of plague has resulted in millions of lives lost to homicides, suicides, mass shooting, accidental and negligent injuries. Although any time a gun is used on a victim it is horrible but what is more appalling is when a youth use a gun on another youth in school and take multiple lives. This is how far we have come as a society in the modern world when everyone is powerless to speak out because of the love affair with guns.

The biblical scripture tells us that God will disarm nations that will fight against his return. The battlefield of Armageddon will become a river of blood. Armored tanks and airplanes and all weapons of war will be consumed in fire. The eyes of soldiers will rot and their flesh will literally melt where they are standing. "Surely in that day there shall be a great earthquake in the land of Israel, so that the fish of the sea, the birds of the heavens, the beast of the field, all creeping things that creep on the earth, all men in the face of the earth shall shake at my presence. The mountain shall be thrown down, the steep places shall fall, and every wall shall fall to the grown; I will call for a sword against Gog throughout all my mountains, says the lord God. Every man's sword will be against his brother. And I will bring him to judgment with PESTILENCE and blood shed. I will rain down on him, on his troops and on many people who are with him, flooding rain, great hailstones, fire and brimstone. Thus I will magnify myself and sanctify myself, and I will be known in the eyes of many nations. Then shall they know that I am the Lord." Ezekiel 38:19-23.

In 2019 Australia showed the world a glimpse of the Apocalypse when brush fires left its destructive path with devastation of life and property. Then after the fires ended the dust storm arrived that made people begin to worry that it looked like the end of days with tremendous clouds of dirt that turned daylight into darkness. Then the hailstorm came with golf ball sized hail damaging cars and homes, people began to wonder have scripture from the pages of the bible come to life?

But it did not stop there, the floods came and the plague locust came that sent most people in search for their bibles that was long ago placed in storage. God has a peculiar way of getting our attention.

WWIII
The Tribulation Period

It is the 25th of March, 2020 at 9:00 am in the morning on a day that most people would be at work but instead my family and I and most others are hunkered down in our bunkers (home). Our everyday routine has been interrupted by an attack by an unseen enemy that is hungry for victims. In any other war we would be listening for the frightening sounds of bombs exploding all around us, unless the bomb found its target. But thank God there are no bombs falling on our cities. Only an unseen enemy that is more deadly than all of the past wars combined without a nuclear war.

As the body count rises the World Health Organization gave us a frightening projection. The enemy will continue to expand enveloping the whole world. The news reporter tells us that if this invisible enemy continues to spread all over the world 1/3 of mankind would be killed. When I heard that doomsday projection I remembered what the biblical scriptures foretold. "And the four angels were loosed, which were prepared for an hour, and a day, and a month, and a year, for to slay the third part of men." Revelation 9:15. We are assured by the scriptures that these days will be cut short, due to the intervention of our Lord and Savior Jesus Christ, if not the whole world would be destroyed. "For then shall be great tribulation, such as was not since the beginning of the world to this time, no nor even shall be, and except those days should be shortened, there shall be no flesh be saved; but for the elect's sake those days shall be shortened." Matthew 24:15-22.

It is day 66 and we are still hunkered down in our homes with no end in sight of the death angel with a mission to kill all humanity if not stopped. Now I know how refugees of war feel when bombs are falling on their cities while they hunkered down in homes, caves, or wholes in the ground. As I gaze into my wife eyes I can see the fear written all over her face. It's a feeling I've never felt or saw in her before. While we act in front of our kids that there is nothing to worry about, anxiety and fear takes over by bed time.

Our government leaders proclaim that we are at war with a different type of enemy that needs no weapons of mass destruction. It is even a war without the use of bullets.

During the time of Moses one of the plagues descended on the city then the smell of death filled the air. Moses directed his followers to go to their homes and stay there before the death angel comes. He instructed them to put blood on their door so that the death angel seeing the blood would past by and choose another house. Moses and his followers were spared certain death because they had God on their side. That event is celebrated by the Jews who call that day the Passover because death past over their homes and their lives were spared.

It is day 90 and the death toll continues to mount as we remain hunkered down in our bunkers. We all wonder if we would be the next victims. Some nights I wake up early thinking about all the people dying without seeing their love one or saying good bye for the last time. I wonder when this nightmare will end. Before we arrived at this horrific moment in our history we were already experiencing a feeling of uncertainty as our government leaders fought it out over what direction they want the country to go. It left all of us divided and spiritually drained from the ego eccentric demagogue.

For the past four years our world has taken on a more sinister atmosphere with our leaders embracing hatred and using fear as a weapon to divide people. From political leaders to news reporters to everyday people they all give the same sentiment that something is abnormal in our world. When a dark cloud is approaching the skies, you are able to predict stormy weather. You observe the calm atmosphere before the storm. Just beyond the horizon, you see lightning bolts flicker in and out of those dark clouds. Then instantly upon you, wind and rain confirms your predictions. The bible tells us that Jesus Christ gave us the insight to be able to see the changing of the atmosphere for better or for worst. He said, "When you see a cloud rising in western parts, at once you say, a storm is coming, and it turns out so. And when you see that a south wind is blowing, you say, there will be a heat wave, and it occurs." Luke 12:54-55.

No one could predict the pandemic of 2020 and saw the devastation of lives that it caused. But it happened when our world was already experiencing a time of uncertainty that made us take notice of a dark side of our politics that threatened to divide us further toward anarchy. All of the elements of the end time scenario are right in front of us. If we had observed the climate of the world, you would have found a demonic presence. You may come to realize that a dark cloud is approaching just beyond the horizon.

The bible tells us that the Great Tribulation period is coming. Is the corona virus the beginning of the biblical prophecy of that tribulation period? The corona virus which enveloped the whole world make the following biblical scripture come to life. Daniel 12:1 "and there shall be a time of trouble, such as never was since there was a nation even to that same time."

Day 98 finds all of us still hunkered down in our homes to escape the invisible monster that searches for its next victim. He will show no mercy. A devoted pastor who loves the Lord Jesus stood in defiance and ignored public officials warning held his service on Sunday morning inviting all his worshipers to attend service. Then told his followers to not be a coward and be afraid of the virus that already killed thousands all over the world. He ignored warnings from government officials and held worship service to show the world that God would protect him from harm. The pastor got infected with the virus and died. Members and friends could not understand why God abandon him at his darkest hour.

Did God really abandon him? Where God is sitting he is able to see things in a higher perspective than the average human mind. Although the family members and friends were over whelmed with grief from the lost of a love one, the pastor in death celebrated in victory. He had run a good race. He had withstood the challenges of life. He had showed the world what a good Christian should be. Then God took him and said, job well done. Jesus Christ left these words for all people who have lost a love one, John 14:1-4. "Let not your hearts be troubled. Believe in God, believe also in me. In my Father's house are many rooms. If it were not so, would I have told you that I go to prepare a place for you? And if I go and prepare a place for you, I will come again and will take you to myself, that where I am you may be also. And you know the way to where I am going."

Christians should hold firm to their faith. Do not let the devil win the victory. In these final days of this world Satan will use every weapon to kill man and attempt to devalue your belief. The Pastor is in the bosom of the Lord. Now, the understanding of what the Pastor taught his followers is on display for the whole world to see. We must remember how the members of the Charleston Church massacre behaved after experiencing a great loss of life. Family members and members of the Church forgave the perpetrator of this despicable act. They showed the world how to turn the other cheek like Jesus Christ taught them.

We must strive to be like Christ and set an example for others to follow. The trials of life help to mold our character into becoming a stronger Christian. The Apostle Peter explains it this way, "In this you greatly rejoice, even though now for a little while, if necessary, you have been distressed by various trials, so that the proof of your faith, being more precious than gold which is perishable, even though tested by fire, may be found in praise and glory and honor at the revelation of Jesus Christ." 1 Peter 1:6-7.

We must never temp God to fulfill an obligation. God saves those at his discretion. God warned Moses to place his followers in QUARANTINE. God did not tell Moses and his followers to stand out in the open and he would save them. He told them to take shelter because his wrath is coming. I believe in God but I still put my mask on to cover my mouth and nose to protect me from the virus.

It is day 100th and the death toll continues to mount as the corona virus wrecks havoc on the bodies of innocent victims. I am exhausted from weeks of tending to people who I've never met but need my help. As I watch many die I become the last person they see so I try to give them comfort when they take their last breath.

This is the 101 day of the virus as I put on my mask and scrubs to prepare to enter the hospital. This day will be different because I will stop by my church and complete my attire for today by putting on the armor of God. I can't help but wonder why this deadly virus has come upon the whole world and killed many. Maybe God is trying to get our attention. I know many of my friends who have sinned. Some do drugs as away to cope with the many hardships of life. Some of my friends are women who go to bed with other women. Some are men who go to bed with other men. Some of my friends do not believe in God. Some of my friends worship sports more than any unseen God. Some believe money is their God.

I wonder is the corona virus here to slow us down so that we can see the important things in life. Maybe we should all take a moment and reflect on the things that is more meaningful. Maybe we should take this time to get to know God. I remember the pastor always tells us that we should REPENT of our sins. Maybe that is why the corona virus is here. To get us to REPENT of our sins before it's too late.

Day 103 has made many of us wonder is this God's judgment on the world. Our world has been turned upside down over night with long lines of people receiving food because they have been laid off their job. This scene of poverty is reminiscent of the Great Depression that struck our country in 1933. Is it something that we did to cause this virus to come upon us after years of prosperity? Isaiah 26:20-21 "Come, my people, enter thou into thy chambers, and shut thy doors about thee: hide thyself as it were for a little moment, until the indignation be overpast. For, behold, the Lord cometh out of his place to punish the inhabitants of the earth for their iniquity...."

This virus is affecting every soul on earth rather it be the rich or the poor no one will escape. Isaiah 24:1-3 "Behold, the Lord maketh the earth empty, and maketh it waste, and turneth it upside down, and scattereth abroad the inhabitants thereof. And it shall be, as with the people, so with the priest; as with the servant, so with his master; as with the maid, so with her mistress; as with the buyer, so with the seller; as with the lender, so with the borrower; as with the taker of usury, so with the giver of usury to him. The land shall be utterly emptied, utterly spoiled; for the Lord has spoken this word." The world must repent of sins and return to the commandments of the Lord.

The Rapture

Is the corona virus the long held belief of some Christians that people will drop dead during the end time and forever be with Christ? The word rapture is no where to be found in the bible but what Christians are eluding to is this event signals the imminent return of Jesus Christ to this earth to redeem the Church. The second coming of Jesus Christ is described in this prophecy by the apostle Paul, 1 Thessalonians 4:13-17. "But I would not have you to be ignorant, brethren, concerning them which are asleep, that ye sorrow not, even as others have no hope. For if we believe that Jesus died and rose again, even so them also which sleep in Jesus will God bring with him. For this we say unto you by the word of the Lord, we which are alive and remain unto the coming of the Lord shall not prevent them which are asleep. For the Lord himself shall descend from heaven with a shout, with the voice of the archangel, and with the trump of God; and the dead in Christ shall rise first; then we which are alive and remain shall be caught up together with them in the clouds, to meet the Lord in the air; and so shall we ever be with the Lord."

Some theologians may say that COVID-19 is not the apocalypse or the rapture. No one can say for sure because they never had to live through it, but tell that to the doctors and nurses around the world in hospitals fighting to save thousands of lives and the many lives who are still suffering at this writing.

The Mask

The mask before you represents movies and plays that describe human emotions an actor must portray. If it's a scene of sadness brought on by some sort of tragedy, the actor's face brings out that emotion in the audience's emotions. This scenario is repeated if the play calls for a face that portrays comedy.

In the real world there are masks used for different occasions that depends on the event. There are masks used by people for bank robbery, terrorist attacks, and Halloween. But the mask that is used by people for protection is the most important. This particular mask has the potential to save many lives if applied. So why in the name of God didn't our leaders inform the public to obtain the simplest thing to avert someone's death? Why did it take three months for the leaders to inform the public to put on a mask for protection after 36,000 people already died and thousand more infected?

From the beginning of the COVID-19 crisis, our leaders placed a stigma on the mask if someone wore it. They said if someone wears a mask then that person must have the virus. It's supposed to be worn to prevent someone from spreading the virus. Why was there so much double talk by our leaders and scientist? They never said how important the mask is if worn to prevent the infection. Why did the leaders and scientist tried to discourage people from wearing the mask early in the pandemic? That stigma about the mask still is in effect at this writing. From the beginning our leaders and Health officials gave a one sided view point concerning the wearing of mask. Even the media continued to pressed the point that you should wear the mask to prevent you from spreading the virus. But never said the mask would prevent you from getting the virus. By promoting the mask that way caused thousands of death to innocent people. They would never tell people that if you wear the mask it will prevent you from getting the virus. The most important fact is to save oneself isn't it?

Many people are reluctant to wear the mask because our leaders and health officials are sending subliminal messages. They were never seen with a mask on their faces until three months past. The leader of the free world refused to wear a mask in public except for a few occasion after six months. The Pied Piper effect is being implemented by our leaders. Their message to the public was for them to do as they do.

When the news media ask a bystander why he wasn't wearing a mask, he said the reason why he is not wearing a mask is because our leader of the free world is not wearing one.

The media ask the leaders "should people begin to wear mask?" The answer from the top health official was a disgrace. He said on CBS news when asked, "that's a great question." With all his knowledge from colleges and being paid top salary he could not determine that wearing a simple thing as a mask would save lives. Unless he was influenced by his superiors not to support the wearing of mask. He could not say that everyone should wear a mask to protect themselves from the virus. Who are these people? They knew about the Spanish flu of 1917. They knew that a mask played an important role of prevention during that time. They always said that the hospitals need the mask more than the public. I disagree. A great leader would have said that the hospital and the public should get mask immediately. They're excuse was a shortage of mask and equipment. Why couldn't this government order the making of N95 for the first responders and the public? That excuse was insane unless there was another motive. I got mask from overseas as early as the month of February 2020. Even a governor got mask and equipment from South Korea. As soon as the CDC said that everyone should wear something to cover their mouth and nose American creativity went into motion.

For the first two months of the pandemic, thousands of people got infected from the virus while the leaders and health officials remained silent about wearing a simple thing as a mask. Why? The leader of the free world even suggested that people infected with the virus should take disinfectant over wearing a mask for protection and treatment. The chief of police in a major city said after loosing many citizens plus fellow officers to the deadly virus if his department dawn mask they would have saved many lives.

Finally, after three months had past and after growing pressure from the public, the CDC and our leaders agreed to inform the public to wear masks made of cloth after 10,000 people died while the body count continued to mount. At this writing there have been 200,000 souls lost and over 6 million infected from the deadly virus. During the same time span of the corona virus in America, South Korea total of death was 269, Japan total of death was 800, and Hong Kong only 4. After 6 months of the pandemic Taiwan with a population of 23 million people have only 400 cases and only 7 deaths. The difference was their government leaders made wearing the MASK MANDATORY AT THE BEGINNING OF THE PANDEMIC.

Why did it take until June 28, 2020 five months later from the start of the pandemic for the top scientist and health leaders to finally report that if you wear a mask it would save you from getting infected from COVID-19? The prominent Health leader said after further study they realize that wearing the mask is an effective tool to combat COVID-19 after 125,000 death and 3.5 million people infected here in the USA. It took 5 months of a deadly pandemic for top health officials and government leaders to figure out that a simple thing as wearing a mask save lives.

As I watched the faces of the top scientist and the government leaders give their updates and plan of attack their smiles turned into the mask of comedy and tragedy. Something sinister was on their faces and only God could see their true story. This poem by Paul Laurence Dunbar sums up this great tragedy:

We Wear the Mask

"We wear the mask that grins and lies,
It hides our cheeks and shades our eyes,
This debt we pay to human guile;
With torn and bleeding hearts we smile,
And mouth with myriad subtleties.

Why should the world be over-wise,
In counting all our tears and sighs?
Nay, let them only see us, while
We wear the Mask.

We smile, but, O great Christ, our cries
To thee from tortured souls arise.
We sing, but oh the clay is vile
Beneath our feet, and long the mile;
But let the world dream otherwise.
We wear the Mask."

Why would a top government official visit a major hospital in the fight to save lives from the corona virus did not wear a mask while top doctors and nurses wore theirs? The hospital has a mandatory policy that all who enter its facility must wear a mask to cover mouth and nose. The government leader went there to see recovering patients from the deadly virus. Why is wearing a mask taboo to some government officials and they seem to have no fear of the virus. If you needed to get food out of a hot oven, the first thing you would do is put on gloves to protect your hands. The government leaders did not feel the need to put on a mask because they already knew that COVID-19 would not effect them.

Top government officials seem to be invincible to the virus. Why? Did they take a secret vaccine that make them immune from COVID-19 and will introduce it to the public in October 2020 just before the elections confirming Nostradamus prediction of a 9 month plague? These questions only heighten suspicion about what they are hiding. They seem to know early on during the pandemic that the virus cannot harm them because they know where it came from and they have certain immunity. Is the corona virus genetically engineered to identify certain DNA? Some government officials do not wear a mask to protect themselves from the virus but if we look closely we see their true mask in their faces.

A political journalist by the name of Michael Gerson says that political hypocrisy is "the conscious use of a 'MASK' to fool the public and gain political benefit." He's not talking about a physical mask but a mask of deception written all over their faces. It is interesting to note, a kitten was born in the midst of this horrific pandemic with two faces. Not two heads with separate faces but one head with two faces. This undoubtedly tells us that smiling faces tell lies. Which face do we trust? Is it the mask of comedy or tragedy?

The physical Mask has become a political weapon by our leaders and is being used to send a SECRET coded message to their constituents that it's okay to not wear a mask in the hopes that other segments of society want wear a mask too in which would result in their desired outcome. The power of suggestion when used can be a powerful tool to convey a desired message. Subliminal messaging is being used by our leader of the free world by using a loaded word that meant to target a certain race that identifies their past. The leader of the free world liken the wearing of a mask to "SLAVERY, CULTURE OF SILENCE, OR SOCIAL DEATH." Which means if you wear the mask you are a SLAVE and is going to die. Does this coded message imply a deliberate scheme to entice black people to not wear the mask so they would easily get infected, which would result in multiple deaths? The message is also directed at white people that it's okay to not wear the mask because most of them would only get sick and recover or for some the virus wouldn't effect them at all.

The more people they see not wearing a mask lessens the value of a mask so that people of color would get infected by the virus which would seal their doom. Everyone knows that the leader of the free world leads by example. So when people see him not wearing a mask they perceive that it is a coded message for them that not wearing a mask is safe and to act like they are warriors because we are at war. No wonder why many people Black and White believe that COVID-19 is a hoax.

Is there a secret coded message floating around that White people know about and Black and Hispanic people did not get the memo? My wife told me a suspicious story on her job that involve her supervisor who is Black had his mask on and was asked by a fellow employee who is white why was he wearing a mask as if to say look at me, I am not wearing a mask because the air is fine. The fellow employee was trying to convince the Black supervisor to not wear a mask so that he would be more vulnerable to the virus.

Even constituents of the leader of the free world is demonizing the wearing of mask. It has been reported that they are sending out coded messages that if you wear a mask you would die and that the wearing of mask is the work of the devil or if you wear the mask you are a democrat and if you don't you are a republican. There is a method to this madness. Is this a true statement? Most democrats are black and most republicans are white. Which American is this coded message targeting? If you are republican and white and is against wearing a mask you are safe from harm? This is all intended for black and brown people to discount wearing the mask in the hopes of them having a high body count. Although COVID-19 has killed white people as well as blacks, the number of death of Black and Hispanic outnumber white people disproportionately.

Why is the leader of the free world promoting a black doctor who says wearing a mask is useless while promoting an unproven drug that the scientific community is against its use. The doctor also said her scientific team have a vaccine made from ALIEN DNA and if you ingest this vaccine it will make you disbelieve religions. As bizarre as this may seem the media reported that top government officials met with this scientific team. It is not so much of importance the message the doctor gave, but what was more important was the black doctor who gave the message surrounded by an all white team of doctors. It was more of an optic for black people being told that wearing a mask is useless and the drug hydroxychloroquine is safe. This TRAGEDY would sound more convincing coming from a black doctor being televised all over the world. Black people were the target of this subliminal messaging.

From the beginning of the deadly pandemic government leaders were concern about the optic of wearing a mask so they were against informing the public to wear a mask for protection. According to CNN sources from the government said it was not a "good look" for government leaders to wear masks. Some of the reasons claimed by government officials is that they did not want to panic people. Tell me which is the lesser of the two evils? To panic me or to die from some deadly virus?

Other countries that were infected by COVID-19 made it mandatory that all citizens wear masks for protection. As early as February, 2020 Asian people contacted relatives here in America and ask why they weren't wearing masks.

If anyone look at the photos of the pandemic of 1918 you will see everyone wearing a white cloth over their mouth and nose for protection. It does not take a rocket scientist to see from that photo that wearing a mask saves lives.

The optic by government leaders to not embrace the wearing of mask has a profound effect on it's citizens. After 8 months into this deadly disease wearing a mask for protection is still a hot issue. This position by government leaders is a deliberate act to lessen the importance of wearing a mask. We can only conclude one sinister reason.

Some representatives of certain states are going as far as suing local governments for enforcing the wearing of mask by making it mandatory. It is interesting to note which political party is against wearing mask to the point of demonizing it. Why is some people in the republican party against wearing mask? Why is anyone against the wearing of mask if it save lives? Unless there is a secret agenda that involves the extermination of certain ethnic groups.

A black man who lost five members of his family from COVID-19 was distraught after hearing doctors in a meeting with government officials in his state walked out of the meeting because they refuse to make wearing a mask MANDATORY. The doctors realized that the best weapon to fight against the COVID-19 pandemic is a simple thing as wearing a mask so they pleaded with government officials to make it MANDATORY in which they refused. The hospital where the black man family members died had 90 percent of black patients all suffering from COVID-19. He said, "if those people wore a simple thing as a mask they would not be sick with that awful disease." Why has wearing a mask or not has become a hot issue especially as the death toll rises to 200,000 and counting with a total of over 7 million infected at this writing here in America.

The United States Postal Service was planning to send 650 million mask to the public in April to help combat COVID-19 but the leader of the free world stopped it in fear that it would cause panic. This blunder allowed thousands of people to die even though they knew that this deadly virus was airborne as early as January the beginning stages of the virus. The masks was designated to be sent to the states with the highest effected area that included people of color.

It is the mix-messaging and the subliminal messaging by the leader of the free world that has caused the most gravest health crisis since the pandemic of 1918. There seems to be a profound motive by government leaders to discredit the only weapon (the mask) from being worn by it's fellow citizens. The leaders of the free world has been criticized by public health experts according to ABC news, "Trump has been criticized by public health experts for failing to aggressively promote the widespread use of masks across the country to help stop the spread of the novel coronavirus." The leader of the free world has only been seen once or twice in public wearing the mask since the outbreak of the virus and continue to discredit the wearing of mask.

The head of the Center for Disease Control and Prevention (CDC) director Robert Redfield testified in front of Congress said that the wearing of mask is the best defense against contracting COVID-19. He even went further and said, "that the mask can give better protection than a vaccine" in preventing the deadly disease. The leader of the free world told reporters, Redfield "made a mistake."

Can you imagine how many souls could have been saved if these words were spoken at the beginning of the deadly pandemic? That the wearing of mask is the best defense. The leader of the free world did not say those words. The head of the CDC did not say those words until eight months later. The top health officials did not say those words. Only God alerted those of us who are still here to put on mask as early as January the beginning of this deadly pandemic. This tragedy falls on the leader of the free world.

Dr. Leana Wen, a public health professor at George Washington University and former health commissioner of Baltimore, told ABC News, "Our entire response has been hampered by mixed messaging. At this point, it's way beyond mixed messaging, we're talking about an absolutely disruptive message that goes against public health."

Wearing the mask has allowed some resemblance of normalcy. It has allowed people to go to work or to the grocery store without fear of contracting the deadly disease. While there is no vaccine at this writing to combat the pandemic, wearing a simple thing as a mask has become the next best thing to prevent the spread of the virus.

If the mask was dawned early on in the pandemic along with quarantining, we would have less people getting infected and less people needing hospitalization. It would not be such a burden on the first responders if wearing the mask was made mandatory by our leaders and most people could have continued working in which would have minimal effect on the economy. City officials had no problem making wearing a seat belt mandatory in order to save lives but a simple thing as wearing a mask has become political. Why did the leader of the free world mock anyone who wears the mask? Something smells and it's not in the fish markets or the wet shops in China.

A Modern Day Search to Kill Jesus A Second Time

What if Satan knew the day when Jesus Christ returns to this earth? He must be shaking in his boots because he knows he has a short time left. What if he tried to kill Jesus by using the COVID-19 virus as a weapon? There is a duality principle at work when you see biblical history repeats itself. Take for example the two most powerful stories in the bible. The stories of Jesus Christ and Moses are similar. Kings during the time of their infancy decreed to kill children in hoping to eliminate them from the earth.

When the Wise Men went to look for the infant Jesus in Jerusalem they encountered King Herod the Great who became paranoid at the news of a coming "King of the Jews." So he decreed to kill children age 2 and below. Matthew 2:13-16 "And when they were departed, behold, the angel of the Lord appeareth to Joseph in a dream, saying, Arise, and take the young child and his mother, and flee into Egypt, and be thou there until I bring thee word: for Herod will seek the young child to destroy him. When he arose, he took the young child and his mother by night, and departed into Egypt: and was there until the death of Herod: that it might be fulfilled which was spoken of the Lord by the prophet, saying, Out of Egypt have I called my son. Then Herod, when he saw that he was mocked of the wise men, was exceeding wroth, and sent forth, and slew all the children that were in Bethlehem, and in all the coasts thereof, from two years old and under, according to the time which he had diligently inquired of the wise men."

Moses was born during the time when his people, the Israelites were slaves and was increasing in population in which Pharaoh feared that they may ally with his enemies. The mother of Moses a Hebrew whose name was Jochebed hid the baby Moses when the Pharaoh ordered that all newborn Hebrew boys to be killed to reduce the population. The story of Moses can be found in the Book of Exodus.

Today we have a leader who has become paranoid because a certain ethnic group will be the majority population in the near future and takes on a mission to bar them from entering the country and has made it known to the world that he only wants people of his race to come but people of different ethnicity should stay out. What if he has developed a secret mission to decrease the population of people of color by using the corona virus as a weapon? What if there is a coordinated effort by some world leaders? Let me remind the reader that this scenario is only conjecture.

Before you holler "that's insane," just take a good look at the numbers of people of color killed by the pandemic. Remember that God works in the principle of duality. The Pharaoh during Moses time decided to decrease the slave population by killing newborn boys. This COVID-19 virus seems to be targeting male more than female. It is also a fact that the virus is attacking minorities in a greater number than whites. The governor of New York did a survey by zip code of minorities and found that 65 percent of the corona virus cases come from those areas inhabited by people of color. Why? Where there is a high concentration of people of color affected city officials give the same reason in each state or county. Reasons like they are essential employees on the front line, they can't work from home so they must leave home or their medical history is riddled with diseases that make them become more of a target. All of these reasons maybe true but there must be another scenario why people of color are taking a direct hit from the virus. Could it be something about their genetic and biological makeup?

Due to the war in Syria we have seen immigration on the rise. Even in America immigrants come with their caravans trying to escape the hard life of oppression by militants. We've witness the horror of men, women and children drown in the oceans trying to escape from harm seeking a better way of life in countries of another race and often turn back because of the color of their skin. We've seen children placed in facilities that look like cages.

The plight of immigration has caused countries to convert back to their tribal nature to prevent escaping immigrants from entering their land. With nationalism and populism on the rise across Europe, it has caused fear and prejudice to take root. In

America our leader has called refugees and immigrants invaders instead of people just trying to find a better way of life. They are seen as parasites instead of fellow human beings seeking to live in peace. Our leader has built a wall that stretches for many miles just to keep out asylum seekers.

Black folks here in America and people of color must never forget the Tuskegee experiment that infected more than 600 black men with the deadly disease called syphilis. The experiment began in 1932 and lasted for 40 years without the participant realizing that they were being studied without their consent.

Those who perpetrated The Tuskegee experiment thought that what they did would not come to light but they did not factor in God's power of revealing secrets. Luke 12:2-3 describes how the hypocrisy of Pharaoh came to light, "For there is nothing covered, that shall not be revealed; neither hid, that shall not be known. Therefore, whatsoever ye have spoken in the darkness shall be heard in the light; and that which ye have spoken in the ear in closets shall be proclaimed upon the housetops."

America was built on principles and rules but when those in power utilizes that power to engage in shams, or schemes to deceive others reveals hypocrisy at its highest level. Those in power did not take in account the all knowing God who balances the scales of justice. Luke 8:17 "For nothing is secret, that shall not be made manifest; neither anything hid, that shall not be known and come abroad." Those in power during the Tuskegee experiment had to confess what they did to an assembly of their peers who stood for justice and awarded those people who suffered reparation for the atrocities committed against them. God's hand was at work. It is revealed in this scripture, Proverbs 26:26 "Whose hatred is covered by deceit, his wickedness shall be showed before the whole congregation."

What if the COVID-19 virus was created in a lab and was dispensed throughout the world to decrease the population of the elderly and people of color. This scenario was first reported by prominent government officials from two countries who blamed each other. At this writing there are many people from different countries who share the same view. With those sentiments in mind let us explore this mind boggling theory by looking at past history of governments using biological warfare.

Let us establish first the fact that viruses was used in the past history of the world by governments who had the will and means. In June 1763 during the siege of Fort Pitt, the British Army used smallpox against Native Americans that left more that one hundred natives dead in Ohio County from 1763 to 1764. In 1789 the British Marines unleashed smallpox on the Aboriginal people in New South Wales, Australia. Dr Seth Carus who is a distinguished Research Fellow, Center for the Study of WMD, National Defense University, Ft McNair, Washington states, "Ultimately, we have a strong circumstantial case supporting the theory that someone deliberately introduced small pox in the Aboriginal population."

During WWI in 1914 thru 1918 the Spanish Flu plagued soldiers even before and after they were placed into battle causing hundreds of death. This happened during the advent of germ warfare and bacteriology was introduced to the world by the Imperial German government. With the development of anthrax and other bio-agents added to the many ways to kill man in a war these lethal weapons created an explosion of sophisticated techniques for use.

By the time WWII began Biological Warfare Program grew in fruition by the Ministry of Supply in the United Kingdom. They effectively weaponized anthrax, botulism toxin, and brucellois and a variety of deadly pathogens. The United States joined with it's British ally and establish a large research program at Fort Detrick, Maryland in 1942. Many facilities spread across the country producing mass production of anthrax spores, brucellosis, and botulism toxins. By 1950 The United States Army Biological Warfare Laboratories enhanced the deadly pathogens called Q-fever, tularemia, anthrax and brucellosis.

Biological weapons are so effective that they could be used on a nation and incubate for a week before the host country can make an effective investigation of where it came from. A technique called Clustered, Regularly Interspaced, Short

Palindromic Repeat (CRISPR-Cas9) is used by taking a DNA SEQUENCE AND CUT IT OFF AND REPLACE IT WITH A NEW SEQUENCE OR CODES for a particular protein or characteristic which shows up in the desired organism. This Biological weapons program can easily be used for genome editing technology in which DNA is inserted, deleted, modified or replaced in the genome of a living organism targeting the insertions to site specific locations.

Could this break through in Biological engineering used in creating COVID 19? Scientist has called this deadly disease the "SMART" virus that can find our blind spots, it can find people with preexisting conditions, it can locate where there is a high possibility of transmission, and most importantly, it could identify your DNA, your genetic makeup, and your race. Synthetic biology is a new technology that is engineered to chemically synthesize DNA to create organisms with novel or enhanced traits, and characteristics.

COVID-19 can even determine what blood type a person is due to their genes makeup. According to the New England Journal of Medicine our genes and blood type can determine whether we get the more severe case of the virus or mild symptoms or no symptoms at all. This journal states, "The two stretches of DNA implicates as harboring risks of severe COVID-19 are known to carry some intriguing genes, including one that determines blood type and others that play various roles in the immune system. In fact, the findings suggest that people with blood type A face a 50 percent greater risk of needing oxygen support or a ventilator should they become infected with the novel corona virus. In contrast, people with blood type O appear to have about a 50 percent reduced risk of severe COVID-19." We've always heard of designer drugs that was created in a lab to target certain people. What if that technology has evolved into a DESIGNER VIRUS CALLED COVID-19?

Some scientist and government officials claim that the COVID 19 virus began when a bat and human came into contact in China's sweat shops. They describe a scenario identical to the way it is described in a movie called "Contagion" where a bat droplet came into contact with other exotic animals and was ingested by humans. This explanation may satisfy some people but looking at the past history of certain governments use of biological warfare gives one the inclination to investigate further.

If COVID-19 virus was created in a lab then what was the method of delivery throughout the world? Entomological warfare is a type of biological warfare that uses insects, bees, wasps, bats and others on an adversary. "The concept has existed for centuries and research and development have continued into the modern era. Entomological warfare has been used in battle by Japan and several other nations have developed and been accused of using an EW program. Entomological warfare may employ insects in a direct attack or as vectors to deliver a biological agent, such as PLAGUE. One type of Entomological warfare involves infecting insects with a pathogen and then dispersing the insects over target areas."

The description of Entomological warfare could be the method COVID-19 was delivered throughout the world. Although the method of delivery is primitive to today's method. Scientist do not need to deliver infected bats to a certain country to bring harm. They can use the DNA of a bat and a well known virus and created a monster. "Most of the biosecurity concerns in synthetic biology, however, are focused on the role DNA synthesis and the risk of producing genetic material of lethal VIRUSES like the 1918 Spanish flu, or polio in a lab." Even COVID 19 could be a suspect with the use of gene editing by the CRISPR/CAS system. This technology has proven to be the most effective way of creating a smart virus that can be delivered throughout the world in weeks and was hailed by the Washington Post as "the most important innovation in the synthetic biology space in nearly 30 years."

How did COVID-19 spread throughout the world so quickly? In comparison to other viruses like SARS, COVID-19 spread across the world with phenomenal speed infecting people in countries across oceans. Let's compare the outbreak of SARS versus COVID-19 and see how the deadly disease infected and killed more people in the same time as it's predecessor. In

2002-2003 for a total of 6 months SARS spread across 29 countries and infected 8,000 and killed over 774 people. COVID-19 began around January 11, 2020 and spread its deadly virus to 125 countries in the same amount of time as SARS (6 months), infecting over 6 million and killing 373,000 people and has now reached hundreds of millions of cases and nearly 7 million deaths at the time of this writing.

COVID-19 virus has eight or more strains that are circling the globe. The strain in China is different from the strain in Europe. Once the virus got to Europe it quickly spread all over moving across the globe with phenomena speed. The strain of COVID-19 in America derived from Europe which devastated the east coast infecting people with a faster pace compared to other pathogens.

Did COVID-19 spread from human to human initially at it's birth or is there another method of delivery? Most scientist agree that COVID-19 spread from person to person but that does now rule out the possibility that it's roots began in a test tube and was administered to the population via airborne. Today's advancement in technology look like something out of a science fiction magazine. We see drones delivering packages to waiting customers everyday. They streak through the sky like birds of a feather that stick together. They have put the gleam in the eyes of many kids and adults when they see their toy rise from the ground to the air in seconds. Some drones has enhanced military arsenal that can reach targets thousands of miles away with pen point accuracy. Was the drone used to deliver COVID 19-virus for targets designated around the world?

Have you ever notice airplanes in the sky that leave a trailing cloud close behind. The cloud remain long after the airplane left the area. I've often wondered why the cloud is necessary in some airplanes and others has no trail of cloud. I remember watching countries who was hit with the corona-virus began spraying the streets and buildings and even cars and buses with some kind of chemical as if something fell from the sky and landed everywhere. This scene was not confined to just one country. Many countries had people with mask and suits cleaning everything throughout the city. I remember Nostradamus prophesied that a FALSE DUST would plague the world. Could this FALSE DUST come from a man made cloud of dust made of the corona-virus?

New York city was hit hard with the corona-virus infecting and killing thousands of people. Even the Bronx zoo was not spared from COVID-19 as it killed lions and tigers and other animals. City officials reported that the animals got their infection from the zoo keeper. Can you imagine a zoo keeper getting close enough to a tiger and dropping droplets on or near him? This scenario maybe possible but it just don't add up. It is more likely that the zoo animals contracted the virus from the environment they live in. The natural air they normally breathe was changed because COVID-19 had infiltrated the air and the building, sleeping area, and the natural habitat where they play. Human to human contact was not the initial way of spreading the virus. What happened to the zoo animals is exactly what happened to the human population of New York and all around the world in my opinion. A cloud of invisible dust like a fog landed on New York and diluted the air and covered everything every where and waited for weeks before revealing it's deadly mission.

What is more mind boggling concerning Nostradamus prediction of a man made cloud of dust spreading around the world is the fact that at this writing of the book (26 June, 2020) it has been reported that a gigantic cloud of dust is approaching the U.S. from the continent of Africa that will effect specific states that has seen a heavy dose of COVID-19 infections. This article states, that "research shows airborne DUST can have adverse effects on health, with one of the most important being pulmonary disease. Inhalation of dust particles into the airways can initiate an inflammatory immune response. Dust is most unhealthy for people with pre-existing conditions like COPD, asthma and allergies, but dust as thick as the plume heading towards the U.S. may even be harmful to otherwise healthy people, if exposure lasts too long."

Can this report be the smoking gun? Read this article very carefully and decide for yourself, it states "another complication posed by this imminent DUST CLOUD is it's coincidence with COVID-19. A recent Harvard University study found that increased pollution, specifically particulate matter, like dust, can lead to higher hospital admissions and death rates from COVID-19. Health officials recommend wearing a mask for protection from inhaling the dust."

Upon further investigation of this cloud of dust I learned that part of the same cloud system had already blanket part of the U.S. a few weeks prior hitting some states that had an increase of people getting infected. The article brings this fact to life that COVID-19 virus could be inside this invasion of an enormous dust cloud. It states "cases of COVID-19 have been on the rise in Florida and Texas, which are in the path of the plume. As the dust overspreads the southeast and then Texas, air quality index numbers are expected to be in the unhealthy range." It has also been reported that an enormous dust cloud spread across the globe in November of 2019 and June of the same year. Is this all a coincidence or is this cloud of dust manufactured in a lab like Nostradamus predicted?

The dust cloud drops particles of dust which acts like pollen on trees which became like an aerosol spray and delivered the virus all over the city while the infected air slowly moved from state to state infecting everyone who did not put on a mask for protection unless you have immunity. This is a highly contagious virus in which caused person to person contact weeks after the dust cloud past.

Upon my further investigation scientist has discovered that the COVID-19 virus could be inside particles of air pollution and travel long distances which increase the infection rate of hundreds of people. This factual account by scientist proves that COVID-19 could have been deliberately placed inside dust clouds and launched from a far distant that was designed to hitch a ride with the jet stream.

Well known journalist Bob Woodward who is the author of the book "Rage" interviewed the leader of the free world at the beginning stage of the deadly virus revealed that COVID-19 is AIRBORNE. From audio tape of the interview the leader of the free world said the virus is "dangerous, airborne, contagious and deadly." He went even further when he said that, "you just breathe the air, that's how it's passed."

Why was this truth withheld from the public? At that moment in time COVID-19 was just beginning to take effect here in America. With the knowledge that the virus was AIRBORNE and easily passed to people from just breathing air people would have no problem dawning a mask for protection. But there was no mention of urgency to alert people to wear a mask for protection. Thousands of lives were lost due to this distortion of the truth.

If the leader of the free world and top health officials knew from the beginning of COVID-19 that this virus was airborne and failed to warn the public then they must be hiding something. Our leaders were discouraging people from wearing the mask even with this knowledge. They did not put on a mask to protect themselves until months later even with this knowledge. Even when top government officials visited a major hospital fighting COVID-19 without wearing a mask that knowledge that the virus was airborne did not matter to them because they knew they were genetically protected.

How did indigenous people who live on remote islands who have no contact with the outside world contract COVID-19? The answer is that COVID-19 is AIRBORNE that traveled across the globe infecting millions of people in a short period of time. It took only a few days for the smoke from the fires in California to reach as far as Europe. A dust cloud filled with COVID-19 would have the same effect spreading it's deadly virus across the globe in a matter of days.

There is a number of other possible ways technological advancement could have delivered the COVID-19 virus around the world. Someone used the microwave technology and delivered it on 21 diplomats in a hotel in Cuba that made all of them sick with brain damage. Experts describe patients experiencing painful sounds, some sort of sonic attacks, viral infections and contagious anxiety according to Douglas H. Smith, the study's lead author and director of the Center for Brain Injury and repair at the University of Pennsylvania. People can be in a building miles away and become a victim of a sound wave that vibrates the ear hitting the head. Another possible technique is the laser beam technology that carries particles or viruses long distance to a designated target. The possibilities are enormous by using the Entomological warfare to deliver pathogens to target areas thousands of miles away can be realized.

Let me add that no one knows for certain how COVID-19 spread it's deadly virus across the world with phenomena speed. My theory is just an opinion that many others has expressed and is not satisfied with the scientific community explanation. It is interesting to note that as soon as China and the World Health Organization mapped out the genetic sequence or footprint of COVID-19 and discovered that the genetic code of the virus in China is different from the genetic makeup in Europe and announced their findings, the leader of the free world dropped membership in the World Health Organization.

There are many conspiracy theories floating around the world of how COVID-19 originated. Some say the deadly virus began in a lab in Wuhan China. Some say the virus began in a lab in America and was delivered to the world by the U.S. Army. No one can say for sure but read this article from Jon Cohen on an article entitled "A WHO-led mission may investigate the pandemic's origin," it states, "Another outstanding question is whether Sri"s team or other researchers in Wuhan manipulated bat viruses in "gain-of-function" experiments that can make a virus more transmissible between humans. In 2015, Shri co-authored a paper that made a chimeric SARS virus by combining one from bats with a strain that had been adapted to mice. But that work was done at the University of North Carolina, not in Wuhan, and in collaboration with Ralph Baric."

Black and Brown People Deliberately Targeted by COVID-19?

In America the black and Hispanic community has been hit with COVID-19 the most. Statistic show that blacks carry the burden of having the largest infection rate and the highest number of death in comparison to other ethnic groups. In every major city that black people live they only make up 13 percent of the population but 23 percent of deaths compared to their white counterpart.

Also the Latino and Asian people has a high number of infections and death as well. It is as if the corona virus are seeking this group out and is leaving them devastated. Why is the United States make up only 5 percent of the population in the world and 25 percent of the corona virus cases. Another disturbing fact is that 300 thousand children at this writing of the book are infected with COVID-19. As reported by CNN the children are 46 percent Black, 36 percent Hispanic, and 7 percent White.

Could the same thing be happening across the world where people of color has a high number of COVID-19 infections and death? The answer is shocking of what I found. Here is an excerpt from the National Health service, "England's Black, Asian and Ethnic Minority groups are two to three times more likely to die from COVID-19 compared to the general population."

The statistics revealed that according to the Welcome Open Research showed data revealing, "out of 16,227 patients who died in hospitals in England and tested positive for COVID-19 between March 1 and April 21, 2020. The data revealed that the risk of death is 3.24 times higher for Black Africans, 2.41 times higher for Bangladeshis, 2.21 times higher for Black Caribbeans, and 1.7 times higher for Indians compared to the general population. The ethnic group with the largest total numbers of deaths was Indian."

It is reported that Black people in the United Kingdom are four times more likely to die from COVID-19 than white people and a number of other ethnic groups. According to the Office of National Statistics black women were 4.3 times more likely than white women and black men are 4.2 more likely to die.

In Norway the infection rate among Blacks are the same as other countries. "When health experts began looking into the backgrounds of those infected by corona virus, they made a startling discovery; people born in Somalia have infection rates more than 10 time above the national average." They reside in a small community in Norway but the infection rate among them outnumber the Norwegian people in an alarming rate. The following graph depicts the plight of ethnics groups around the world with Black people taking a greater hit from COVID-19 virus.

The following statistics are from America and England courtesy of the APM Research Lab and the Institute for Fiscal Studies.

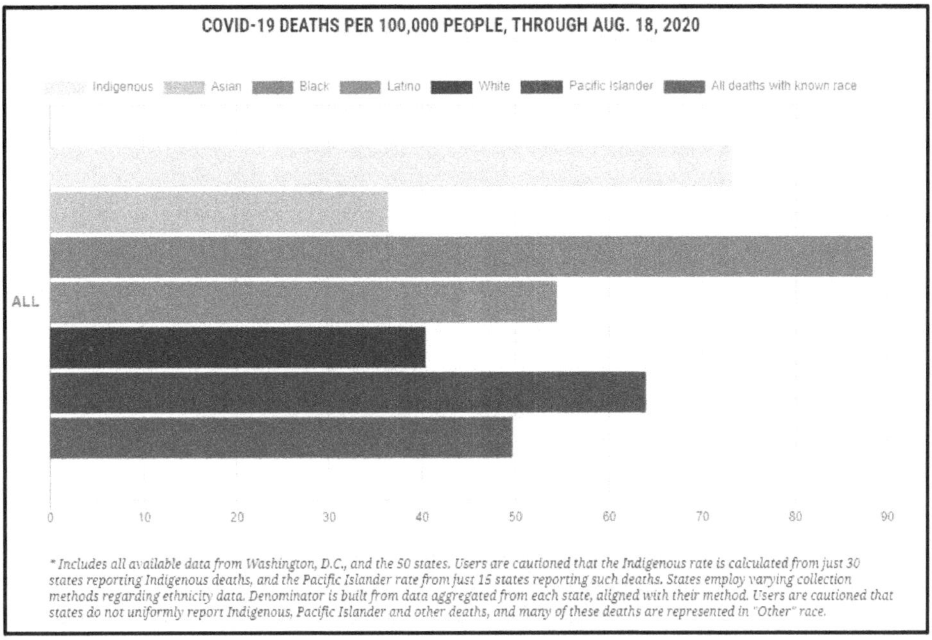
COVID-19 DEATHS PER 100,000 PEOPLE, THROUGH AUG. 18, 2020
Indigenous
Asian
Black
Latino
White
Pacific Islander
All deaths with known race
ALL
0
10
20
30
40
50
60
70
80
90
* Includes all available data from Washington, D.C., and the 50 states. Users are cautioned that the Indigenous rate is calculated from just 30 states reporting Indigenous deaths, and the Pacific Islander rate from just 15 states reporting such deaths. States employ varying collection methods regarding ethnicity data. Denominator is built from data aggregated from each state, aligned with their method. Users are cautioned that states do not uniformly report Indigenous, Pacific Islander and other deaths, and many of these deaths are represented in "Other" race.

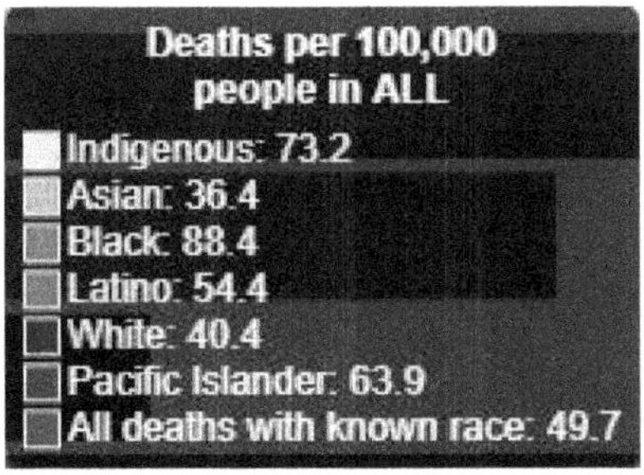
Deaths per 100,000
people in ALL
Indigenous: 73.2
Asian: 36.4
Black: 88.4
Latino: 54.4
White: 40.4
Pacific Islander: 63.9
All deaths with known race: 49.7

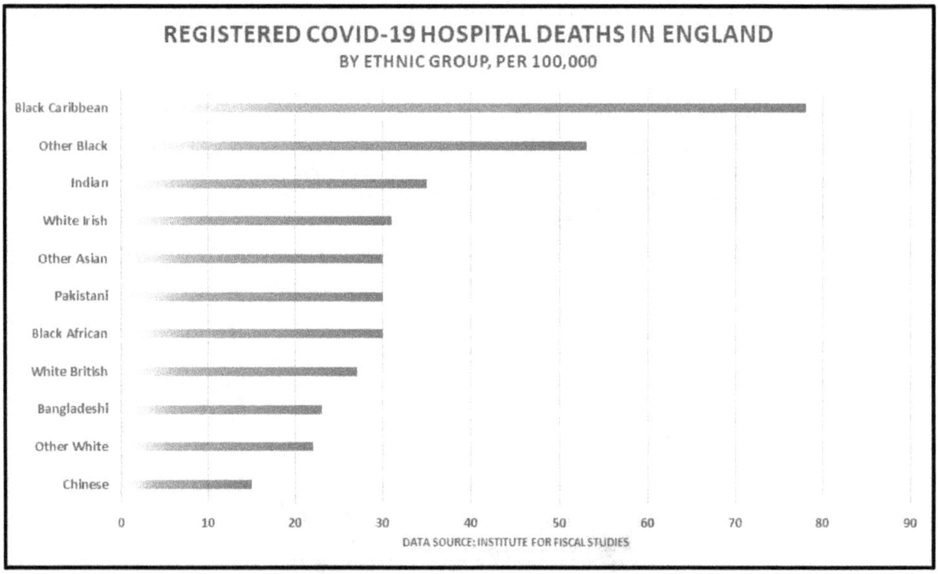
REGISTERED COVID-19 HOSPITAL DEATHS IN ENGLAND
BY ETHNIC GROUP, PER 100,000
Black Caribbean
Other Black
Indian
White Irish
Other Asian
Pakistani
Black African
White British
Bangladeshi
Other White
Chinese
0
10
20
30
40
50
60
70
80
90
DATA SOURCE: INSTITUTE FOR FISCAL STUDIES

How can the same explanation of why Black people are dying from COVID-19 around the world stand as a reasonable answer without investigating further? The following explanation is given in America and the U.K. and other countries that have a high death rate of Black people caused by COVID-19; "The disparities are partly a result of socio-economic disadvantage and other circumstances, but a remaining part of the difference has not yet been explained, the study said even after taking into account age, demographic factors and measures of self-reported health problems, black people were still almost twice as likely to die from COVID-19 than white people."

Our leader of the free world is labeled a war time president. Is the COVID-19 virus the beginning of WWIII? At this writing of the book COVID-19 has caused more casualties and death than the Vietnam war and WWI.

During war the generals plan their method of attack by considering the number of casualties versus the enemy that also include collateral damage. The generals ponder the idea if a thousand of our soldiers may die but we will kill hundreds of thousands of theirs, that will be a good day. Is this scenario being played out in cities around the world with black people and other ethnic groups taking a direct hit from COVID-19?

Whether or not COVID-19 was created in a lab or an act of God it has affected every living soul here on earth. The virus has caused all of us to stop the normal activity of life and realize what's more dear to us is family. The virus has also pushed some of us to seek out the Lord Jesus Christ and has made us think about our world maybe coming to an end. I personally feel that God has given us this moment in time to get ourselves ready for his return to earth. This maybe our last chance to repent of our sins and finding peace in believing in our Lord and Savior Jesus Christ.

We are experiencing a time of sorrow. A period where everyone will be affected directly or indirectly. Everyone will know someone who has been diagnosed with COVID-19 or lost a friend or relative. This is the reason the biblical scriptures call this time period "The Tribulation Period."

The Church's Mission in the Tribulation Period — Stamp out Racism

Does the color of a person's skin play a significant role in biblical history? If racial injustice is prevalent throughout the whole world then you better believe that racism has infiltrated the church as well. Racial discrimination seems to be prevalent even as early as the first bible was created. Why was the book of Enoch not added to the King James version of the bible? It is a historical fact that King James omitted and added scripture to the widely read and most popular book in history.

In the book of Enoch there is a story about a biblical character called Lamech who became the father of Noah. I found this story so fascinating because it describe a direct reference to skin color of a person in biblical history. In the King James version, the story of Lamech was shortened and only told the story of his two wives but in the Book of Enoch the story is told in more detail of how Lamech left his two wives alone while he went on a journey and when he returned found one of his wives pregnant. After the baby was born Lamech watched the little lad grow but then notice that something was different about this little boy. Lamech describe the boy as being white as snow from his hair to his toes. Later in the story Lamech is told by an Angel that this boy was sent by God who became Noah.

There are many multicultural stories throughout the bible. In the past history historians purposely omitted achievements by black people and left a legacy that people of color did not contribute anything to the world. Racism was done in the Church as well when we see pictures of Jesus as white, and pictures of black saints destroyed. Even biblical characters are portrayed as white when there is plenty of evidence that show those people were people of color. For example Moses was married to an Ethiopian woman by the name of Zippora, and other biblical patriarch married people from Africa. Black people has always played an important part of the bible but due to deception that knowledge was kept hidden.

In the book of Genesis a description of the Garden of Eden that identifies the land of Cush, Havilah, and Asshur which is located near the borders of Eastern Sudan, Ethiopia, and Eritrea is further evidence that black people played an important role in biblical chronology. The oldest human remains were found in Ethiopia in 1974 which makes Africa the birthplace of humanity.

The story of King Lalibela did not make it in the bible but it's significant enough to be told for black people to know that they have a rich heritage in the gospel of Jesus Christ waiting to be discovered. In the 12th century King Lalibela fearing that the original Jerusalem would be destroyed gave orders to his followers to build a "New Jerusalem" after Muslim conquest stopped Christian pilgrimages to the holy land. In the heart of Ethiopia eleven churches were carved out of a mountain that can only be appreciated when viewed from the air. The Church is built deep down below the surface of the rock. The intriguing thing about these churches is that they are in the image of a majestic CROSS like the one that was displayed in my backyard on Crossview Ln.

Some legends about this Church made of stone explain how angels from heaven cut and carved the image of the Church out of the rock by night and the Ethiopians build on it by day. The other fascinating thing about the Church of Lalibela is rumors of the elusive Ark of Covenant is hidden under the chambers of the churches. No man from the outside world can enter it's location or view this important relic of biblical history but priest who stand guard there hold this secret with their life.

Why is the Church of Lalibela built deep in side the ground and most churches are built so that it can be seen above the ground? Why is the cross on most churches are standing straight up on top of structures but the Church of Lalibela's cross can only be appreciated when viewing from a position in the air?

Some historians believe that the Church of Lalibela was built under ground to evade Muslim conquerors from finding its location. This theory is most likely true but the reason for the cross meant to be viewed from the air opens up an intriguing possibility. This scenario opens up the possibility of space flight during the 12th century. When worshipers stand on the ground gazing at the church the cross's splendor cannot be appreciated but when seen from the air the majestic cross of Lalibela stand looking up at you. The same effect was realized when viewing the Nazca lines of Peru.

In the Peruvian landscape of the Andes is the ancient city called Nazca. If you are in an airplane looking down at the landscape you will see lines in a geometrically design in a perfect formation that looks identical to our airports landing scripts. When you stand on the ground in front of these lines you cannot see the order and how they are parallel to each other that runs for 37 miles long and 1 mile wide and is surrounded by trapezoidal landscaping. There are gigantic drawings of animals on the face of mountains that can only be viewed in it's glory from high up in the air. Were these drawings made by the ancient Peruvians identifying marks for in coming space craft?

The tools that the Ethiopians used to build the church of Lalibela out of a portion of a mountain was not primitive. A hammer and chisel could not build a structure with precision that rivals builders of our day. Evidently the Ethiopians had help from the angels who came from the sky and left them a message for all humanity.

There are many black people of today who do not know this historical site exist. It is very important to reveal this knowledge so they could pursue a christian life without fear that Jesus is only for white people.

The fate of the world is moving back to the place where it all began. Racial tension is on the rise along with a thirst for separatism and division lead by forces and principalities in high places. This strife originated in the Garden of Eden in Africa where the children of Adam rebelled against the children of the fallen angels who would rather die than to give up earth to God's pride and joy, the first man called Adam, a black man.

Although my view is a fresh way of looking back at the biblical story in Genesis, it promotes the archaeological proof that the black man was the first human in Africa which supports the theory that Adam's race is black. With continued growing tension between the races this strife fast forward the world back to Africa where the people and the country itself is in a spiritual war with dark and evil forces that is bringing the world to a climatic battle the bible calls Armageddon.

The story of the Church of Lalibela must be told in order to get the true meaning of Christianity and how it's beneficial to man. Christianity must embrace all races of people and let them tell their part of the story so that the record and history can be found to be true for future generations. The black man does have an important role to play and the Church of Lalibela proclaim this truth.

The Church of Lalibela,
Located in the heart of Ethiopia,
The New Jerusalem

The Christian church must remain the moral and ethical guide posts so that the world will stay focus on what is pleasing to the eyes of God. It must not stand silent any longer while a bible waiving demagogue in the image of Hitler display his dividing tactic a few feet from Saint John Episcopal Church. He turned holy ground into a battle ground where innocent protesters were gathered to display their discussed with racial injustice.

The murdering of George Floyd by the police reminded me of the Roman soldiers torturing Jesus. The policeman who put his knee on the neck of Mr. Floyd seemed to be getting pleasure from the ordeal. The Roman soldiers put a crown of thorn on Jesus forehead that drew blood from the sharp edges while they laughed and joked. While Jesus lay dying on the cross he called out to his father. In contrast Mr. Floyd called out to his mother in which all mothers felt his pain. People all over the world was able to see the connection between how Jesus Christ died and how George Floyd died that left all of us wondering what kind of animal would show no mercy.

A few pastors spoke out against racial injustice after peaceful protesters marched in Lafayette Park in Washington DC. But the church remained silent while the leaders distort the truth. Either the church become a champion for justice and march along side by side with protesters or continue to be silent and become irrelevant in today's world.

My message to all christian churches around the world who remain silent when racial injustice is being perpetrated by the establishment; when Jesus comes he will be an Alien. When Jesus comes he will look like an immigrant or refugee. When Jesus comes he maybe a person of color. It is better to stand up for great causes and be a drum major for justice like Martin Luther King Jr. preached or sit silently and allow a divider mold the church in his image.

United States Space Force In the Tribulation Period

The Antichrist and his armies will annihilate millions in the coming battle in WWIII. Dead bodies will be stacked high among themselves. Blood will flow like a river. Nations will be left desolate by the destructive power of a nuclear explosion. Then suddenly the war will end. It will not end because one of the warring parties surrendered, but the war will end because their eyes will be focus on the sky. Nations who are in involved in the war will stop fighting each other and form an alliance with the Antichrist to make war with an invasion of gigantic space ships descending from the skies. These space ships will descend on the fields of Armageddon. For that day will be the day of our Lord and Savior Jesus Christ.

The warring nations will be convinced by the Antichrist to stop fighting and form an alliance with each other to fight the forces of Jesus because they will see the returning Christ as aliens from another world and is arriving to conquer the people of earth.

Was the United States Space Force created to fight against an invasion of extraterrestrial? The Space Force was signed into law December 20th, 2019 as part of the 2020 National Defense Authorization Act. The creation of a military force in space was visualized years ago by President Ronald Reagan when he introduced Star Wars space plan.

While former President Reagan was in office, he made a startling revelation concerning an invasion of UFO's from another universe. He asked this revealing question, "What if our world was invaded by extraterrestrials would we be able to defend ourselves"? The Washington Post at that time in history stated that the president opened up a can of worms when he made that statement.

Did former President Reagan unwittingly predict the end time scenario when he stated, "God has a plan for everything. In our obsession with antagonisms of the moment, we often forget how much unites all the members of humanity. Perhaps we need some outside universal threat to make us recognize this common bond. I occasionally think how quickly our differences worldwide would vanish if we were facing an ALIEN threat from outside this world. What could be more alien to universal aspirations of our peoples than war and the threat of war?" President Reagan made this statement on September 21st, 1987, at the United Nations General Assembly. Were our government preparing for an invasion of extraterrestrial from another world?

To our world leaders when Jesus Christ and his Armies return to earth it will look to be an invasion of alien beings from another planet. Matter of fact, that scenario has already been established in the negotiations between former President Ronald Reagan and Mikhail Gorbachev who I pointed out as the "man of sin." At a Survival of Humanity meeting on February 16, 1987, at a conference at Grand Kremlin Palace in Moscow, Gorbachev said, "At our meeting in Geneva, the U.S. President said that if the earth faced an invasion by extraterrestrials, the United States and the Soviet Union now known as Russia would join forces to repel such an invasion."

Now we have a military force designed specifically for repelling an invasion of alien beings from another world. The 2019 Space policy Directive-4 states, "The Department of Defense shall take actions under existing authority to marshal its space resources to deter and counter threats in space, and to develop a legislative proposal to establish a United States Space Force as a sixth branch of the United Armed Forces within the Department of the Air Force. This is an important step toward a future military department for space."

CHAPTER 5

THE CHURCH

On any bridal wedding day, you will find a jubilant woman dressed in her beautiful white dress complimenting the building that she is standing in. This particular building becomes an exceptional place to be on this special day due to the event that holds the imagination, hopes, and dreams for all in attendance at this grand occasion.

From her stunning white dress to the groom's million dollar smile, the building is brought to life just like Christ designed it to be over 2000 years ago.

Jesus Christ founded this building called the Church. The Church is the body of Christ that has every human being's fate wrapped in its destiny. In the New Testament, the word Church is spoken by Christ when he says to Simon Peter, "I will build my Church," Matthew 16:18.

Christ is returning to earth for his bride, the Christian Church. I began this chapter with a visualization of a bride at her wedding wearing a sparkling white dress symbolizing her purity, pageantry, and the majestic building she is standing in.

The Christian Church must become like the bride and purify itself from the corruption and many unclean events that have shattered the credibility and integrity of the Church. Before Christ returns for His bride, the Christian Church must cleanse itself. I do not mean that we should literally clean a building. The cleansing must begin in the hearts and soul of the congregation including priest, bishops and ministers. Do we as Christians want Christ to return and find the church in the state that it is in today?

How do people view the Church after being rocked by scandal? Church scandals threaten to destroy the image and credibility of the Church. If we destroy the Church, we kill Christ. That is why the Church is killing Christ a second time.

How to Restore the Integrity of the Church

We must first establish and acknowledge that there is a problem in the Church that needs to be fixed. In order for the Church to become the vital instrument Jesus Christ intended it to be, we must begin by cleaning God's house of corruption, child sex abuse, blatant disregard of scriptures, changing scriptures to satisfy a certain understanding, and silence when the world needs guidance.

In this chapter, I will point out to you some scriptures that the Church leaders have ignored. Are the Church leaders afraid of being wrong when the Holy Scriptures teach us to step out on faith? Did God intend for priests to practice and maintain celibacy throughout one's life? Is homosexuality accepted by God?

If you didn't know, God hates homosexuality. He destroyed Saddam and Gomorrah for doing this unnatural act. Romans 1:26-27, "For this cause God gave them up unto vile affections: for even their women did change the natural use into that which is against nature: And likewise also the men, leaving the natural use of the woman, burned in their lust one toward another; men with men working that which is unseemly, and receiving in themselves that recompense of their error which was meet."

Today, many church leaders are grappling with the decision whether to let homosexuals attend church service and even perform marriage ceremonies that involve men marrying men and women marrying women.

The acceptance of gay marriage is being promoted by secular beliefs all over the world. Many church leaders have succumbed to the movement that changes the nature of God's image. Romans 1:25, "Who changed the truth of God into a lie, and worshiped and served the creature more than the Creator."

Bishops from the Methodist Church has decided to divide its congregation into two different denominations creating two distinct Churches under the name of Methodist. One denomination will be for those who want to marry homosexuals and become gay ministers and the other church will be for the congregation who follow God's laws.

Homosexuality in the eyes of God is not accepted. The biblical scriptures tells us that those who partake in it will be dealt with in a harshly manner. When the day of our Lord and savior Jesus Christ return to our world, it will be like during the time of Moses when Pharaoh harden his heart which brought the wrath of God upon him. Luke 17:34-36. "I tell you, in that night there shall be two men in one bed; the one shall be taken, and the other shall be left." "Two women shall be grinding together; the one shall be taken, and the other left."

Ministers, pastors, and religious leaders, hold firm your conviction. Do not waver or bend your teachings for the trickery of Satan. You must remember this is Satan's world that dwells in uncleanliness.

Although we see these unnatural things occurring every day, we cannot judge them. Let God be their judge. Romans 2:1, "Therefore thou art inexcusable, O man, whosoever thou art that judgest: for wherein thou judgest another, thou condemnest thyself; for thou that judgest doest the same things."

We as Christians cannot condemn them. We can only pray for them. We must come to realize that God created them too for His purpose and plan so that Christians will know what sin looks like.

We must remember the Godhead, the true holy trinity made up of a man, woman, and child. Therefore, gay marriage cannot be recognized by the Church as a Christian union. It must be condemned at every pulpit. Church leaders cannot straddle the fence and say they believe in the word of God then condone gay marriage. They must uphold the integrity and credibility of the Church and God's laws.

Celibacy and Confessions

The practice of celibacy by priests promotes homosexuality and bad sexual behavior. The Church is riddled with horror stories of child sex abuse and nuns having abortion to hide their sexual needs. There is no law by God that decree such a thing as celibacy.

There are many atrocities that were perpetrated in the past by the Christian Church that painted a picture of unlawfulness by the religious leaders. Therefore, the Church itself must confess and ask for forgiveness. The Church must tear down its walls and rebuild again.

The True Name of the Church

In order for the Christian Church to begin restoring its credibility in the world, it must become holy again. The Church must start anew by unifying all branches and denominations under one tree. We must call this tree of life the CHURCH OF GOD as it was named by Jesus Christ from the beginning as outlined in the Holy Scriptures.

That means all Christian churches must change their name. Churches like Catholic, Jehovah's Witness, Protestant, Presbyterian, Lutheran, Methodist, and Baptist, all must be renamed The CHURCH OF GOD. The Christian Church must appear unified to its parishioners and to nonbelievers.

All who worship in the Christian Church must "speak the same thing" and follow the inspiration of the Apostle Paul. 1 Corinthians 1:10, "Now I beseech you, brethren, by the name of our Lord Jesus Christ, that ye all speak the same thing, and that there be no divisions among you; but that ye be perfectly joined together in the same mind and in the same judgment." There is only one true Church and that is the Church of God founded by our lord and savior Jesus Christ which glorifies the father. Christ stressed the point that this Church must keep the father (God) intact.

Here's a listing of some of the scriptures that identify "The Church of God" as the true name Jesus Christ intended for all churches to be called.

1 Thess. 2:14, "For ye, brethren, became followers of the churches of God which in Judaea are in Christ Jesus."

2 Thess. 1:4, "So that we ourselves glory in you in the churches of God for your patience and faith in all your persecutions and tribulations that ye endure."

1 Corinthians 15:9, "For I am the least of the apostles, that am not meet to be called an apostle, because I persecuted the church of God."

1 Corinthians 1:2, "Unto the church of God which is at Corinth, to them that are sanctified in Christ Jesus, called to be saints, with all that in every place call upon the name of Jesus Christ our Lord, both theirs and ours."

1 Timothy 3:5, "For if a man know not how to rule his own house, how shall he take care of the church of God?"

1 Timothy 3:15, "But if I tarry long, that thou mayest know how thou oughtest to behave thyself in the house of God, which is the church of the living God, the pillar and ground of the truth."

God said the following statement to Moses at the burning bush. Exodus 3:5, "And he said, Draw not nigh hither: put off thy shoes from off thy feet, for the place whereon thou standest is holy ground." The Christian Church should adopt this practice in order to cleanse itself. Shoes should be left at the door before entering God's house so that the church can become holy again.

This one true Church has one body and is ruled by one government. The Church of God aids in the restoration of the government of God. The Church will rule with Christ at his second coming aiding him in bringing salvation to the world.

I stress the point that today's churches must break away and form one Church with one body. The Church cannot afford to have different belief systems, doctrines, and names. The Church cannot continue to be divided and form other branches that end up polarizing each other.

The Church must follow God's formula like He outlined in 1 Corinthians that reveals how He wants his Church to operate. 1 Cor. 12: 4-6, 12-14, 20, 25, "Now there are diversities of gifts, but the same Spirit. And there are differences of administrations, but the same Lord. And there are diversities of operations, but it is the same God which worketh all in all. For as the body is one, and hath many members, and all the members of that one body, being many, are one body: so also is Christ. For by one Spirit are we all baptized into one body, whether we be Jews or Gentiles, whether we be bond or free; and have been all made to drink into one Spirit. For the body is not one member, but many. But now are they many members, yet but one body. That there should be no schism in the body; but that the members should have the same care one for another."

My goal and purpose is to unify and restore the Church to the way it was from the beginning including honoring festivals and the Sabbath day and to become one body in the Spirit of Jesus Christ.

Changing of Scriptures

The Catholic Church changed the wordings of the Lord's Prayer from "lead us not into temptation" to "do not let us fall into temptation." They feel that the original wording is saying that God is leading us into temptation and that it is a bad thing. In Rome, the changes stand as the true word of God in hoping that the rest of the Christian world follow suit. This is an example of how the religious leaders of today are not able to comprehend the understanding of God's words. They still have to learn how he operates.

Here is an example of how God moves a person in the right direction by using the negative to bring about the positive.

Isaiah 45:7, "I form the light, and create darkness: I make peace, and create evil: I the Lord do all these things." God uses evils, snares, and traps so that you can be moved toward the greater good. He uses the adversary so that we can see God. We must understand the basic principles of good versus evil as it is outlined in the book of Genesis. It is the same reason the religious leaders of today cannot identify the "man of sin" even after being pointed out. Romans 11:7-10, "Let their tables become a snare, and a trap, and a stumbling block, and recompense to them. Let their eyes be darkened so they shall not see and ears so they shall not hear to this day."

The Pope said when referring to the Lord's Prayer, "It is not a good translation because it speaks of a God who induces temptations," he told Italy's TV 2000 channel in 2017 per The Guardian. "I am the one who falls. It's not him pushing me into temptation to then see how I have fallen." Pope Francis has not looked deeper into what God is trying to reveal to people he wants to move in a specific direction. Matter of fact God is pushing you towards temptation to teach you a valuable lesson. God is the one who set up traps and snares. God is the one who is leading us into temptation so that you will become battle worthy and to know when to put on the armor of God.

The Lord's Prayer

"Our Father who art in Heaven
Hallowed be thy name,
Thy kingdom come, thy will be done,
On earth as it is in heaven.
Give us this day our daily bread.
And for give us our trespasses,
As we forgive those who trespass against us.
LEAD US NOT INTO TEMPTATION,
BUT DELIVER US FROM EVIL.
For thine is the kingdom, the power
and the glory, for ever and ever, Amen.

It was God who placed obstacles in front of Jesus in the wilderness by using the adversary (Satan). It was God who brought Jesus to the wilderness to be tempted in the first place.

Matthew 4:1-3, "Then was Jesus led up of the Spirit into the wilderness to be tempted of the devil. And when he had fasted forty days and forty nights, he was afterward an hungred. And when the tempter came to him he said If thou be the Son of God, command that these stones be made bread." God brought Jesus to the wilderness to be tempted by Satan. "Lead us not into temptation but deliver us from evil." God creates traps and snares to prepare Christ for the road that he must follow. This was done in order to move Christ in the right direction so that Christ would go to the word of God for protection.

God uses evil to move people in the way he wants them to go. God is willing to lead us into temptation if it teaches us a valuable lesson. Experience is the best teacher when applied to the trials and tribulation of everyday life. A pastor of a church can preach a great sermon from written material, but a person who actually experiences what's written can give an even better analogy of a certain topic.

The obstacles of my life helped to mode me into the person I have come to be. God put adversity in my path so that I could be moved in another direction that was better suited for me. That is why it is important that I put on the armor of God for protection.

If one word from the written scriptures is changed to meet a certain understanding, then the whole Bible is thrown into validation. Pope Francis has opened up a Pandora's Box when he authorized his fellow religious leaders to uphold the change, therefore rendering the Holy Bible as just another book and not the sacred literature that it was intended to be, and that is the word of God.

The Church in Government

We have reached a pivotal moment in world history where the Christian Church and those who love freedom of democracy are threatened by the forces of evil on a grand scale. It is no coincidence that all of these things are happening at the same moment in history. Anti-Semitism, xenophobia, racism, bigotry, nationalism, atheism, white supremacy, Nazism and the COVID-19 pandemic are some of the evil forces that have been magnified all across the globe.

The Christian Church with its broad influence on millions of people all over the world has not been spared by an ongoing assault on Christian values. Take a look at the recent scandal by the Catholic Church that threatens to destroy the credibility of all Christian Churches. This act alone has weakened Christian values and is helping to kill Christ a second time.

From the Churches silence on major issues affecting everyday life to changing the word of God in the Holy Scriptures, this proves to all who love Christ that it is time to wake up.

The Christian Church must become a viable instrument in God's Kingdom if it wants to remain relevant into today's ever changing world. When our civic leaders in the past history voted to keep the Church out of government affairs it rendered the Church's function only for ceremonial and pageantry. This situation must change in order for the Church to become a powerful force to be reckoned with.

The Christian Church must be a part of the legislative branch of the Supreme Court and have a voice in decision making. The Church cannot continue to survive in silence and remain muted. It must get into the fight and prove to the world that God has the right answer for everything.

The Church must become an equal part of government and have the power to render an opinion that is crucial to everyday decision making. It is an injustice to people in society who believe in the teachings of Jesus when there is no representative on the Supreme Court to render a verdict.

The very reason why moral issues that is related to biblical scriptures are being magnified today is because the Christian Church has been rendered invisible. When the integrity of one's character is not important when selecting our religious leaders, we are loosing the credibility of the church. When homosexuality dictates what marriage can be the Church has been rendered useless. When greed is allowed to run rampant by our institutions while the Church is dead in silence. When hatred and bigotry is allowed to have a voice while the church remained silent, the church has been rendered out of service. All these things are killing Jesus a second time by the Christian Church.

I stressed the point of the churches relativity in the world, it must become an equal branch in government affairs. We as Christians must live up to the words "In God we trust" if we believe in the teachings of Christ. As a society under God we must prove our worthiness. We must practice what we preach.

Why can't the Church distinguish between what is right or wrong based on the principles that is outlined in the bible? The more secularism invade the mine of fellow believers it takes away from the principles religious leaders were taught. That is why they can't make sound decision based on Godly principles.

A few years ago an issue arose that religious leaders should have come to the rescue or even voice their opinion on a bakery shop owner who refused to bake a wedding cake for a gay couple. When the gay couple complained to the media the incident got world wide attention. People on both side of the issue made their opinion heard but the Church remained silent.

Does the bakery owner who is a devoted christian have the right to refuse a person's request simply because of their sexual preference? Is this situation like the days of the civil rights movement when black people were refused by white business owners their service? Like any hard problem that may materialize we must take it to Jesus. The Holy Scriptures is just waiting for you to open up its pages.

Based on the scriptures the answer to the question, does the bakery owner who is a devoted christian have the right to refuse a persons request? The answer is, because you are a christian you should bake the cake for the gay people. Although the bakery owner do not believe in gay marriage like I do, we should not judge them for who they are. We should not discriminate against anyone. The scriptures tells us that Paul said in Romans 2:1 "Therefore thou art inexcusable, O man, whosoever thou art that judgest; for wherein thou judgest another, thou condemnest thyself, for thou that judgest doest the same things."

No one knows how it feels to be discriminated against unless you walked in their shoes. We Christians can be as prejudice as anyone without the right teachings from the word of God. This is why the Church must intervene at certain moments in history in order to show its relevance.

The Final Era of the Church Before Jesus Returns

The Christian Church began on the day of Firstfruits called Pentecost, in June of A.D. 31 where the Holy Spirit descended from heaven and interacted with 120 disciples gathered to worship. This supernatural event is described in Acts 2:2. "And suddenly there came a sound from heaven as of a rushing mighty wind, and it filled all the house where they were sitting."

In the year 2007 I visited the Philippines and stayed in a house that will forever be remembered as the day I experienced my first encounter with the Holy Spirit. I experienced the same supernatural event like was described in Acts 2:2. At the time of this event I did not understand what it was but now after experiencing other miracles in my life I must attributed it to God's way of teaching me. The Holy Ghost's job is to teach one the way's of the Lord.

My wife and I experienced this supernatural event together in which she helped me realize that God has a mission for me to perform. We heard together the mighty wind blowing so hard as if the roof of the house was being torn off. Then the loud noise sounded like a locomotive or a jackhammer pounding out of no where. We were frightened out of our minds. In chapter 6 of this book I explain the whole story.

This supernatural event helped me realize my mission to uplift the Christian Church in Jesus name. I had come to realize that the Church is where I must begin to alert Christians of the final warning before Jesus Christ returns to this earth.

Jesus Christ built his Church under the rule of the Roman Empire. At its inception in the world the church was persecuted by the Romans. But that wasn't the only adversity the church had to endure. False Prophets threatened to distort the message Jesus preached. In Corinthians 11:3 the apostle Paul tells us to beware of wolves in sheep clothing. "But I fear, lest by any means, as the serpent beguiled Eve through his subtilty, so your minds should be corrupt from the simplicity that is in Christ. For if he that cometh preacheth another Jesus, whom we have not preached, or if ye receive another spirit, which ye have not received, or another gospel, which ye have not accepted, ye might well bear with him."

The endurance of the Christian Church has been tested through time with people like the insane Nero who in A.D. 64 blamed the burning of Rome on the Christians and persecuted many using horrific methods.

During that same period Jews of Palestine fought against Roman authorities and was defeated and Jerusalem destroyed in A.D. 70.

After Jesus Christ founded his Church and sent his apostles out to spread the word of God through out the world Satan reared his ugly head in the persona of Simon Magus who tried to incorporate his pagan religion using the name Christianity to fool believers of Christ that his doctrine was the real deal. He supplanted his own version of the Christian Passover with what we call today Easter.

The apostle Paul urged followers of Christ to remained steadfast in their belief and study the word of God and not listen to the false doctrine of prophets distorting the truth.

During this period those who called themselves Christians were persecuted by the Romans and suffered because they did not want to follow the Romans pagan God's.

The Christian Church must abolish the name Easter and return this celebration as it was intended to be from the beginning and renaming it The Christian Passover. For too long the name Easter was allowed by religious leaders to flourish in disguise as the true Christian celebration and hide the fact that it was derived from a pagan god and not our Lord and Savior Jesus Christ.

This must be done as part of the cleansing of the Christian Church. Laws that are decreed by God must be obeyed.

The Seven Eras of the Church

In the book of Revelation the apostle John records seven messages sent to seven Churches that existed in Asia Minor. The churches are Ephesus, Smyrna, Pergamos, Thyatira, Sardis, Philadelphia, and Laodicea. They were located near the Roman Empire. The messages that were sent involved encouragement to continue what was taught by Jesus Christ while he was on earth.

The messages revealed prophecies of the true Church of God on how it would perform from the day of Pentecost, A.D. 31 until the last message to be sent proclaiming the second coming of Christ. The message would outline seven distinct eras of the church describing its weakness and strength, trials and tribulations and the assurance of God's word would be passed on from era to era.

After enduring unspeakable persecution God's message was passed on to the era of the Ephesians to the Smyrna era of God's church. They also endured persecution from the Roman Empire until Constantine saw a cross made of light shinning bright in the sky which prevented him from becoming like his predecessors. He mixed his pagan religions with the teachings of Jesus which created a false Christianity. It was named the Babylonian Mystery religion being disguise as Christianity.

Due to the Roman Emperor Constantine brave decision to teach the word of God among the other pagan religions the teachings of God survived.

After Roman Emperor Constantine's death in A.D. 337 his followers began living with religious freedom for a time became the persecutors. This false Church caused true believers to be put to death. If one did not agree to their doctrine they were doomed.

Christians of the Smyrna era church fled from persecution to be free to worship Jesus the way they were taught originally. They suffered many attacks from those who hated them. The message came from Jesus himself encouraging them to keep the faith, he said, Rev 2:9-10. "I know your works, tribulation, and poverty....Do not fear any of those things which you are about to suffer....Be faithful until death, and I will give you the crown of life." This message passed from the Smyrna era to the Pergamos era.

After enduring much persecution the Pergamos Christians passed the message of Christ to the Thyatiran era. They also had to endure persecution from non-believers. Christians who called themselves the true Church of God and kept the sabbath although small in numbers kept the teaching of Jesus alive until the message of God was past on to the end time Churches.

The Sardis era in Revelation 3:1-6 is described as being weak in promoting the message of God. They new that in Matthew 24:14 proclaim "this gospel of the kingdom of God shall be preached in all the world for a witness unto all nations; and then shall the end come."

Revelation 7 to 13 describes the Philadelphia era which reveals an angel or messenger will come in today's world to restore the Christian Church. In Malachi 3:1-5 and 4:5-6 that God would raise up someone in the likeness of Elijah, just before the return of Jesus Christ. It is prophesied that this messenger would "truly shall first come, and restore all things." Malachi 3:1-5. "Behold, I will send my messenger, and he shall prepare the way before me:" and the Lord whom ye seek, shall suddenly come to his temple (the Church)............."

The Christian Churches must examine carefully the message I am presenting. There is not much time to squander over petty squabbles that serves no one.

The Churches hierarchy must take this small window of opportunity to debate the validity of my proposition. I hold no political office or have a degree in theology. You may want to ask me on what authority I have. The same question was asked to Jesus.

The Counterfeit Christianity

Who was Simon Magus? Was he Satan in disguise? From the beginning of Christ ministry Satan was on the prowl. He plotted to kill Christ as he stalked him, and waited for the right moment to attack the Son of God. Satan tried desperately to disqualify Christ as the true heir to the throne of earth. He was relentless in his attempt to destroy Jesus even to this very day. Satan soon realized he could not defeat Jesus one on one so he went after the prize of Jesus, his Church. Satan infiltrated the church to counterfeit it and mold it into a false Christianity.

After the day of Pentecost, when Jesus created his Church the apostle Peter and others followed the instructions of Jesus and went out into the world preaching the gospel of the kingdom of God.

Simon Magus, also known as Simon the Sorcerer was a Samaritan, allegedly asserted that he was an incarnation of God who boasted that he had magical powers and had the gift of flight. The opinion that this person from the bible is Satan is my own assertion. After studying this man's life and comparing his deeds to the wiles of Satan I felt strongly that he has the credentials of Satan and had a strong influence on the Christian Church. What happened to the Christian Church during the ancient world has greatly influence the existence of the Church for 2000 years due to the infiltration of a false doctrine created originally by Simon Magus, the Sorcerer.

His story begins this way. Phillip went into the city of Samaria to preach the word of God to it's citizens. While there he healed the sick and caused demons to come out of those who were possessed.

Simon was there in the same city performing miracles displaying his magical powers in front of huge crowds. After seeing Simon worked his sorcery, the people said that "this man is the great power of God." The people of Samaria became familiar with Simon's sorcery and became bewitched.

Phillip who was a man of God was preaching to the people of Samaria at the same time Simon was showing them his magical powers. While Phillip was preaching the things concerning the kingdom of God, and the name of Jesus Christ, Simon noticed that his audience was leaving him and was being drawn to the power of God. As Phillip baptized many men and women in the audience, Simon believed in what Phillip was saying and was baptized too. He joined Phillip in the mission and while journeying throughout the city he watched with amazement and astonishment at the miracles and signs Phillip was performing.

When the apostles heard that the people of Samaria had accepted and believed in the word of God, they sent Peter and John to minister to them. The apostles knew that the people of Samaria was only baptized in the name of Jesus and needed to have the Holy Ghost come upon them. Then Peter and John laid their hands on the people, and they received the Holy Ghost.

When Simon saw the apostles laid their hands on the people and the Holy Ghost was received Simon was so amazed at the power of God he offered money to the apostles, saying, "Give me also this power, that on whomsoever I lay hands, he may receive the Holy Ghost." But Peter said unto him, "Thy money perish with thee, because thou hast thought that the gift of God may be purchased with money. You have no part in this ministry, because your heart is not right before God. Repent of this wickedness and pray to the Lord. Perhaps he will forgive you for having such a thought in your heart. For I see that you are full of bitterness and captive sin." Then Simon answered, "Pray to the Lord for me so that nothing you have said may happen to me." Acts 8:9-24.

The story of Simon Magus is the plight that the Christian Church finds itself in. His story incorporates the classic battle between Satan and God. As we examine Simon's obsession with being equal to God notice the battles he chooses to wage.

He was known as a God by the people of Samaria and only wanted the gift of God for his own selfish reason.

Simon waged a diabolical war using magic against the power of God. It was that old classic battle that consists of magic versus miracles, and good versus evil. As Simon used magic to win over the people, the apostle Peter invoked the name of Jesus Christ when he performed miracles. But that did not stop Simon from challenging Peter to a dual in front of the citizens of Samaria. In the Acts of Peter we find a great example of this historic battle; "Following Peter's exceptional demonstration of miraculous ability, Simon found it necessary to indulge in greater prodigious feats in an attempt to win back Peter's converts (and to convince the disciples that his faith was ill-founded)."

This scenario of a monumental battle between Simon and the apostle Peter is the same battle being waged between God and Satan. What's so mind boggling about Simon is how he used his power to infiltrate the Christian Church and has influence it until today. Is it a coincidence that Satan and Simon share the same goal?

The colossal battle between God and Satan is when Satan tempted Jesus to perform miracles. This single battle is the cornerstone of the world we live in where Satan is in a tug of war with God to see how many souls will follow him or God.

After Simon lost his followers to Peter's God, he challenged Peter to a contest to see which power is the greatest in order to win back his followers. This dual between Simon and Peter is the same challenge as Jesus and Satan waged when the devil tempted Christ. Matthew 4:1 "Then was Jesus led up of the spirit into the wilderness to be tempted of the devil. And when he had fasted forty days and forty nights, he was hungry. And when the tempter came to him, he said, If you be the Son of God, command that these stones be made bread. But he answered and said, It is written, man shall not live by bread alone, but by every word that proceed out of the mouth of God."

The dual between Simon and Peter and Satan versus Jesus is what we all go through in our daily living experiences. We are faced with choices that will determine which God we serve.

We should ask ourselves whether to follow the teachings of Jesus or submit to the cunning of Satan. What if this proposition was ask of you, "all these things will I (Satan) give to you, if you will fall down and worship me." Matthew 4:9. Whom will you choose?

Simon the Sorcerer started his great false church called Christianity in A.D. 33 two years after Jesus Christ founded his church on the day of Pentecost. Simon who began the Babylonian mystery religion in Samaria was proclaimed "from the least to the greatest, saying, This man is the great power of God." Acts 8:10.

So, from the beginning Satan had infiltrated Christianity and the Church via Simon the Sorcerer. The name Christianity derived from the pagan Babylonian mystery religion and has drawn believers of Christ still to this very day. Simon aspired to turn his pagan religion, who he named Christianity into the premier political power in the world. Although he did not live to see this happen but other religious leaders gained political control over the Roman Empire which became the Holy Roman Empire.

Every year we celebrate Easter not knowing that this name derived from Simon the Sorcerer who tried to turn the true Christian Passover into Babylonian ceremony now called Easter after the goddess Ishtar.

A great controversy began between the true Church of God and the leader of the Church started by Simon the Sorcerer. The Passover/Easter controversy between the bishop of Rome and a follower of Christ by the name of Polycarp became a heated theological battle that was won by the Church of Rome because the Church of God members were out numbered.

The Christian Church today is riddled with the effects of Simon the Sorcerer in the persona of false prophets, and false churches headed by Satan. Some examples of this are the Reverend Jim Jones who tricked his 900 members to drink poison in the belief that it was the will of God. The Heavens Gate members were under the spell of a cult that convinced its members to drink poison because they would board a UFO that would take them to heaven.

Simon the Sorcerer tried to pay for the blessings of God and was turned down by the apostle Peter but his aspiration lived on in today's world with the advent of the mega Churches which brings in millions of dollars in the name of Jesus Christ. The talk of money rules the pulpit instead of the biblical scriptures being taught to fellow worshippers. Ministers with their bibles in one hand and their thirst for money have replaced the gift of God with the roots of all evil and the hunger for riches instead of gaining one's soul.

The Christian Church has evolved with many different tentacles branching out and has incorporated all different belief systems that threaten to destroy what God intended for his Church. Churches that worship snakes and has put them in their ceremonies is a testament of where Christianity is going without the direct intervention of Jesus Christ.

The apostle Paul warned the early Christian Churches that they were in danger of succumbing to false teaching from counterfeit ministers. He warned that the Christian Church that was founded by Christ was being infiltrated and diluted with false belief of the pagan God's, the Babylon and Persian belief that was began by whom else, Simon the Sorcerer.

As time went by the original apostles encouraged the followers of Christ to stay strong in their belief. Jesus brother Jude encouraged members to remember what was taught to them by Christ. The apostle John gave his members the same sentiment as Jude reinforced the word of God as the true testimony of Jesus and assured his followers to not listen to false doctrines.

Where is the true Church of God today? It is in the hearts of people who follow the teachings of Jesus Christ and obey his laws. The redemption of the Christian Church will restore Christianity to the way it was originally intended to be by our Lord and Savior Jesus Christ. If Jesus Christ can change the apostle Paul after he persecuted Christians, he will have no problem transforming the Christian Church into the Kingdom of God.

The Christian Church duty today is to prepare itself to help Jesus in developing his government to come. Jesus came to this earth to deliver his message from God called the gospel. This message is the good news that the kingdom of God is coming and that he will rule over this government here on earth.

Jesus Christ needs the Christian Church help in administering his authority to carry out his will. That is why he said in Matthew 16:18 "I will build my church."

The Church will play an important role in the new government to come. This is why the Christian Church must rid itself of corruption and make the church holy again. It must start today and restore what was lost from the beginning.

Jesus is the head of the Church and he is returning for his bride, the Christian Church. He is not returning to a church that has been marred in scandal. He is not returning to a church that is scattered in disarray. He is not returning to a church that is swallowed in paranoia. He is not returning to a church that its tongue has been rendered mute. For the Christian Church must prepare itself for a grand wedding and follow the example that was laid out for us in Ephesians 5:22-30 "Wives, submit yourselves unto your husbands, as unto the Lord. For the husband is the head of the wife, even as Christ is the head of the church; and he is the savior of the body. Therefore as the church is subject unto Christ, so let the wives be to their own husbands in everything. Husbands love your wives, even as Christ also loved the church, and gave himself for it; that he may sanctify and cleanse it with the washing of by the word, that he may present it to himself a glorious church, not having spot, or wrinkle, or any such thing; but that it should be holy and without blemish. So ought men to love their wives as their own bodies. He that loveth his wife loveth himself. For no man ever yet hated his own flesh; but nourisheth and cherisheth it, even as the lord the church; for we are members of his body, of his flesh, and of his bones."

We must begin the process of cleansing the Christian Church so that it will shine as bright as a diamond. The cleansing of the church must extend its reach into all governments who profess the love for our Lord and Savior Jesus Christ. The church can no longer be sidelined by segments of society who are atheist. For too long the churches administration has been stifled by civic leaders who want to continue the separation of church and state. Iron and clay cannot hold together as the scriptures proclaim, and atheism and Christianity cannot stick together but only righteousness is the glue that binds the soul.

Still, there is a major task that the Christian Church must perform in order to become worthy of the return of our Lord and Savior Jesus Christ to his holy temple. Even after the Christian Church change everything about itself in order to please God, it won't matter if that one major task is not performed by the Christian Church. The biblical scriptures warned us in 2 Thessalonian 2:3-4 "Let no man deceive you by any means, for that day(the day Jesus Christ return to this earth) shall not come except there come a falling away first, and that man of sin be revealed." The Christian Church must point him out to the world. The man of sin must be revealed by the Church otherwise this world will be destroyed by Jesus Christ.

The count down has already begun. The atomic clock is ticking its last minutes. The virus is taking lives one by one, family by family. Gun violence is ravishing inner cities across the globe. Wars and rumors of wars is waiting to explode. Morality and integrity is just words that have no meaning when civic leaders and government officials substitute it for political gain. Racism and hatred against your fellow man is on the increase. All of these evil forces is being magnified in order to bring destruction to this world and these forces will not stop until God commands it to stop.

Focus on the World Through the Eyes Of God

Some of us may want to argue that there is no indication or evidence that God is working in our everyday affairs. That may be true if you don't focus your attention on the world through the eyes of God. Take for example the political arena where civic leaders abandon the idea of what's right and wrong and instead they adopt their own way of explaining reality. In their world it is a place where good and evil has been relegated to the eye of the beholder. With that thought in mind it is by choice how you want to shape your world. Do you want a world that has godly things or a world where there is no God?

If you think that God is not important in our world just look at the way our politicians use God as a political weapon. When the leader of the free world stand in front of a church holding up a bible to take photos while peaceful protesters near by are being gas by policeman, God is really the target.

When the leader of the free world attacks someone's religious belief and pit one group against another even God is being politicized. Especially when you accuse someone of being against God and guns as if God condones shooting someone.

I wrote this book to prove to the world that God is at work every single day in our world. Today people are focusing their attention on the political arena due to the horrific deaths from the corona virus and the coming elections. It was in the political arena where I discovered the "man of sin" from the biblical scriptures. I could not have found him if I wasn't focus on the world through the eyes of God.

From the beginning of my life I established a relationship with God, so when I saw the evidence implicating Mikhail Gorbachev as the "man of sin" from the bible I had to let the church know. At that moment I had an important message to give and I felt the evidence was to compelling to keep it all to myself.

While I was writing the book I realized that the message I kept and the Christian Church is involved in a great mystery. That message was so important that it would redeem the church and would be the key to the return of Jesus Christ. I couldn't have realized this if I wasn't focused on the world through the eyes of God.

Why are the two leaders whom I identified as biblical related different than any other historical figure? Some may say Adolf Hitler was the Antichrist or "man of sin" whose deeds were diabolical. Yes, he was a proponent of evil but he did not fulfill biblical prophecy that is displayed throughout the biblical scriptures. Even Napoleon did not measure up to the candidates I identified. The candidates I've chosen have something in common that no one in history has. They both have a "Messiah complex."

CHAPTER 6

THE MESSENGER

A JOURNEY OF DISCOVERY

Sitting on a ledge of a mountain in the Philippines jungle crying my eyes out from the experience of being there seeing my wife washing her clothes at the well below. While sitting there on the mountain visions of the story of Moses appeared in my mind when he met his wife at the well. My fiancé's family member looked up and saw me crying and climbed a short distance up the mountain to investigate what happened to me. I told him I felt the presence of God at that moment and his spirit overwhelmed me to the point of jubilation and amazement.

Just before we arrived at the well, I saw a group of naked children playing in the river with a waterfall in the background. I thought we were in heaven.

I came down from the mountain and my wife to be began washing my feet which at that point I realized I actually was in heaven.

From that point in my life I realized that I must stop running away from God and begin to listen to what people were saying about me. They all had the same message from God for me. That message to me was, "God has something important for you to do." It was the same message I heard many times in the U.S. before I arrived in the Philippines.

The next day my wife to be and her family members took me to the beach. It was a perfect day for going to the beach and as we arrived I could see the beautiful blue waters of the ocean coming into view. As we entered the entrance of the beach the sound of loud music coming from a house caught everyone's attention. To my surprise and astonishment, the music from the motion picture "The Ten Commandments" was playing extremely loud so that whom ever comes to the beach would here that particular music. No other music was being played. At that moment I realized just the day before I was sitting on a ledge of a mountain with visions of the prophet Moses finding his wife at a well. I must remember that God works in duality. What happened thousands of years ago is repeated.

I realized at that moment that God was talking to me and that is not all that happened on that day. As the family members and I got settled, they brought out food to grill and broke open many coconuts that were particularly refreshing. After we all finished eating, we walked to the ocean with some going directly into the water while I stood on the bank watching the family members including my wife to be playing in the water.

As I was watching my fiancé swimming I noticed a man running in my direction. He looked like he was coming toward me. At that moment, I knew he didn't know me because I had just arrived in the Philippines two days ago. To my surprise, he came up to me and said, "God sent me to you. Please pray for me and my family." Startled, I said to him, "Sir, I am not a minister." He then said, "I am a minister and my church is the Church of God." He said, "God told me to come to you."

Without hesitation, I told him to gather his family and meet me in the water. He, His wife, his three children, and I formed a circle in knee-deep water. As we held hands, I recited the Lord's Prayer. My wife to be and her family looked on with amazement at me and the strangers praying in the water.

From that moment I knew I had to stop running away from what God was directing me to do. I remember the biblical stories of characters running away from God. The prophet Moses was ordered by God to do his will and Moses protested and said to God, "I am not the one because I stuttered." The Apostle Paul who killed many followers of Christ ran away from the teachings of Christ until Jesus stricken him with blindness so that he could see and realize his calling.

Jeremiah rebelled against God's commandment when he told God he was too young. Jeremiah 1:7, "Do not say, I'm only a youth; for to all to whom I send you, you shall go, and whatever I command you, you shall speak." Jonah attempted to run away but God convinced him to obey God's message.

They are all the prophets who at first ran away from God's commandment. It took some convincing from God before I yielded to his orders. I continued to doubt my worthiness and found excuses to not listen to God's calling.

My story of discovery didn't start there in Philippines. The Philippines only served as a place of confirmation that God has something important for me to do. It was not until my second trip years later that confirmed everything in a supernatural way.

My story of discovery really began at an early age of 7 when my parents sent me and my brother to Sunday school. I had two great parents who loved the Lord and attended Church with two boys in tow. So, the blessing of church attendance stayed in my heart throughout my youth.

Before I entered the military, my mother gave me a bible to read for protection. That particular bible stayed with me until today. It served as a reminder for me to look to the lord for comfort and advice. Make the right choice, my mother would always say.

After I got out of the military, my brother and I joined a gospel group. We traveled around our city singing in different churches. While we were singing, we saw the faces of the young and the old who saw us as rock stars.

While attending church during those early years of listening to the minister preach about different bible stories, one story stayed in my mind. The story of the man of sin, or Antichrist, left an impression on my heart for many years to come. I began to look for him in our world believing one day he would show up in the political arena. I would listen to the news and read books and articles on the subject hoping to find evidence of the man of sin's arrival. None of the politicians I saw at the time fit the description.

Most of my life I spent enjoying life but in the back of my mind was this yearning to discover the Antichrist, or man of sin. After years of not pinpointing this character from the bible, in 1986 I hit the jackpot. The moment Mikhail Gorbachev came on the scene a bell went off in my head. Then a voice said, "he is the one". Without any evidence to prove he was the one I was looking for, I knew in my heart he had to be.

People with Biblical Names who Ministered to Me

While I worked in the medical hospital, my coworker whose name was Elijah, a member of 10th Street Baptist Church, taught me scriptures from the bible. After 10 years of working beside him, a new coworker on a different job site came into my life. Her name is Mary, who was a member of Jehovah's Witness, who also taught me scriptures from the bible. I affectionately called her my mother, which she acted just like my mother.

Then came into my life Mr. Adams who is a member of Iglesia ni Cristo Church of Christ ministered to me the Holy Scriptures and became my best man at my wedding. Then come John and Mr. Amos who I called Moses who motivated me to write a book about what I experienced.

While working at the medical hospital, strangers came to my office and told me that God had something important for me to do. Different people would come. One identified himself as a minister and said to me, "It's almost time for you to do what God is asking of you." Puzzled, I said to myself, "What in the world is going on?" This continued for years and I dismissed them as lunatics.

I was still convinced Gorbachev was the man of sin from the bible. I would read anything about him that would give me a clue to his identity. Then, bingo, the evidence began to pour in. With this much evidence the first thing that came out of my mouth was that I had to inform the church. That sentiment can be found in the Holy Scriptures. God searches the heart for those people who have strong convictions. With the evidence in hand I began to write a draft copy of a book I would later call "Mikhail Gorbachev is Gog and Magog: The Biblical Antichrist." Then I put the manuscript on a shelf to collect dust.

Then came the second trip to the Philippines with the book far away from my mind. I was still running away from God knowing there was something strange happening around me. Strangers would still walk up to me claiming that I had a mission from God to take care of.

The Supernatural

Here is a true story my wife and I experienced together while visiting the Philippine Islands in 2006. Like most people, I never experienced the supernatural or paranormal. Although I've read about these things or saw a movie based on the subject, these events were far away from my mind as someone's imagination. My wife and I are firm believers in Jesus Christ and this event tested our faith.

Our friend here in America offered us to stay in his recently purchased home in the Philippines while we visited my wife's relatives. At first glance the house was very appealing with a gated fence yard and a geometric walk way designed by Germans. At the time of our visit it was only occupied by a caregiver who attended to the chickens for cockfighting, so we were the only guests.

The house had no furniture and no running water, so the Well became our only source of water for cooking and washing ourselves. Upon entering the house, the first thing that struck my attention when I walked up the stairs to store our suitcases was a rosary cross hanging at the top of the staircase, and I immediately thought to myself that it is peculiar to see a rosary left by someone hanging in an empty house.

As my wife and I settled in an empty room, we noticed what looked to be sawdust sprinkled over our suitcases and on the floor and inside the wall cabinets. This would be our first night stay and we were very tired from the airplane trip, but my wife and I began to clean and sweep the sawdust up thinking to ourselves where did it come from?

The next morning, we got up from sleeping on the floor all night and went to visit my wife's relatives. When we returned to the house that afternoon, we entered the room and to our surprise piles of sawdust were spread all over our belongings including the floor and wall cabinets. This was only the beginning of strange happenings in that house.

We would go to bed at 9 o'clock every night, and like clockwork the house revealed its secrets. As my wife and son fell asleep, I would stay up alone with only the candle light flickering in the darkness. Then I would hear someone moving about downstairs in the kitchen with the sound of forks and spoons and dishes falling to the floor and footsteps walking up the stairs.

I quickly get up from the floor and leave the room to go downstairs to investigate the noise. I enter the kitchen and see no one. The dishes and forks and spoons still lay where my wife left them.

Each day the sawdust would return as fast as my wife and I would clean it up. The noise in the kitchen and footsteps continued each night as I alone continued to investigate it. For weeks my wife and I did not discuss the events because I did not want to frighten her or my son. Then one day, I told her that I kept hearing noises in the house after we had gone to bed. It happens as soon as everyone is asleep. To my surprise she said she heard the same noise too, but was reluctant to mention it because she did not want to frighten me.

After staying in the house for about a month, I was convinced that something strange was going on and this was no ordinary house. As family members came to stay with us, the strange events continued each night but no one would discuss what they heard until I made a decisive request. I asked my wife to stay up with me past 9 o'clock and listen together to the peculiar sounds.

Everyone went to bed at exactly 9 o'clock, but my wife and I stayed up together to listen to the noise. At 9:05 pm, we heard the noise in the kitchen of someone moving about. Then we heard the dishes falling to the floor. Then someone began walking up the stairs. I quickly investigate and see no one. Then the frightening show begins. The wind begins to blow with no rain and the trees sway side to side. It sounded like a roaring tornado or hurricane or train. It was a deafening noise. At that precise moment a loud stomping noise like a jackhammer was heard by us coming from the attic above us. A repetition of boom! boom! boom! lasted for hours. Doors began to open and shut by themselves. It sounded like the roof of the house was being torn off. My wife and I stood motionless. I ask her, 'what is that noise?' We both were visibly shaken and frightened to death.

The room was very dark and the candlelight provided only a glimmer of light as the noise became louder and louder. There was a tiny hole in the ceiling where a light fixture would be leading to the attic, so I shined my flashlight into the hole to investigate the noise. As soon as I did this, we heard a popping noise like pop! Pop! The only light in the house that provided light to the stairs cut off as if it was telling me, "you shine the light in my domain, I turn off the light in your domain." Was this some type of communication? I noticed the neighbors house lights were still on, but our house was the only house without power.

By 12 midnight, the noise began to subside simultaneously as the wind stopped blowing. The house had an eerie quietness about it as my wife and I held each other throughout the night.

The next morning, we were eager to leave the house and return to a hotel. I went outside to survey any damage but there was none. The roof of the house was still intact. There were no shingles on the ground and no debris. It was as if nothing happened that night.

I asked my wife's relatives if they heard any noise in the house last night, and to my surprise they did not hear a thing. So whatever happened to my wife and me that night was only confined to the room we stayed in. As we walked through the village we met the previous owner of the house who asked us a peculiar question. He asked, "Did you experience anything unusual in the house?"

To many people this story is of a haunted house possessed by a ghost. But to me and my wife, it was a visitation from the Holy Ghost. For those who do not have faith or believe in Jesus Christ, it was as it may seem, just a ghost story. This paranormal and supernatural event strengthened and enhanced our belief in Jesus Christ. It is how a person perceives an event when it is presented. If you are looking at the world through the lens of God, he will open up to you the wonders of the universe.

After Jesus Christ ascended to heaven, the twelve disciples were visited upon them by the Holy Ghost. Observe the scriptures; Acts 2:2-4, "And suddenly there came a sound from heaven as of a rushing wind, and it filled the house where they were sitting. And there appeared unto them cloven tongues like as a fire, and it sat upon each of them. And they were all filled with the Holy Ghost, and began to speak with other tongues, as a Spirit gave them utterance."

This supernatural event that is recorded in the biblical scriptures reminds me of the supernatural event that happened to my wife and me. To the twelve disciples, this supernatural event was confirmation that Jesus Christ was who he said he is, the Son of God. To my wife and me, it was confirmation of what we already believe, that Jesus Christ is the Son of God.

ANALYSIS

1. The ghost did not appear until I "ACKNOWLEDGED" that it was there in the house.

2. The ghost appeared only to the "OBSERVER."

3. The ghost communicated in an "UNUSUAL OR UNIQUE" way.

4. It was never "SEEN."

5. The ghost was only "HEARD."

6. It made a non-believer of ghosts become a "BELIEVER."

Using the same analogy of a non-believer in ghosts, an atheist can become a believer in Jesus Christ.

TRANSITION FROM AN ATHEIST TO A BELIEVER

1. Jesus Christ will not come to you unless you "ACKNOWLEDGE" his existence.

2. You will not see Jesus Christ until you begin to search or "OBSERVE" him.

3. God will speak to you in mysterious and "UNUSUAL" ways.

4. Although you will not be able to see him, his presence is always there.

5. Listen to the voices of the Christian community and "HEAR" those wonderful sounds of joy.

6. You will become an advocate for Jesus Christ, a "BELIEVER."

I personally did not believe in ghosts until I was shaken and frightened beyond belief. Sometimes we need a shock to the system or a kick in the pants in order to see the unbelievable. We must come to the realization that there is something else that is going on around us that we cannot see with the naked eye. Sometimes we can see more in life using our other senses.

To many people this story is of a haunted house possessed by a ghost. But to me and my wife, it was a visitation from the Holy Ghost. For those who do not have faith or believe in Jesus Christ, it was as it may seem, just a ghost story. This paranormal and supernatural event strengthened and enhanced our belief in Jesus Christ. It is how a person perceives an event when it's presented. If you are looking at the world through the lens of God, he will open up to you the wonders of the universe.

The Battle with Satan, a Test of Faith

After leaving the Philippines and returning to the U.S., I felt at that moment what I experienced in Philippines was enough confirmation to write and publish my first book. The Holy Spirit's job is to help and direct you to fulfill God's plan for you. Little did I know what was to come later made me realize that the journey of discovery was not over, in fact, it was just the beginning.

As my family and I settled in from the long trip from the Philippines, I began writing my book with excitement. A steady flow of information coming from the spirit of God motivated me to write more. Eventually, I completed writing the book and published it in 2010. Life at that moment was great. Summer vacation was over and my wife went back to work. We were back to a normal routine of family life.

By Thanksgiving holiday, I received the first copies of my book titled "Mikhail Gorbachev is Gog and Magog." We were all happy and excited that I accomplished my goal. My wife announced on Facebook that Gorbachev is the Antichrist and that everyone should read my book. From that moment, I noticed a change come over my wife's face. Her face appeared puzzled and scared.

My boys and I went to bed at normal time because they had to attend school the next morning. I was awakened by my wife around 2:30 in the morning telling me she saw my dead relatives, but she did not come to bed. She stayed up long past bedtime on the computer. I immediately told her to come to bed. We both had to get up early the next morning.

I went back to sleep and when I awakened, my wife was beside me sleeping. So I thought to myself she just needed some sleep. I took the boys to school and when I returned and went up to the bedroom to check on my wife she was standing up on top of the bed with both hands raised up to the ceiling. Startled, I asked her to please get down from the bed. She then asked me do I see the bright light coming from the ceiling?

At that moment, I knew my wife was in trouble. After an hour on the bed, I finally convinced her to get down. After she got down from standing on the bed, she informed me that she got confirmation about my book. She said Jesus told her my book is true and Gorbachev was that Antichrist. What came next scared the living daylights out of me. She didn't recognize me at that moment and said she hears a voice in her head telling her he is going to destroy her.

I knew my wife was in trouble and begged her to go to the hospital with me. She rebuffed that idea and continued to resist my demand. I went and got help from her best friend. We both convinced her to go with us to the hospital. She didn't even recognize her best friend. They admitted my wife to the hospital after a night of her telling the doctors that voices in her head kept making demands and that she felt that she was possessed by a demon.

When I got back home, I was distraught and worried to death about my wife's state of mind. I immediately called one of my relatives and told her the bad news about my wife. While I was on the phone with my cousin talking about demonic possession, out of no where a third person interrupted our conversation with a heavy voice, speaking in an unknown language, and with static and a hurricane-like noise in the background. The hair on my arms and legs stood straight up. A scary feeling came over me. Whoever this is, it's not human. My cousin said the same sentiment. My cousin asked me did I hear that? I said yes. My cousin told me, whatever is going on, it sounds to be biblically related.

Friends of ours got the news and told me my wife needed confirmation of the book. I realized the same thing but was puzzled why she was possessed by a demon. So I called another cousin who is a minister. He informed me that this battle is for me to perform through Jesus Christ.

I went straight to the bible because I knew the answers were in there on how to fight Satan. I had to make sure it was a demon and not just an illness. How can I know for sure? The answer was found in Job 4:15, "Then a spirit passed before my face; the hair of my flesh stood up." At that moment I recalled the phone call with my cousin whom we both heard a demon speak which made the hair on my body stand straight up.

I felt that Satan was going to attack my family because of the book. If what I said about Gorbachev was true, then Satan was coming. What I didn't know was in what way or how. By attacking me, it would prove the validity of the book.

The attack by Satan on my family was confirmation for me to protect myself with the armor of God. Ephesians 6:10-12. "Finally, my brethren, be strong in the Lord, and in the power of his might. Put on the whole armor of God, that ye may be able to stand against the wiles of the devil. For we wrestle not against flesh and blood, but against principalities, against powers, against the rulers of the darkness of this world, against spiritual wickedness in high places."

At an early age, I learned to go to the bible and read scriptures in times of trouble. The scriptures instructed me on how to go about solving my problems. I knew it could not have happened without the love of Jesus Christ. 2 Timothy 3:16-17, "All scripture is given by inspiration of God, and is profitable for doctrine, for reproof, for correction, for instruction in righteousness: That the man of God may be perfect, thoroughly furnished unto all good works."

While the doctors administered to my wife in the hospital, I prayed to Jesus Christ to lift the curse upon my wife and make the demon flee from her body. But the battle didn't begin in that moment. He put an obstacle on the battlefield that I didn't see coming.

In order for my wife to be released from the hospital, I had to appear in court in front of a judge to argue why I felt she was ready to be released. While in court, my wife and I sat side by side while her doctors and social worker sat across the table ready to give the judge their opinion. The social worker spoke first while I took notes. She gave reasons why my wife should stay in the hospital. The doctor had the same sentiment.

Then it was my turn to argue on behalf of my wife. I began discrediting the doctor on a technicality. My wife stayed in the hospital for nine days and not once did the doctor confer with me about her diagnosis, condition, or a plan of recovery. The doctor didn't even acknowledge my phone calls. Not once. As the records revealed, the social worker never spoke with my wife or examined her. No records of the social worker's diagnosis were written anywhere in the hospital files. The judge concurred and released my wife immediately. Case closed.

It's been 8 years since the attack on my wife. There has been no other incident like what she experienced. Not one day of illness. Not one day of possession. Praise be to Jesus Christ, my savior, my salvation.

All the battles we experienced were for a purpose designed by God to strengthen and train us on how to find him in times of need. There was no reason for me to keep running away from God. There is an old saying, "You can run, but you sure can't hide from the Lord." Realize it or not, you will fulfill your destiny that was predestined by God. I stopped running from God and realized my mission to identify the man of sin and send this message to all the Christian churches. Once this prophecy is revealed, the obstacle that kept Christ from returning to earth will be removed, therefore preparing the way for the return of Jesus Christ to his church. 2 Thessalonians 2:3-4, "Let no man deceive you by any means: for that day shall not come, except there come a falling away first, and that man of sin be revealed, the son of perdition; Who opposeth and exalteth himself above all that is called God, or that is worshipped; so that he as God sitteth in the temple of God, shewing himself that he is God."

I still needed confirmation that this tall task would be mine alone, so I searched the scriptures to see if someone in the bible sent a message like this to the churches and would this scenario be written in the scriptures? Malachi 3:1, "Behold, I will send my messenger, and he shall prepare the way before me: and the Lord, whom ye seek, shall suddenly come to his temple, even the messenger of the covenant, whom ye delight in: behold, he shall come, saith the Lord of hosts."

Shocked and amazed, I researched further when I found another pastor's interpretation of the scriptures describing this messenger appearing just before the end time. Pastor Herbert Armstrong states, "It is revealed in Malachi 3:1-5 and 4:5-6 that God would raise up one in the power and spirit of Elijah, shortly prior to the second coming of Christ. In Matthew 17:11 Jesus said, even after John the Baptist had completed his mission, that this prophesied Elijah 'truly shall first come, and restore all things.' Although it is plainly revealed that John the Baptist had come in the power and spirit of Elijah, he did not restore anything. The human leader to be raised up somewhat shortly prior to Christ's second coming was to prepare the way—prepare the Church—for Christ's coming, and restore the truth that had been lost through the preceding eras of the Church. Also a door was to be opened for this leader and/or the Philadelphia era of the Church to fulfill Matthew 24:14: 'And this gospel of the kingdom shall be preached in all the world for a witness unto all nations; and then shall the end come.'"

Nostradamus predicted over 500 years ago that a person will come before the end time and restore the entire Christian church. The biblical scriptures proclaimed the same thing when

Jesus Christ said, Matthew 17:11, "And Jesus answered and said unto them, Elias (Elijah) truly shall first come, and restore all things." This book proclaims the same message to be sent to all the Christian churches. Get your house in order because the government of God is coming. Prepare the way for the second coming of Christ to marry his pride, the church.

If God's messenger is here on earth, that means that Jesus Christ's second coming is imminent. He is coming to his temple (the church) to build the kingdom of God. It will be a unified government that will envelop all nations. It will consist of one government, one state, and a unified church all run by the government of Jesus Christ.

Growing up I had no idea that I would be the one who would do something of this magnitude, but God knew that I would be the one. In fact, he's the one who predestined it. Read this scripture and see how God sets everything under the sun in motion. Romans 8:29-30, "For whom he did foreknow, he also did predestinate to be conformed to the image of his Son, that he might be the firstborn among many brethren. Moreover whom he did predestinate, them he also called: and whom he called, them he also justified: and whom he justified, them he also glorified."

If you get a calling from God, he has a will and plan for your life. God's plan for you was put in motion before you were born. I thank God for choosing me to serve him.

CHAPTER 7

NOSTRADAMUS PREDICTS THE MESSENGER

What if one of the most talked about and popular prophets described you in his well known visions called quatrains? Then when you read particular prophecy you would know without a doubt he is talking about you. Or would you consider it to be coincidence or would it be your intuition that Nostradamus could actually be talking about you?

It is one thing to read Nostradamus famous predictions and be amazed by his astounding accuracy, but it is another thing when that prophecy could be describing certain characteristics about you that only you could know.

Over 500 years ago Nostradamus became known as the king of all prophets and seers due to his ability to predict future events with astounding accuracy. His full name is Michel de Nostradamus and was born on December 14, 1503 in St. Remy-de-Province. He was so successful in his predictions that historians labeled him the man who could see into the future.

In this chapter we will examine prophecy's that the famous seer left us to ponder over and decipher with a hint of a spiritual awakening. With Nostradamus religious background at work, you will see the seers vision of the end time scenario of our world that includes Russia, "the man of sin," the Christian Church, the messenger and possibly the biblical Antichrist appearing at the same moment in history.

The author/interpreter Peter Lemesurier interprets Nostradamus prophecy in a letter to King Henry II shows how in 1917 Russia began its quest for world dominance in the Russian Bolshevik Revolution. This act by Russia plunged the world into darkness with its proclamation of atheism.

"In the month of October a great revolution shall take place, so profound as to convince people that the earth has ceased to move naturally and has descended into everlasting darkness. Following warning signs the previous spring, extraordinary changes shall occur, kingdoms will be turned upside down..."

For 73 years the old Soviet Union now Russia held its grip on kingdoms with the spread of communism around the world that resulted in the building of the Iron Curtain that suppressed freedom of religion just like Nostradamus predicted. "This shall last no more than 73 years and seven months. At that time, from the stock that has so long been barren, originating in the 50th degree, shall come one who shall restore the entire Christian Church. Then a great peace shall ensue."

The interpreter Peter Lemesurier writes in his interpretations that the passage of 73 years brings us to the year 1991 when the old Soviet Union was collapsing due to the reforms of Mikhail Gorbachev who I identified as "the man of sin" from the bible. It is interesting to note that Gorbachev and the person who restore the Christian Church arrive at the same moment in history according to Nostradamus.

Nostradamus and the biblical scriptures are identical when describing the characteristics of the person who restores the Christian Church. The key word that joins both Nostradamus and the biblical scriptures together is the word "restore."

The bible describes this person who restores the Christian Church as the Messenger. The late pastor Herbert Armstrong describes this person this way.

"It is revealed in Malachi; 3:1-5 and 4:5-6 that God would raise up one in the power and spirit of Elijah, shortly prior to the Second Coming of Christ. In Matthew 17:11 Jesus said, even after John the Baptist had completed his mission, that this prophesied Elijah 'truly shall first come, and restore all things.' Although it is plainly revealed that John the Baptist had come in the power and spirit of Elijah, he did not restore anything. The human leader to be raised up somewhat shortly prior to Christ's Second Coming was to prepare the way—prepare the Church—for Christ's second coming, and restore the truth that had been lost through the preceding eras of the Church."

Somehow the moment I read Nostradamus prophecy concerning the Messenger I knew immediately that it could possibly be me due to certain characteristics of his description. Although the prophecy could be anyone with these characteristics, my actions toward the belief in Christ confirmed my conviction that I must identify that "man of sin." A strong feeling came over me that compelled me to warn the Christian Church.

Let us examine Nostradamus prophecy and see why I felt strongly that he could be talking about me. "From the stock that so long been barren," the word stock could very well mean people. Slaves and their descendants were looked upon as being barren or unproductive. I am a descendant of slaves. "Originating in the 50th degree." This is the birth date of this person circa 1950. I was born in the year 1950.

Nostradamus also gives the month and date of my birth date and describes what happens to this person in the near future.

"Mars and the Scepter will be in conjunction, a calamitous war under cancer. A short time afterward a new King will be anointed who will bring peace to the earth for a long time." The Scepter represents the planet Jupiter, say astrologers. This will appear June 21, the month and day of my birth date.

Erika Cheetham who is a well known interpreter of Nostradamus prophecies says after reviewing that particular prophecy, "there is a future for the world after the millennium, with a promise of "REDEMPTION." In the second chapter of this book is the letter I sent to all Christian Churches asking the question; what if the REDEMPTION of the Church rest solely on identifying "the man of sin"? I did not know Erica Cheetham's interpretation until years after I sent letters to all the Christian Churches. I am like any human being who had doubts at times until the miracle of the sun, a cross made from the sun, the symbol of Christianity appeared in my backyard confirming my conviction. I will discuss the Miracle of the Sun in chapter 8. Shortly after 1991 I began writing my book and naming Mikhail Gorbachev as the "man of sin" from the biblical scriptures fulfilling Nostradamus prophecy that after 73 years of Russian aggression would come someone who will restore the entire Christian Church. At the same moment of Nostradamus prophecy being fulfilled the biblical scripture 2 Thessalonians 2:3-4 was also fulfilled by me who revealed to the world who the "man of sin" is.

Nostradamus Predicts the Man of Sin

Nostradamus specifically points to this world figure in his prophecy naming him as MABUS. By using anagrams of his real name Mikhail Gorbachev, his arrival on the world stage place him in the prophecy's time frame.

"Mabus will soon die and there will happen a dreadful destruction of people and animals. Suddenly, vengeance will appear, a hundred hands, thirst and hunger, when the comet past."

The comet of 1986 (Hailey's Comet) arrived in our skies at the same moment in history as Mikhail Gorbachev arose to power. Then in 1991, he received a death blow to his political career and died a political death. Immediately following his removal from the president of Russia, the wars in the former Yugoslavia began, America went to war with Iraq and ethnic cleansing perpetrated by the war in Bosnia was reminiscent of WWII.

Both the biblical scriptures and Nostradamus point out the fact that the "man of sin," will die.

Rev: 13-3 "And I saw one of his heads as it was wounded to death, and his deadly wound was healed."

Rev: 13-14 "A wound by the sword and did live."

Nostradamus: "Mabus will soon die and there will happen a dreadful destruction of people and animals."

The biblical scriptures and Nostradamus prophecy's are in further agreement with each other when they both predict the arrival of Mikhail Gorbachev to the world stage with a sighting by mankind of a comet or star in the same year 1986 the year of Gorbachev meteoric rise to power.

Nostradamus: "Suddenly, vengeance will appear, a hundred hands, thirst and hunger, when the comet past."

Hailey's Comet arrived in our skies in 1986 as Gorbachev begins his reign as president of the old Soviet Union now Russia.

Revelation 8:11 "And the name of the star is called WORMWOOD; and the third part of the waters became wormwood; and many men died of the waters, because they were made bitter."

In 1986 as Gorbachev took control of the old Soviet Union there was a Nuclear power plant meltdown at CHERNOBYL in Ukraine in which the explosion and radioactive fallout spread contamination for thousand of miles that reached land in Russia, Belarus, and Ukraine. Many people died and one third of the water turned bitter due to nuclear radiation.

If the nuclear waste was not stopped from spreading, lakes, rivers, and the ocean would be contaminated infecting the whole world.

Mikhail Gorbachev was responsible for the CHERNOBYL nuclear power plant and gave orders to limit press information in particular the body count total was gravely unreported. The bible points to Mikhail Gorbachev as that "man of sin" from the biblical scriptures in a way that can't be denied. CHERNOBYL in Ukraine means WORMWOOD, the name of the star that is poison to the third part of the waters in Revelation 8:11.

This is another example of how the Christian Church has adopted a blind eye to biblical prophecy being deciphered. It is how the Christian Church is killing Jesus Christ a second time.

Russia Returns

America has been in a war with Islamic radicalism that began with Osama Bin Laden for the past 20 years at this writing. The Middle East has become a ticking time bomb waiting to explode into all out war since Mikhail Gorbachev brought the old Soviet Union now known as Russia crashing down.

For the past 20 years The Russian bear has been in hibernation and stayed out of world affairs until today. They have returned to the world stage with vengeance.

For the first time in history, Russia has interfered in America's election system and put soldiers in the Middle East to protect the Syrian government, which has gotten the attention of the NATO Alliance. The other important fact is Russian troops are now located just a few miles from Israel, the apple of God's eye.

Nostradamus has given us a glimpse of the future with his epistle to Henry II where he writes a startling prediction. The return of the Antichrist to the world stage brings destruction.

"The Antichrist returns for the last time...All the Christian and infidel nations will tremble... for the space of twenty five years. Wars and battles will be more grievous than ever. Towns, cities, citadel and all other structure will be destroyed...

So many evils by Satan's prince will be committed that almost the entire world will find itself undone and desolated."

What if the dreaded arrival of the Biblical Antichrist and the "Man of Sin" is not a man alone but both man and country? The bible makes reference to a beast with two heads, and one of his heads is wounded to death. The bible also makes reference to a country coming from the far north that will destroy Israel. DAN: 9:26 "and the people of the prince that shall come shall destroy the city."

Nostradamus predicts a great war is coming before the man of peace arrives on earth. This calamitous event is being played out at this very moment in the Middle East and the plague. All the end time players have been set in motion.

"False Dust"

At this writing the corona virus has begun to threaten stability in the world. As the death toll continue to rise and the number of infected cases sky rocketing helps to heighten fear of end time predictions of total annihilation of the human species. The World Health Organization along with top scientist labeled the corona virus as a pandemic and is scrambling to lesson world panic.

What if this doomsday scenario was foreseen by Nostradamus? Well, this amazing prediction was prophesied by the famous soothsayer 500 years ago according to Erica Cheetham who is a famous interpreter of Nostradamus prophecies. What she uncovered is an astounding prediction that involves the United States, China, Russia, Turkey and Kurds all combining to reveal the plight of our world at this crucial time in world history.

Nostradamus claims the corona virus was manufactured in a lab and distributed throughout the world to affect the economic condition of world governments. The question is which government would benefit the most in this insane endeavor?

He even gives us a time span of this "FALSE DUST" as he describes it that last for a short duration.

While the U.S. is involved in a Trade War with China, conspiracy theories began to manifest with both sides blaming the other for some type of biological warfare. A prominent American senator said that the corona virus began in a lab in China. The Chinese diplomat said that the U.S. military created the virus and deployed it on Wuhan Province. The ambassador for China said on national TV that claims of the deadly virus began mysteriously in Wuhan Province but officials are still investigating.

Century V

NOSTRADAMUS: "In the Cyclades, in Perinthus and Larissa, in Sparta and all of the Peloponnese, a very great famine, plague through FALSE DUST. It will last nine months throughout the whole peninsula."

ERICA CHEETHAM INTERPRETATION: "False dust implies a chemical agent of some kind. Is Nostradamus trying to imply here that the plague and famine are artificially introduced? There appear to be a widespread disaster throughout the whole of Greece and the southern Balkans. This quatrain may tie in with those that predict trouble in the Middle East. Perhaps it may be a reference to the deaths of many thousands of Turkish and Iraqi Kurds."

This interpretation of Nostradamus prophecy can be found in Erica Cheetham's book published in 1989 titled "The Final Prophecies of Nostradamus". As you can plainly see Ms Cheetham's interpretation is identical to events of our world today right down to the wars in the Balkans in 1991 to the wars in the 21st century that involves Russia, Syria, Turkey and Iraq and Iran that has taken thousands of Kurdish and Iraqi citizens lives. Ms Cheetham was able to interpret that the deadly virus or "False dust" as Nostradamus describes it was created by man and deliberately administered to the world. Will the spread of this deadly disease (Plague) last for 9 months?

Century VI

NOSTRADAMUS: "In a short time the colors of the temples, the two will be intermingled with black and white, the red and yellow ones will carry off their possessions. Blood, earth, (PLAGUES), hunger, fire, maddened by thirst."

ERICA CHEETHAM INTERPRETATION: "Religion will become confused, unable to distinguish between right and wrong, the red and yellow people may well then refer to the Russian Communist and the Chinese who, when they carry the day, bring in their wake all the PLAGUES, famines and wars that are forecast."

This book is written because of the way the Christian Church has become complacent in ceremonial and pageantry and has lost the will to challenge everyday problems. When religious leaders see things that are wrong based on scripture from the bible and cannot distinguish between what is the right way to behave then the Church must be admonish. This is why the Christian Church is killing Christ a second time because they can't distinguish between what is right from wrong based on Christian values. Religious leaders have become confused by secular belief introduced by Satan's lies.

Nostradamus is speaking about our time in the 21st century when the Christian Church has been rendered useless and cannot render a verdict in today's affairs. Nostradamus was capable of seeing my written text from this book alerting the Christian Church over 500 years ago. In Century VI he said that the Church is unable to distinguish between right and wrong. I wrote the exact same sentiment in the first chapter of this book without any knowledge of Nostradamus opinion. Was he able to see in the future what I've discussed in this book?

The famous seer was capable of visualizing scenes of man made viruses, China, Russia, America and the Church heading for a showdown with God Almighty.

Although the corona virus may have began in China, Nostradamus also describe a country made up of black and white people that seems to imply the mixing pot of America and the color red that represents Russia and yellow being the nation of China. All three countries are associated with a plague. He describe this FALSE DUST or deadly disease materializing doing the time when Russia reasserts itself in world affairs, specifically sending troops to help Syrian Leader Assad massacre thousands and caused thousands more to become refugees and the annexing of Ukraine that resulted in the death of thousands of Ukrainian due to the war with Russia.

From the wars in the former Yugoslavia (The Balkans), the Gulf war, war with Iraq, war with the Taliban in Afghanistan, even Osama Bin Laden and his terror campaign can be found in Nostradamus prophecies. The following is a chronology of wars beginning in 1991 the year Mikhail Gorbachev died a political death just as Nostradamus predicted in his epistle to Henry II: Note: all prophecies are interpreted by Erica Cheetham and Peter Lemesurier except names identified by me in which I filled in the blanks.

"In the Adriatic there shall be such great conflict that those who were united shall be torn apart and, to a house, cities will be destroyed..."

"Great discord in the Adriatic (Italy), Yugoslavia and Greece, warfare will arise...unions will be split apart...including England and France...

In that time and in those countries an inferno power will rise against the Church of Jesus Christ..."

In these prophetic visions by Nostradamus, you are able to see Bosnia being torn apart by war and thousands of lives lost to ethnic cleansing. The Bosnia-Croat-Serb war threatened to spread all over Europe and plunge the world into WWIII. This war began in 1991 the same year Mikhail Gorbachev resigned from office after a coup de tat.

This war also happened the same year Osama Bin Laden rose to power as Nostradamus describes for us "an inferno power will rise against the Church of Jesus Christ." It is the same year Osama Bin Laden proclaimed a holy war or Jihad against America and all Christians and Jews.

From that moment in time Islamic radicalism grew in numbers spurned by the hatred of Osama Bin Laden that caused the ending of the 20th century to become a horrific time of terror, and the Middle East waiting to explode into all out war.

Nostradamus describes this new evil leader coming from the Middle East and specifically identifying the country of his birth, Saudi Arabia. Observe this prophetic prediction by Nostradamus;

"In the fortunate country of Arabia will be born one powerful in the laws of Mahomet."

"He will be born of the gulf and the immeasurable city, born of dark and obscure parents. He will wish to destroy the power of the great, revered King throughout Rouen and Eureux."

As Osama Bin Laden terrorizes the world with his brand of Islamic fundamentalism, the other evil tyrant (Saddam Hussein) invades Kuwait which results into the Gulf war, that war also began in 1991.

"The King of Europe will come like a giffon, accompanied by those of the North. He will lead a great troop of red and white. They will march against the King of Babylon." (CX Q86)

The North is represented by the red, white and blue stripes of the American flag that symbolizes the U.S. military force, and a Coalition of nations coming to rescue Kuwait from the jaws of Saddam Hussein, the King of Babylon. That war is called the Gulf War.

As the world watched America and a coalition of nations chase back Saddam Hussein threat of destroying the oil fields the other evil tyrant begins his reign of terror as he calls for a holy war or Jihad against America and Israel, and all Jews. Nostradamus points out to us Osama Bin Laden's thirst for terror as he calls for the death to all Christians and Jews in this prophetic quatrain.

"From Fez, the kingdom will stretch out those of Europe. The city blazes, the sword will slash. The great man of Asia with a great troops by land and sea, so that the blues perse, will drive out the cross to death." (CQI Q80).

As the rise of Islamic terrorism continued to spill over into the 21st century, Nostradamus gives us a powerful vision of a dramatic event taken from today's news. This only event that I am about to describe could only happen in our day and age because 500 years ago there was no television. Observe this prophecy;

"The blue leader will inflict upon the white leader as much evil as France has done them good. Death from the great antenna hanging from the branch. When he is seized, the King will ask how many of his men have been captured." (CII Q2).

America and a coalition of nations went to war with Iraq a second time in 2002 but this time Saddam Hussein is seized hiding in a whole in the ground. After about a year into the war, Saddam Hussein is captured by U.S. troops and while in captivity he asks his captors, "how many of his men have been captured?"

The broadcasting of Saddam Hussein's death was seen by millions of people around the world on television (antenna) just like Nostradamus prophesied over 500 years ago. After Saddam Hussein's death the Shiite's (blue turban) and the (Sunni (White turban) struggled with each other, sometimes with deadly violence to become the dominant sect.

The accuracy of Nostradamus prophecies is astounding. How was he able to see television being broadcast all over the world and during that event see Shiites and Sunni's clashing while the death of their leader (Saddam Hussein) is broadcast all over the world on national television? Nostradamus even describes the method of punishment, death by hanging. He said, "death from the great antenna hanging from the branch." Even the Europeans call their TV stations "antenna."

Erica Cheetham and Peter Lemesurier interpreted these prophecies by Nostradamus many years before the invasion of Iraq and Saddam Hussein's capture. They did not realize at that time these particular quatrains were talking about Bin Laden or Saddam Hussein or even Iraq. They made it easy for me to fill in the blanks and identify names because these prophecies can only be fulfilled through time. Even Mikhail Gorbachev was not named by Erica Cheetham or Peter Lemesurier as "the man of sin" from the bible or Nostradamus predictions. These names can only be seen when looking back through time specifically in the last 25 years of major events that Nostradamus beckons us to take notice.

Nostradamus has given us most of the major players in the end time scenario. He even reveals God's messenger and "man of sin" and describes to us the plight of the Christian Church. For more than 500 years these prophecies were sitting in archives waiting to be interpreted. These end time prophecies are telling us that after 6000 years of mankind's toiling in the sun, Jesus Christ will return to this earth bringing with him the Kingdom of God.

The accuracy of Nostradamus' prophecies is astounding. How was he able to see television being broadcast all over the world [illegible] with [illegible] of the [illegible][1] [illegible] television [illegible] describes the method of punishment: death by hanging. [illegible]

[illegible]

CHAPTER 8

REFLECTION,

THE MIRACLE OF THE SUN,

ON CROSSVIEW

On the cover of this book is a photograph of a phenomenon that I experienced at my home in my backyard on 10-13-19 at 8:40 am. That event brought tears to my eyes as I witnessed the power of God and realized that he chose me out of the whole universe to reveal his awesome way of expressing himself.

In this chapter we will explore the different meaning of the word reflection so that we will be able to see the many shades of our life. Once God shines his light on you it would be up to you to reveal what type of reflection you shine back at the world. Will your reflection be of lightness or of darkness?

The miracle that happened at my home was created by the hand of God. The cross made of sun light that materialized from the sun in my backyard was viewed by many of my friends, relatives and strangers. At the moment of this majestic cross made of sun light's appearance in my backyard it did not occur to me that my address and place of resident bare the name of this miracle. My home is located on CROSSVIEW. Is this a coincidence or divine intervention?

Is there a scientific point of view that we can examine explaining how a reflection can create this miracle? How did the sun rays single out my house and backyard with pin point accuracy to make a cross made of light and place the image at my view point a few feet from my back door? I have lived in this house for 14 years and have never seen anything like a cross made of light shining as bright as the sun on the lawn of my backyard.

When we examine the Cross of Light to see where it could possibly come from we figured out if we stand inside the Cross of Light while taking a camera and pointing it toward the direction of my house we discovered a brilliant ball of light as bright as the sun hovering in front of one of the windows of the house. This event was done after encouraging my son to not look directly at the object because the light was so bright it may cause blindness. Matter of fact my son closed his eyes while taking a camera shot of the house.

This brilliant light served as the source that created the image in the yard. The ball of light appeared to look like a mini sun hovering over the window. At that moment it appeared to be two suns, one in the sky and the other hovering over the window. While the image of the sun is hovering in front of the window, it reflects a Cross of Light that has a dimmer light surrounding it for accent which means 'look at me, I am here, I am Jesus, I've heard your prayer. This cross made by the sun was not a cross made by humans like neon signs, etc. It was a cross made of sun light that represents Christianity, the face of Jesus Christ.

This was no ordinary reflection that appeared in my backyard. The cross made by the sun was done in stages. It was like a spotlight or hologram being shined at a specific target. The image first appeared as a bright diamond shaped light with a brighter diamond shape light in the middle on the fence of my backyard. I watched the image move from the fence to the lawn within seconds as if being directed from above. God made an adjustment of the cross of light from one area to another to place it within my point of view. As I stood in awe at the site of the image of the cross it developed into a perfect cross of light right before my eyes. A random reflection cannot do that unless it's being directed from some form of intelligence. The cross made by light was surrounded by a lesser light with a pentagon shape which made me realize this event is from God.

God created the image of the cross on my lawn to get my attention. He wanted me to focus on the task at hand. To call on him when needed, and to complete the mission. Malachi 3:10 "I will send my messenger...."

How can a clear window create such a splendor that has never happened before? My window reflected exactly what it saw from the sun's image, the crucifix. The sun and the earth had to be in perfect harmony to create such an event. It happened just like an eclipse of the sun that amazes scientist and stargazers all over the world.

This supernatural event that occurred at my home could not have happened without prayer. The previous year my family had to endure a lot of pain and sorrow due to the many lost of love ones. Prayer was the only consolation that helped us through those difficult days. This particular incident became the catalyst that motivated me to ask God for help. I ask God to perform a miracle. My wife's sister was murdered one year exactly from the date of the Cross of Light appearing in my backyard. When I saw the Cross of Light appear I knew it was God answering my prayer.

While writing this book I needed confirmation that I was worthy and have authority to write a book of this magnitude. After I completed writing 5 chapters of this book I felt that I needed to hear from God directly so I prayed to Jesus that I would not write another word until I hear from God himself. I needed God to show me a sign.

When I saw the Cross of Light in my backyard two months later, it was enough convincing. I knew then that it was a sign from God. Not only did I listen to my own thoughts, my friends, relatives and even strangers told me the same sentiment that it was an act of God and this was a sign and a miracle.

From that moment on I had come to realize that God was answering my prayer and he communicated with me in his own divine way. I had to interpret the meaning of the cross of light and the brilliant ball of light that look like a mini sun hovering in front of my window.

While viewing the cross made by sun light it appeared as a shield with its pentagon shape surrounding it. With further investigation of the cross of light it becomes obvious that the brilliant cross is a symbol of Christianity but because it's embroidered in a pentagon shape light it reminds me of shields used by ancient warriors but without the cross as a symbol.

The pentagon shape surrounding the cross made by light has a spiritual meaning. The pentagon's interpretation means it's the highest form of divinity in man. This is what landed in my backyard and has forever changed my life. Praise be to God. Hallelujah!

The mini sun that hovered in front of one of my windows was the image of God in dramatic glory shinning as bright as no man made image could duplicate. It was Jesus Christ himself who came to answer my prayer personally as I requested. He said to me, Psalm 84:11-12. "For the Lord God is a sun and shield: the Lord will give grace and glory: no good thing will be withhold from them that walk uprightly. O Lord of host, blessed is the man that trusteth in thee."

The appearance of Jesus Christ confirmed my belief and assured me to continue writing my book and uplift his holy name. Only God can prove the validity of what I was writing about and I would be protected and shielded from haters, doubters and those who do not believe.

Over 100 years ago while the world was experiencing a deadly pandemic three children witnessed the Virgin Mary appear and were told on 13 October 1917 there will be a miracle performed. Over 70,000 people witnessed the "Miracle of the Sun."

On October 13, 2019 exactly one hundred years later on the anniversary of the "Miracle of the Sun" a cross made of sun light appeared in my backyard for the whole world to see. A few weeks later a deadly pandemic materialized killing hundred of thousands of people as the death toll continued to mount. Examine the seven photos of this miracle for yourself and see the wonders of the universe being displayed in dramatic glory.

As the sun hovers over the window, it projects its rays like a spotlight toward the yard.

An image of a diamond-shaped light appears on the fence, but this is not the desired target being directed by the hands of God.

As the diamond-shaped image moves from the fence to the yard, a shadowy figure appears nervously, mine.

With desired target found, God transforms His creation right before my very eyes.

The majestic cross of light molded by the hands of God appears for the whole world to see, but it is not yet complete. It is still evolving.

"For the Lord God is a sun and shield: the Lord will give grace and glory." Psalm 84:11

Behold the Glory of God.
"Behold, I will send my messenger, and he shall prepare the way before me." Malachi 3:1

The symbol of the cross is a powerful statement for Christians who hold firm to their faith. Throughout the ages this symbol has carried the belief in Jesus Christ all over the world and serves as a beacon of light for millions of followers. These photos of the cross made of light is for people whose faith is dimming and serve as proof of the many ways God is willing to reach out to us if only we believe. It is because I chose to uplift his holy name is the reason he appeared to me.

There are many people who have doubt in the existence of God. Prominent and educated people like doctors, lawyers, policeman and others do not believe in God but hold firm to their belief in atheism. God's answer to those who do not believe is stated in Psalms 14:1. "The fool hath said in his heart, there is no God." This scripture is a plain and simple answer that if not obeyed will have dire consequences.

There are many people who has committed murder and gotten away with it so they think. The disobedience of people all over the world has shown a great disrespect to the laws of God. Atheism is on the rise as people shy away from the words of wisdom from the pulpit. Our world is moving toward a world of an unbelieving world where God is relegated as a fairy tale. The biblical scriptures talks to us about this in prophecy; it said in 2 Timothy 3:1-7. "But realize this, that in the last days difficult times will come. For men will be lovers of self, lovers of money, boastful, arrogant, disobedient to their parents, ungrateful, unholy, unforgiving, malicious gossips, without self control, brutal, haters of good, treacherous, reckless, conceited, lovers of pleasure rather than lovers of God, holding to a form of godliness, although they have denied its power; always learning and never able to the knowledge of the truth."

This scripture from the pages of the bible describes the state of our world today. As the headlines from newspapers and television reveals to us it's a carbon copy of recent news events of greedy corporate leaders and corrupt politicians who leave their victims with broken dreams and empty pockets.

People who do not believe in God think that no one is watching and can get away with anything that is unlawful. My message to those who think they have gotten away with murder you better re-think it. The Sun was projecting itself as a Cross. Therefore, when you look at the Sun you are looking at the face of God. For God is the Sun. You can run but you cannot hide from the Lord. What's done in the dark must come out into the light.

Reflection — Bad Behavior

The way we are taught by our parents and school officials reflects good or bad behavior. If a child is never taught the difference between good and evil the consequences can be devastating for him, his family and community. That is why parents must inject the belief in Jesus Christ as guidance. Why does people who do evil deeds do not reflect on the danger to themselves or others before committing a heinous crime? If they had reflected on the teachings of Jesus, they would be compelled by the will of God to refrain from evil thinking. The fear of God must be taught at an early age.

Our sun shines its rays on earth everyday and every human being or anything that lives benefit from its majestic rays of light. When the sun rays strike a person who has evil intention his evil doings will manifest in the light. His reflection will be seen as darkness. The Bible explains the battle between light versus darkness this way, "No man, when he hath lighted a candle, putteth it in a secret place, neither under a bushel, but on a candlestick, that they which come in may see the light. The light of the body is the eye; therefore when thine eye is single, thy whole body also is full of light; but when thine eye is evil, thy whole body is full of darkness. Take heed therefore, that the light which is in thee be not darkness. If thy whole body therefore be full of light, having no part dark, the whole shall be full of light, as when the bright shining of a candle doth give thee light." (Luke 11:33-36). Those people who perpetrate evil never allowed Jesus Christ to grow and be nurtured in their decision making. Christ is the light of the world and those people who ignore his teachings will forever be in darkness.

Different Shades of Reflection

On a beautiful sunny day Billy prepares his clothes for the upcoming event that he has been reflecting on for months. He chose April 20th as the day to commit the unthinkable. That date is the birth date of Adolf Hitler. Why has Billy chosen the most evil tyrant in the 20th century to imitate? Why did he choose a swastika over the cross to follow?

Billy's attire for that day was a black trench coat with a swastika on his arms, and he called himself, "The Black Trench coat Mafia." Their motto, "Insanity is healthy." Those lyrics were used during the time of Hitler.

If Billy had the right training at the beginning of his life, he would have been able to think clearly and reflect on Christ. Billy did not know Jesus; therefore, he grew up with Satan as his master. On that faithful day, he asked a fellow student "do you believe in Jesus Christ?" and the student answered and said "yes." He responded by pulling the trigger of his gun, killing the student instantly.

The Good Shepherd

John 10: 11-18; Jesus said, "I am the good shepherd. The good shepherd lays down his life for the sheep. He who is a hired hand, and not a shepherd, who doesn't own the sheep, sees the wolf coming, leaves the sheep, and flees. The wolf snatches the sheep, and scatters them."

Jack is a man of God who grew up in church and sang his heart out in the choir. He was eager to join the military because he wanted to continue the family's tradition.

On a rainy day in Vietnam, Jack and his platoon were under heavy gunfire from the enemy's barrage of bullets streaking over their heads. As he and his comrades took over a trench hole, a grenade thrown from afar landed beside them on the ground. With certain death imminent, Jack picked the grenade up and tossed it back, but it exploded the moment it left his hand.

Jack survived but lost his arm. He saved his fellow soldiers that day and because of his brave act it reflected credit on his character due to his upbringing in church.

God's Light Shine on Me

After years of reflecting on my life and pondering about the mysteries of the universe, it's only fitting that a cross of light made by the hands of God would put the exclamation mark on the sum total of what I've become. The cross of light confirmed to me what I already believed: that I am a child of God who carries him in my heart. Proverbs 27:19; "As in water reflects face, so the heart of man reflects the man."

The moment my mother placed a small bible in my hand and sent me and my brother to Sunday school, that event became the motivating factor that helped me fall in love with all the biblical characters and stories. So when God shined his light on me, it was no accident. He knew me before I was born.

The two characters that I wrote about were based on true events. God shined his light on both men which reflected two different outcomes. They both had the opportunity to seek God. That is the determining factor which set them on different paths. "Seek ye the kingdom of God, and all things will be given to you." Matthew 6:33.

History of People who Saw a Cross Made by the Sun

Over 2,000 years ago, Jesus Christ was put on a wooden cross and died for the sins of man. Before Jesus hung on the cross on that horrible day, he was tormented by the people of Galilee. Not only was he persecuted by the King of Galilee, people inflicted wounds on him that caused him to suffer much pain and agony before he arrived at the place called the Skull. Not only did he have to carry his own cross to his death, he was spat on, cursed, kicked, and sharp edge thorns were placed on his forehead. After suffering much pain and agony, he died on the cross that very day. Then after three days, he arose. Jesus was resurrected.

That event sparked the flame of Christianity to be born. It has left Christians with a heavy heart filled with the will to glorify and uplift the name of Jesus.

Throughout the ages, the CROSS has become the symbol of Christianity. When people see the cross they immediately focus their attention on Jesus Christ providing that they are believers. So when the cross appears in apparitions or someone's dreams, it has a powerful effect on people's psychology. Whether people believe in apparitions or not, the event of seeing a cross gets Christians or even non-believers attention, although non-believers have skepticism. Personally, I have a zero tolerance for hoaxes. It serves to discredit the will of God and has no place in this book or what I'm promoting to fellow Christians and non-believers.

The cross of light that I saw at my home is a legitimate miracle of the sun. No gimmicks or smoke and mirror were done. When a cross of light was sighted ages ago, it was viewed as a sign from God and made a great impact on Christianity. Take for example Constantine the Great, Roman Emperor from 324 to 337 A.D. who became a crusader for Christianity and allowed worship to flourish in a hostile environment. For the first three centuries, the Christian Church endured persecution from the Roman Empire. So, what caused the Roman Emperor to stop persecuting Christians and become a Christian himself?

The other amazing event that is similar in nature comes straight from the biblical scriptures when it identifies the patriarch Paul who persecuted Christians until he saw Jesus Christ in a radiant light and changed his belief and became the greatest crusader for Christ.

So, what event caused the Roman Emperor Constantine to convert and embrace Christianity? "He said that about noon, when the day was already beginning to decline, he saw with his own eyes the sign of a cross of light in the heavens, above the sun, and bearing the inscription, ‘by this symbol you will conquer.’ He was struck with amazement by the sight, and his whole army witnessed the miracle.”

During the days of the Roman Empire, there were many Romans worshiping idols. So why did Roman Emperor Constantine have a different belief? Remember the two examples of men who had different paths to follow due to the belief or disbelief in Jesus Christ. Well, Constantine’s father believed in God and trained his son to follow in his footsteps.

God shined his light on Roman Emperor Constantine and his reflection energized him to become one of the greatest men to uplift the Christian Church and advance Christianity in the ancient world.

Constantine was so amazed by the sighting of the cross of light, he ordered his men to build a banner in the image of a cross in gold and stones. This cross would be carried in wars and would be the symbol of salvation to those who fought alongside him and be a deterrent to his enemies and energizing the cross as a symbol for Christianity to this day.

Saint Francis of Assisi

St. Francis of Assisi is the Italian founder of the Franciscan Order. He was born at Assisi in Umbria in 1181 and died on October 3, 1226. He is well known as ‘the little poor man of Assisi’ and became a great saint in the religious world of Catholicism. He displayed great compassion for the poor which made him unique amongst his peers. St. Francis of Assisi was a great humanitarian and set an example for those of us to follow him with love for our Lord and Savior Jesus Christ.

God visited St. Francis in a dream one night before he began his journey to fight in a war. This is the dramatic turning point in his life that would set the course of his golden life of passion for Christ.

With a pending career of war on his mind the night before, he had a dream that would change his life forever. In the vision, “he saw a vast hall hung with armor all marked with the cross. 'These,' said a voice, 'are for you and your soldiers.'" From that point on his life changed forever. He decided to put down the weapon of war and pursue a life of serving our Lord and Savior Jesus Christ.

The Miracle at Fátima

In 1917, one of the greatest miracles in recorded history occurred at Fátima, Portugal. Over 70,000 people witnessed what was called the "Miracle of the Sun." Before this amazing event occurred, the miracle was prophesied by three children who witnessed the appearance of the Virgin Mary. The children were told by the Virgin Mary of coming events that would change the world and that a miracle would be performed so that the whole world could see and believe in her. The people who witnessed this event on October 13, 1917 were stunned and shocked to see the sun move from one area to another then begin to dance in the sky as onlookers became hypnotized by this extraordinary spectacle. The Catholic Church declared this event as a miracle.

In the book "The UFO Phenomenon" by Time-Life Books describe the events this way; the largest crowed ever to witness a UFO event gathered at Fátima. "In 1917 on the rainy afternoon of October 13, a crowd of 70,000 people in Fátima, Portugal watched in amazement as the clouds parted to reveal a huge silver disk spinning like a windmill and dancing about the sky. The object gave off heat, and some of the witnesses would later state that their rain-soaked clothes had dried in minutes from exposure to it. After plunging toward the earth, the disk climbed back into the sky and disappeared into the sun."

Today millions of people view this event as a miracle sent by God. "The Miracle of the Sun" alerted the world to a new form of evil that would shake the foundation of the Christian faith. This form of evil would be universal and instituted a profound rejection of God. The "Miracle of the Sun" happened at Fátima, Portugal, on October 13, 1917, exactly one month later a revolution in Russia materialized that caused millions of people to reject God. This is the year that Russia began its quest for world dominance with communism as its official doctrine. Communism is an official doctrine that promotes atheism.

Confirmation

As I reflect on my life, the cross of light confirmed my conviction to fulfill God's prophecy and reveal the man of sin. 2 Thessalonians 2:3-4; "Let no man deceive you by any means, for that day (the day Jesus Christ returns to earth) shall not come except there come a falling away first, and that man of sin be revealed."

The Christian Church must acknowledge that Mikhail Gorbachev is that "man of sin" and be redeemed which will remove the restrainer that keeps Christ from returning to earth.

The cross of light also confirms for me that I'm that messenger God sends at the end time to prepare the way for Christ to return by removing the obstacle and restore the credibility of the Church. Prepare ye the way, for the Lord of host is near.

If the cross made by the sun was placed in another area of the yard I would have never seen it. It had to be placed in my point of view. God knew in advance where I would be standing when viewing the yard. He knew exactly what I would be looking for. If you listen to the world's POINT OF VIEW you will never see God. God already knew my Point of View. He placed me and my family exactly where I could be found, on Crossview.

CHAPTER 9

RUSSIA IN PROPHECY

If anyone would read the pages of the holy scriptures the name Russia will not be found. But the bible makes it clear that a powerful country that promotes atheism will come from the far north of Israel that will bring destruction to the world. Ezekiel 38:14-16 states, "Therefore, son of man, prophesy and say unto Gog, Thus saith the Lord God; In that day when my people of Israel dwelleth safely, shalt thou not know it. And thou shalt come from thy place out of the north parts, thou, and many people with thee, all of them riding upon horses, a great company, and a mighty army; and thou shalt come up against my people of Israel, as a cloud to cover the land; it shall be in the latter days, and I will bring thee against my land, that the heathen may know me when I shall be sanctified in thee, O Gog, before their eyes." As we examine Ezekiel's prophecy the atheist nation of Russia has become the country most theologians agree that measure up to his prophecies especially when we look at Mikhail Gorbachev's identity in which the former Soviet Union now Russia is his home. It is not a coincidence that the former head of the old Soviet empire has made Ezekiel's prophecy of GOG and MAGOG and 2 Thess. 2:3-4 which proclaim the "man of sin" come to life.

Although Mikhail Gorbachev was president of the old Soviet Union almost 30 years ago he has left us a lasting legacy that biblical scholars must pay attention to. The bible makes it clear that the people of the prince will destroy the city. Daniel 9:26 states, "and the people of the prince that shall come shall destroy the city."

The bible teaches us that just before the end of the world all the military powers will be divided into four superpowers. They are called the King of the North, the King of the South, the King of the East, and the King of the West. Today they are identified as Russia, the King of the North, the Arab countries the King of the South, China, the King of the East, and America the King of the West.

The prophet Ezekiel outlined the countries that will be a part of the Islamic coalition of nations that is heading toward a showdown with Israel. These Arabs countries have a unique relationship with Russia. Let us first examine Ezekiel's prophecy. Ezekiel 38:5-6 "Persia, Ethiopia, and Libya are with them, all of them with shield and helmet; Gomer and all the troops; the house of Togarmah from the north are with you."

For the first time in history Russia has put troops in the Middle East to protect the Syrian regime. The leaders of Israel is so worried because Russia's soldiers are just a few miles from their homeland they have dispatched envoys to the president of Russia many times expressing their concerns. They fear that the war in Syria will escalate bringing the conflict to their doorsteps.

In Ezekiel's prophecy he identifies Persia now Iran as one of the countries to join Russia in a coalition of nations heading toward a showdown with Israel. Russia and Iran has a unique partnership and shares a common goal. Both countries have formed a partnership in building nuclear weapons in Iran. According to journalist Jephraim P. Gundzik of Time Online said, "In the past several years a number of...Russian companies have faced U.S. sanctions for selling missiles and missile technology to Iran. Rather than slowing or stopping such sales, the pace of missile acquisition and development in Iran has accelerated...Russia's relationship with Iran have also advanced considerably in the past 18 months. In addition to increase investment in Iran by Russia and burgeoning arms trade between the two countries, Russia has been heavily involved in Iran's nascent nuclear energy industry. After much wrangling and repeated U.S. intervention, Russia and Iran finally signed, in February , a deal clearing the way for the shipment of Russian nuclear fuel to Iran's nuclear power plant at Bushehr."

The other reason why Iran is forming an alliance with Russia is because their ambition to destroy Israel can be realized with a friendship with the world superpower. While Russia's eye is on the oil fields in the Middle East, Iran's hatred for Israel is no secret.

There will be many nations that will join the coalition with Russia coming against Israel. Some will be Islamic and some pro-Islamic. It will be a massive army the likes the world has never seen. This enormous Army will spread its wings throughout the Middle East and the battlefield will not be limited to just the tiny country of Israel. Joining Russia in this diabolic attempt to control the holy land will be influenced by what the bible call "the three frogs." In the book of Revelation it describes this satanic trinity consisting of Satan's chief son the Antichrist; the False prophet and Satan.

REVELATION: 16:13-14-16 "And I saw coming out of the mouth of the dragon (Satan) and out of the mouth of the beast (the Antichrist) and out of the mouth of the false prophet (the Church) three unclearn spririts like frogs; for they are spirits of demons, performing signs, which go out to the kings of the whole world, to gather them together for a war of the great day of God, the Almighty...And they gathered them together to the place in Hebrew called Har-Magedon."

This massive army will invade Israel while its people are enjoying a time of peace due to the covenant signed by Israel's leader, the American and Russian leader, and the Biblical Antichrist. The American leader will be under the influence of Russia and broker a seven year peace accord with Israel. While Israel is enjoying a time of peace due to the covenant with America and Russia, the Antichrist will break the treaty after three and a half years. DANIEL 9:27 “And he shall confirm the covenant with many for one week; and in the midst of the week he shall cause the sacrifice and the oblation to cease.”

How Will America Respond?

When we look at the war in Syria and wonder why didn’t America intervene in that war reveals to us America’s unwillingness to get involve in a war with Russia. The world was horrified to see the atrocities perpetrated by the Syrian regime and Russian soldiers against fellow citizens that caused the death of thousands of lives.

The other shocking reason is how the American leader will make moves to benefit Russia and allow that atheist country to continue its aggression and influence in the Middle East. This action by the American leader will allow Russia to break the covenant with Israel and join with Iran and a coalition of nations to invade Israel. The countries joining in this effort will be the King of the South (the Islamic nations), the King of the East (China). America and her allies will not be in this war until later when they finally realize their calling from the Lord of Heaven. The invasion of Israel is described in the bible this way;

“You will come up against my people Israel like a cloud, to cover the land. It will be in the later days that I will bring you against My land, so that the nations may know me, when I am hallowed in you, O Gog, before their eyes.” EZEKIEL 38:16

It is “the people of the prince” that will invade Israel. God is dragging Russia and her allies into a showdown with Israel. It will be the people of Mikhail Gorbachev who God will make an example of for all nations to see.

Yet, while the invasion is taken place America and the Western superpowers will not intervene due to America’s sudden alliance with Russia. This alliance is caused by the diabolical influence of Satan that will last for a short duration due to the appearance of our Lord and Savior Jesus Christ.

Although the invasion of Israel by Russia and their allies is of their own accord, God is actually the one who is putting "hooks into their jaws" dragging them into battle as outlined in Ezekiel 38:4.

As the world is headed towards WWIII the outcome has already been decided by our Lord and Savior Jesus Christ. Ezekiel describes how God will destroy the armies of Russia.

"And I will turn thee back, and leave but the sixth part of thee, and will cause thee to come up from the north parts, and bring thee upon the mountains of Israel." Ezekiel 39:2, kjv

Armageddon is a place in Israel where many past wars were fought. In Hebrew the word Harmageddon means,"the mount of Megiddo or the Mountain of Slaughter. It is a mountain located in Israel and only a few miles from Jerusalem.

The "man of sin" whom I identified as the biblical character the biblical scriptures is referring to plays an important role in the invasion of Armageddon. Although Gorbachev is not seen in world politics today, his people (the people of Russia) is identified in Ezekiel's prophecy. God is against him and calls him by name. God draws him and the nations of the world to a specific place, Israel. "Behold, I am against you, O Gog, the prince of Rosh (Russia), Meshech, and Tubal, I will turn you around, put hooks into your jaws, and lead you out, with all your army, horses, and horsemen, all splendidly clothed, a great company with bucklers , shields, all of them handling swords, Persia, Ethiopia, Libya are with them, all of them with shield and helmet, Gomer and all its troops; the house of Togarmah from the far north and all its troops-many people are with you. Prepare yourself and be ready, you and all your companies that are gathered about you; and be a guard for them." Ezekiel 38:1-7.

What Role Will the Church Play When Russia Invades Israel?

The Christian Church will continue to remain silent and will be against the return of Jesus Christ. The nations and Churches will be angry at Jesus because the forces of Satan will convince them that Jesus Christ is the Antichrist. This is why the Christian Church cannot omit certain scriptures when teaching upcoming prophecy's to be fulfilled.

It is because of these omissions of scripture the Christian Church is killing Christ a second time.

The biblical scriptures identified two beasts that will appear at the end time. The first to appear is "the man of sin"; the second will be the Biblical Antichrist. I've already identified the "man of sin" who is outlined in this scripture, 2 Thessalonians 2:3-4.

In Ezekiel's prophecy "the man of sin" is called Gog and Magog. God stresses the point that he is angry with him and will make an example of him for the whole world to see. "Son of man, set your face against Gog, of the land of Magog, the prince of Rosh, Meshech, and Tubal, and prophecy against him." Ezekiel 38:1-2.

The prophecy of the "man of sin" and the Antichrist can be found in Revelation 13:1-18. "And I stood upon the sand of the sea, and saw a beast rise up out of the sea, having seven heads and ten horns, and upon his horns ten crowns, and upon his heads the name of blasphemy." Here the scriptures is describing a figure coming out of the seas which is interpret as someone coming out of the political arena. "And the beast which I saw was like unto a leopard, and his feet were as the feet of a bear, and his mouth as the mouth of a lion, and the dragon gave him his power, and his seat, and great authority. And I saw one of his heads as it were wounded to death; and his deadly wounded was healed; and all the world wondered after the beast." In chapter 2 of this book I identified Mikhail Gorbachev as the "man of sin" fulfilling this prophecy. Revelation 13 also describe a second beast who is connected to the first beast. "And I beheld another beast coming up out of the earth; and he had two horns like a lamb, and he spake as a dragon. And he exerciseth all the power of the first beast before him, and causeth the earth and them which dwell therein to worship the first beast, whose deadly wound was healed……."

The second beast that Revelation 13 is describing is the Antichrist. The irony of these two beast is that they both have a diabolical relationship with Russia and have a messiah complex. Let us examine some of the scripture that gives clues to his (the Antichrist) identity. This chief son of Satan will have supernatural and demonic power and will be able to thrive on magnetizing people's greatest fears and hatred. Daniel 8:23-25 "and in the later time (the end time) of their kingdom, when the transgressor are come to the full, a King of fierce countenance, and understanding dark sentences shall stand up."

This chief son of Satan will make a seven year peace treaty with Israel and break the accord within three and half years. "and his power shall be mighty, but not by his own power, and he shall destroy wonderfully, and shall prosper and practice, and shall destroy the mighty and holy people."

This chief son of Satan will have an enormous ego and a thirst for money and power. The prophet Ezekiel gave us a clue to look for when he gives us a history of the past Antichrist who was the king of Tyre. Daniel 8:23-25 "and through his policy also he shall cause craft to prosper in his hand, and he shall magnify himself in his heart, and by peace shall destroy many; he shall also stand up against the Prince of princes, but he shall be broken without hand."

This chief son of Satan will lead the world to Armageddon and oppose the second coming of Jesus Christ. He will amass a mighty army and try to fight Christ upon his arrival. He even proclaims that Jesus Christ is the Antichrist which draws other countries to join him in fighting against Christ.

The omission of these vital scriptures by the Christian churches will lead to the demise of the church, killing Christ a second time.

Armageddon

Jesus Christ will not be welcome with open arms. How will the Church recognize Christ if biblical scripture is being distorted? Pastors must engage with people more on a daily basis. Not just on Sunday morning. They must tell their congregation that the end time is approaching and you must be ready. Show them the scripture that relates to the second coming of Jesus Christ with all power and glory. Remind them that he will be returning to reside in his holy temple, the Church.

World trouble is escalating and is spinning out of control. With never ending wars that kills thousands every year, to gun violence that take innocent children lives, to murders and mayhem occurring on a daily basis. If this keeps up its going to take God to intervene if not the whole world will be destroyed. Matthew 24:22 “And except those days be shortened, there should no flesh be saved, but for the elect’s sake those days shall be shortened.”

The biblical scriptures speaks of a time in our world in the future when the world military powers enter a situation where they can’t pull back from. A situation so dire that it was compared to the time of Jacob’s Trouble that took place two thousand years ago. Jeremiah 30:7 “Alas! For that day is great, so that none is like it: it is even the time of Jacob’s trouble; but he shall be saved out of it.”

Jesus Christ called this time period the Tribulation Period. It will be a time when nations are concern more with luxury and wealth. It will be a time when self gratification and pleasure is more important than morality. It will be a time when integrity by our leaders becomes the thing of the past. It will be a time when truth is not truth anymore. It will be a time when music idols and sport figures becomes their God’s. It will be a time when men marry men and women marry women. It will be a time of immoral and sexual gratification that distort rational thinking. It will be a time when violence is accepted as part of the norm. It will be a time when the name Jesus Christ has been relegated to myth and mythology. It will be a time when the Christian Church is smeared in scandal.

A grave time is coming when a single world leader will catapult the nations toward Armageddon. He is described in Revelation 13 as the second beast who is the chief son of Satan.

When the first beast dies (the "the one who was wounded to death") the second beast will pay homage to him. As I stated in my letter to all Christian Churches naming the 1st beast as Mikhail Gorbachev the former president of the Old Soviet Union which is now Russia. His death will be viewed by Russia and the leader of the free world (America) as a saint. Together the two superpowers will build a statue in his image to honor him and demand that the world should worship him.

Although this scenario is only conjecture, it could very well happen the way I've described it. Revelation 13 describe this scenario with a vivid scene of the 1st beast who has fallen and the second beast builds an image to honor the 1st beast that causes all humans to be effected.

REVELATION 13:11-18 "And I beheld another beast coming up out of the earth; and he had two horns like a lamb, and he spake as a dragon. And he exerciseth all the power of the first beast before him, and causeth the earth and them which dwell therein to worship the first beast, whose deadly wound was healed. And he doeth great wonders, so that he maketh fire come down from heaven on the earth in the sight of men. And deceiveth them that dwell on the earth by the means of those miracles which he had power to do in the sight of the beast; saying to them that dwell on the earth, that they should make an image to the beast, which had the wound by the sword, and did live. And he had power to give life unto the image of the beast, that the image of the beast should both speak, and cause that as many as would not worship the image of the beast should be killed. And he causeth all, both small and great, rich and poor, free and bond, to receive a mark in their right hand, or in their foreheads. And that no man might buy or sell , save he that had the mark, or the name of the beast, or the number of his name. Here is wisdom. Let him that hath understanding count the number of the beast; for it is the number of a man; and his number is Six hundred threescore and six."

Revelation 13 is revealing to us an economic wizard will appear bringing to the world Satan's monetary system that will subject people to bow down to that all mighty dollar. This type of monetary system has already begun in today's society with the invention of a cashless way of buying and selling. With the invention of credit cards, micro chips implants, thumbprints and electronic transfer funds, and even banks are now requiring people to implant chips into people forehead and hand brings Revelation 13 to life.

Could COVID-19 be the method that brings the world economical system to a halt and usher in this new world order where Satan's monetary system "causeth all, both small and great, rich and poor, free and bond, to receive a mark in their right hand, or in their foreheads"?Revelation 13:16.

The identity of the Biblical Antichrist is hidden in numbers that the biblical prophets sealed for a certain generation to decipher. This particular person will have these numbers 666 written all over him. The place where the infamous meeting between Russian agents and American officials that began the Mueller Report took place in Building 666 that will forever be associated with treason allegedly perpetrated by the American officials.

It is important to note here that the day before election (2nd November 2020) of the next president of the United States of America there will be a gigantic meteor approaching very close to earth bringing the following biblical scripture to life, Revelation 13:13-14 "And he doeth great wonders, so that he maketh fire come down from heaven on the earth in the sight of men. And deceiveth them that dwell on the earth by the means of those miracles which he had power to do in the sight of the beast......" Whomever this persona is will be the biblical Antichrist.

The Seven Year Peace Treaty With Israel

During the cold war with Russia former President Ronald Reagan and Mikhail Gorbachev developed a friendship that ended the cold war. Today Putin the Russian president and the leader of the free world are joining in a peculiar way. This friendship between the two superpowers are compromising the NATO alliance that held communist aggression intact. This is the moment the world should beware because the bible foretells a coming peace accord with Israel that will be negotiated between Israel, Russia and America that will catapult the world into Armageddon. When we see the leader of the free world withdraw troops from Syria leaving the Kurds unprotected at the wish of President Erdoğan and the blessing of Russia makes one wonder.

When I served in the U.S. Army during the cold war my mission was to fight against communism and the old Soviet Union now known as Russian aggression. Today that mission seem to be just a mirage that faded into a distant memory. But something seems awry with our moral compass and some of our leaders who must have amnesia. Personally I'm pleading to our leaders to not fall asleep and allow this brazen attack on our precious democracy.

Today our leaders are more willing to start a war with our citizens than the adversary who has always had a mission to destroy democracy and what we hold dear to our heart and that is in "God we Trust." Even our allies has been targeted by our leaders as a lesser companion and Russian interest seems to be promoted.

Why has former military generals come out in public to announce their displeasure with the present leadership here in America? When words like fascism and Nazism floating around it sounds like we are at war, but not with our common enemy, but with ourselves. This time period must be a critical moment in world history because of what is at stake. We cannot be fooled by the rhetoric by our leaders. There is a profound trickery going on that is diabolical in nature.

Not only is democracy under attack but the biblical end time story is interwoven within our daily lives that's pushing us towards the Apocalypse. When you see former generals from our military voice their opinion against the leader of the free world we should not take this lightly. Something serious is going on that even the generals are spooked.

Prominent former government officials always ask this question pertaining to the leader of the free world. They ask, what does the President of Russia have on our leader that makes him act as a pulpit? Are we becoming the second head of a two headed beast? This is the reason why we must look at current events through the lens of God. Over 25 years ago Mikhail Gorbachev the former president of Russia "the man of sin" made this intriguing statement, he said, "An alternative between capitalism and communism is in the offing." Which means the creation of a New World Order can be realized as the alternative. It is a world that include Russia as a member of the G7.

In Daniel 8:23-25 prophesied that a man of fierce countenance and understanding dark sentences shall stand up. This individual will attempt to bring peace to the holy land by resolving the dispute between Islam and Israel. In the biblical scriptures this individual is called the Antichrist and will be the one who will create a covenant with Israel.

With this covenant the leaders of Israel will be confident that their protection by America would prevent any adversary from an invasion. But what if that scenario is compromised by a devoted friendship between America and Russia who the bible predicts is the country coming from the far north that will destroy Israel?

The seven year peace accord brokered by America, Russia and the European Union will be interrupted within 3 and a half years by an invasion by the country located from the far north of Israel. How long will the friendship last between Putin and the leader of the free world when Russia/Iran invade Israel and the leader of the free world sit silently and allow it?

The Withdrawal of U.S. Military from Europe

During the Cold War with the old Soviet Union I was deployed in Germany to fight against an impending invasion of Russian troops who threaten the stability of Europe. My deployment to Germany was a very good reason back then and it still is today with our military poised to counter any attack from Russia. But why would our present leader of the free world is threatening to withdraw 10,000 troops from Germany? Presently there are 35,000 United States troops in Germany with a mission to deter any attack but if troop amount is lessened it would give Russia the motivation they have been hoping for.

Today the world is facing a more aggressive Russia with sending their military forces to fight a war in Syria to help their president Assad and the on going war with Ukraine, and the interference in the American elections reveal to us that this country is the very country that could cause WWIII.

How our leader of the free world deal with Russia will determine what direction countries who believe in democracy will have an easier path to victory over demagoguery, nationalism, racism, xenophobia, and separatism. Or will our leader of the free world make it easier for those forces to spread across the globe? We must never forget what former President Ronald Reagan said concerning Russia, he said "They preach the supremacy of the state, declare its omnipotence over individual man, and predict its eventual domination of all peoples of the earth-they are the focus of EVIL in the modern world."

CHAPTER 10

THE FINAL WARNING

What if God asked us this question, "is there anyone on earth capable of seeing that the end time prophecy is being fulfilled and cared enough to investigate?" How would God react to the reality that the Christian Church remained silent because they were afraid of being wrong? What if no one came forward and revealed the "man of sin?" The biblical scriptures warned us of what God is going to do in the event that no one on earth would fulfill the prophecy. God warned us in Malachi 4:1. "For behold, the day cometh, that shall burn as an oven; and all the proud, yea, and all that do wickedly, shall be stubble; and the day that cometh shall burn them up, saith the Lord of hosts, that it shall leave them neither root nor branch."

I believe if I didn't step out on a limb and reveal the "man of Sin" God would destroy our world. Malachi 4:5 states, "Behold I will send you Elijah the prophet before the coming of the great and dreadful day of the Lord. I am just someone like Elijah of old who was inspired by God almighty to be a vessel to do his will.

The other important factor in this scenario is that if the Christian Church did not receive my end time message and refuse to acknowledge that Mikhail Gorbachev is that "man of sin" the world will be destroyed by the return of our Lord and

Savior Jesus Christ. Malachi 4:6. "And he shall turn the heart of the fathers to the children, and the heart of the children to their fathers, lest I come and smite the earth with a curse."

This book is the FINAL WARNING to the Christian Church before the return of our Lord and Savior Jesus Christ. In the early history of the Church of God the true gospel that Jesus Christ proclaimed was silenced and infiltrated by a false gospel that omitted the commandments of God. Today the Christian Church must return to the commandments God decreed and do not disregard scripture that is meant for followers of Christ to be aware of the fulfillment of prophecy. The statement by many ministers that the scripture 2 Thess. 2:3-4 is not taught any more is no excuse. This important scripture of it's fulfillment hinges on the return of our Lord and Savior Jesus Christ to this earth. It states, "Let know man deceive you by any means; for that day (the day Jesus Christ return to our world emphasis mine) shall not come except there come a falling away first, and that man of sin be revealed."

The Christian Church must get God's house in order. The Church must act as though Jesus was returning next year. Jesus Christ is coming to rule all nations. But he will not rule his Kingdom all alone. The Christian Church will help in implementing his laws and commandments.

When Jesus Christ returns to earth the separation of Church and state will not continue. This argument between government officials has caused the Church great harm in rendering it voiceless. The Kingdom of God is coming with a new government that will consume all nations. The Christian Church will play an important role in this effort. Jesus Christ will combine the Church and state under his direction. The world will worship one God, there will be only one government and only one religion, and one church.

For six thousand years of mankind rule on earth has proven that he is incapable of bringing peace to the world. Today many governments suffer from gun violence, wars and strife. They have no solution to the many problems facing society as the world spins out of control. In Isaiah 59:4, 7-10 speaks of our world this way, "None calleth for justice, nor any pleadeth for truth: they trust in vanity and speak lies; they conceive mischief, and bring forth iniquity....Their feet run to evil, and they make haste to shed innocent blood; their thoughts are thoughts of iniquity; wasting and destruction are in their path. The way of peace they no not; and there is no judgment in their going; they have made them crooked paths; whosoever goeth therein shall not know peace."

In the Kingdom of God there will be no corrupt politicians who only want to satisfy their pockets and leave people yearning for deliverance from poverty. In the Kingdom of God there will be no minister or priest who uses the pulpit to further alienate people from God by so called progressive thinking. In God's Kingdom elected officials have to earn a Pulitzer Prize by working for God instead of expecting to receive praise for who they are.

It will be the duty of the Church in the coming Kingdom of God to teach believers to become leaders and assist Jesus in molding the citizens of earth into a utopian civilization. This government will not be run by the will of man but by the will of God Almighty.

To many people the Church is insignificant in their lives. Even the belief in an unseen God is far from their reality. The only time some of the people attend church is when someone dies and they attend their funeral or attend a family or friend's wedding ceremony. So, what is the purpose of the Church? When we look at the stars in heaven they all must have a purpose. We all may not know what billions of stars are doing but we know without our sun in which is a star there would be no light to give the earth daylight. Without its brilliant light we would all be in darkness.

The Christian Church has a purpose just like the billions of stars in the universe. Its purpose is to illuminate the name of Jesus Christ. Although people do not attend Church on Sunday they are still aware in their mind that the Church is visible and seen all over the world so it must have a purpose in the scheme of things.

As a warning the Christian Church must adhere to the commandments of God and worship on the Sabbath and holy days. It must return to the true name The Church of God and alert people that the Kingdom of God is coming with the return of Jesus Christ.

Signs

In the middle of downtown New York City, in the midst of skyscrapers and vendors, a lonely derelict shouts a doomsday message that no one amongst thousands of people pay any attention to. As pedestrians and cars go back and forth, the derelict shouts out a disturbing message, "the apocalypse is coming! The end of the world is near!" As you already know people just don't take what he is saying as being serious. Surely, a derelict on the street does not know what he is talking about.

This scenario is repeated in every country all over the world. Most people ignore his disturbing plea as just another lunatic on the streets. When we get warning signs from God why don't we listen? We read signs everyday and obey the traffic signals, stop signs, posters and advertisements when it's at the appropriate time, but when it comes to biblical prophecy it is looked upon as fable.

In 2004 a tremendous tsunami struck Indonesia and other neighboring countries that caused shock waves around the world. It was so powerful the earth wobbled according to scientist. Hours before the earthquake and tidal waves occurred Indonesian elephants and other animals began running toward higher ground. They were able to heed the warning signs and were spared certain death. How did they know that certain death was imminent?

It did not fair well with humans who subsequently drown due to the enormous amount of water that overcame them. They did not see the signs of impending doom which caused thousands of lives lost to the over flooded cities and villages.

We must take heed of the warning signs that God has given us. The derelict on the street has completed his mission. The ministers and prophets that are labeled crazy have completed their mission. They have earned the treasures in heaven. But the atheist and non-believers who refuse to listen to the signs will have to deal with a shrewd awakening by the hand of God.

There are specific signs that warn us of the conclusion of this age. Jesus Christ predicted there will be earthquakes, wars and famines. Also the "preaching of the Gospel of Jesus Christ throughout the world for a witness to all the nations; and then the end will come." Mathew 24:14.

Pestilences

Luke 21:11 "And great earthquakes shall be in divers places, and famines, and pestilences; and fearful sights and great signs shall be from heaven."

Everyday we hear on the news the report of earthquakes destroying the peace of communities all over the world. Many countries, from Haiti to Italy and Japan, have felt the pain of human lost and the devastating destruction of cities. Earthquakes were not the only destructive force that Mother Nature brought on humanity. Fires spread quickly across major cities with horrendous destruction reminiscent of bombs dropped on cities in WWII.

It is heartbreaking to see poverty stricken communities around the world. From Sudan to Zimbabwe, malnutrition has spread across the African continent. Not only in the African continent but other countries are experiencing poverty that threatens to ravish the land and its people. A total of 5 billion people in other parts of the globe are suffering from the lack of food.

Super organism that was once dormant has awakened and poses a grave threat to humanity. These super organisms have a strong resistance to antibiotics and have built an immune system that has defeated new technologies and advances in medical sciences. Diseases like the Corona virus that spread across the world has left thousands dead and the world health organization scrambling to find a cure. With outbreaks of typhoid, cholera, malaria, diphtheria, and anthrax, these diseases have left health officials in dismay. With new inventions of antibiotics and vaccines, doctors will not be able to save us from the super diseases.

Signs Reminiscent of the Days of Noah

Luke 17:26-29 "And as it was in the days of Noah, so shall it be also in the days of the Son of man. They did eat, they drank, they married wives, they were given in marriage, until the day that Noah entered into the ark and the flood came, and destroyed them all."

Signs that we are presently living in the end times are all around us. It is the same conditions of the world that is described in the bible during the time of Noah when the world was destroyed by a flood.

I can imagine how difficult it was for Noah to warn people of an impending doom when people probably saw him as being crazy and a lunatic. Some of the people were busy in the pursuit of money, some were drowning in lust, and some were literally getting away with murder while others were blind and deaf to the truth.

While there are many signs of the end time today the one I am going to bring our attention to is the removal of a plaque containing the laws that Jehovah God gave to Moses (The Ten Commandments). This is a sign that our world is headed in a direction away from God. The plaque was displayed in the halls of the state capitol right here in America when our government officials protested its viewing by the public.

The following scriptures describe the world Noah lived in:

GENESIS 6:5 "And God saw that the wickedness of man was great in the earth, and that every imagination of the thoughts of his heart was only evil continually."

GENESIS 6-11 "The earth also was corrupt before God, and the earth was filled with violence."

GENESIS 6-13 "And God said unto Noah. The end of all flesh is come before me; for the earth is filled with violence through them, I will destroy them with the earth."

Boom! Boom! Boom! Boom! Run, what's wrong mommy? Just keep running. Boom! Boom! Boom! Someone yell's run, hide! Victims fall in front of mommy and child. Blood flows like a river on the floor as mommy and child run for their lives. They hide in a storage room with the door locked. They can hear the shooter ask a question. Do you believe in God? The victim who is a young girl responds yes. Then instantly rapid shooting begins again. Boom! Boom! Boom! The girl lay dead.

Can we distinguish which world I am describing? Is it the world that God destroyed during the time of Noah? Or is it the description of our world today?

My hope is after viewing the cross made by light by people of all faith that it alerts us to the fact that time is running out and one day it will be too late to come to God. Our world has become a VIOLENT place to inhabit and God is angry.

Tribulations

MATTHEW 24:8-9 "But all these things are merely the beginning of birth pangs. Then they will deliver you to tribulation, and will kill you, and you will be hated by all nations on account of my name."

The persecution of Christians, and Jews and other religious groups who follow our Lord and Savior Jesus Christ fulfills this prophecy. The massacre at Christ Church, New Zealand is a horrific example of how this prophecy is being fulfilled in today's world. The mass murder of Jews perpetrated by Hitler and the slaughtering of millions of people by Joseph Stalin left the 20th century as the century when the world went mad. Now that the 21st century has arrived, the murder rampage continues to plague the world with violence.

Our world is plagued with wars and rumors of wars on a daily basis just as the bible describes it. There are wars in Afganistan, Ukraine, Iraq, and Syria that threatens to bring the world closer to WWIII. Due to the invention of nuclear weapons the world experienced a false sense of peace that caused evil to manifest in other ways. Excerpt from the book, "History of the Modern World" from 1917 to 1980's. by Paul Johnson tells us that evil magnifies itself in many shapes and forms, he said, "It may be that, after the seemingly inevitability of two wars, the creation of nuclear weapons was an admonitory gift, which spared us a third clash of great nations and introduced the longer period of general peace, albeit a peace of terror, since Victorian times....What had gone wrong with humanity? Why had the promise of the nineteenth century been dashed? Why had the twentieth century turned into an age of horror or, as some would say, evil." The answer is written in biblical prophecy, "woe for the earth and for the sea, because the devil has come down to you, having great anger, knowing he has a short period of time." Revelation 12:12.

Now that the 21st century is here the world continue to be plagued by relentless wars that have caused millions of refugees suffering from murder and mayhem perpetrated by the weakness of man who thinks wars are the answer. Why does mankind choose to go to war instead of finding peace. Excerpt from the book "Religion of Man" that dramatizes the choices man makes instead of finding peaceful solutions.

"ONE WHO WOULD GUIDE A LEADER OF MEN IN THE USES OF LIFE WILL WARN HIM AGAINST THE USE OF ARMS FOR CONQUEST. EVEN THE FINEST ARMS ARE AS INSTRUMENT OF EVIL; AN ARMY'S HARVEST IS A WASTE OF THORNS."

Why does man's transgression escalate into war? Although his choices are plain and simple (Good versus Evil) he chooses the path of destruction. He realizes no one can really claim victory. There is great loss on both sides. But yet he chooses evil. He chooses the dark side of him to solve problems.

"IN TIME OF WAR MEN CIVILIZED IN PEACE TURN FROM THEIR HIGHER TO THEIR LOWER NATURE. BUT TRIUMPH IS NOT BEAUTIFUL. HE WHO THINKS TRIUMPH BEAUTIFUL IS ONE WITH A WILL TO KILL. THE DEATH OF A MULTITUDE IS CAUSE FOR MOURNING; CONDUCT YOUR TRIUMPH AS A FUNERAL."

Only when man recognizes that all men are a vital part of his own body will he come to realize that we as a human race are of one mind, one spirit, and one God.

Israel Recognized as a State

JEREMIAH 23:7-8 "Therefore behold, the days are coming declares the Lord, when they will no longer say, as the Lord lives, who brought up the sons of Israel from the land of Egypt, but as the Lord lives, who brought back and led back the descendents of the household of Israel from the north land and from all the countries where I have driven them. They will live on their own soil."

In 1948 Israel was established as a state fulfilling the prophecy. The return of the Jewish people to the land of Israel was decreed by Jehovah God over two thousand years ago.

The Preaching of the Gospel Throughout the World

MATTHEW 24:14 "And this gospel of the kingdom shall be preached in the whole world for a witness to all nations, and then the end shall come."

The spreading of the word of God has been accomplished throughout the world. With the advent of television, computers, radio and the translation of the bible in may languages serves to speed up the process of enlightenment. With the invention of the internet God's words are delivered to people in an instant.

The cross of light that appeared in my backyard is a warning sign for the 21st century. It is meant for the Christian Church to prepare itself for the return of Jesus Christ. It is also meant for people all over the world who has lost faith and need proof that God exist. It is also meant for the non-believer who sees the world only through the eyes of a sparrow.

Why is Demagoguery on the Rise?

Demagoguery is rising in many countries around the world that threatens democracy in a way that if not stopped America and all other democracies will fall. Is Satan mounting his last effort to maintain a firm grip on the world by using his most lethal weapon and that is demagoguery? We must examine how the characteristics of Satan play a major role in our elected officials who is put in charge to lead us in a direction away from God.

The leader for the free world has shown us how his characteristic of Satan is being adopted by other leaders around the world. On national TV let me remind you that he announced to the whole wide world after looking up at the sky he said, he is "THE CHOSEN ONE." Following his announcement broadcasters coined him in the likeness to the second coming of

Christ. They said that he was the King of the Jews and the King of Israel.

The rise in populist demagoguery among other nations can be seen in countries like Hungary, Poland and even in Europe when Brexit became a victim of this. Former Polish Prime Minister Jaroslaw Kacynsky who is a right wing demagogue is a defender of conservative values, embraces Christian values, nationalism, and anti-migrant is on a mission to save his nation from foreign invasion. He see's himself as the savior of the world and is seen by some religious leaders as the "CHOSEN ONE." Why is the leader of the free world and a former prime minister display a "MESSIAH" complex?

For those people who think that this world is not about God but a world where atheism rules better think again. Obviously the two leaders are being led by an unseen presence that can only be revealed in their characteristics. Their action speaks louder than words.

There is only one messiah that the world awaits his return. Jesus is the only messiah the biblical scriptures talk about that is God almighty. Satan is the one the bible says, wants "to be like the most High." Isaiah 14:14. The irony here is that both leaders have Christian values and uses Jesus Christ as an image. Both leaders want to be like the most High and they make sure we know it.

Both leaders have the same characteristics illuminating their belief system. They both have been called homophobic, polarizing, xenophobic, a slanderer, accuser, and a chronic liar and lawless, immoral and unethical, and hater of the truth. All of these are the characteristic of Satan.

The rise of demagoguery has spread to other countries that could breed people like Adolf Hitler who exploited people's economic hardship and hatred for Jews that resulted in millions murdered. Today the influx of migrants has become the enemy just like the Jews were seen as in the 1930's.

Populist demagogues use fear and racism as a weapon to stir up hatred toward a certain race. The far-right movement sees refugees as invaders instead of people needing help. This tactic is being used right here in America against a certain ethnicity.

The refugees are labeled as terrorists and have diseases that make their entry unwelcome. It is sad to think that the leader of the free world is influencing European's right wing nationalist to rise up and maintain solidarity.

Demagoguery and Satan is working together to bring about a certain end. They both have the same goals and that is to rule the world as the savior. As history reveals demagogues have infiltrated democracies and reshaped it according to its insane doctrine. Satan uses demagoguery as a tool to win over political leaders and mold them into his likeness.

Democracy has reached a crucial point in history where its survival is at stake. Christianity has reached a crucial turning point in its survival where it must choose to become a vital voice in the world or succumb to the cunning of Satan. If democracy fails Christianity will fall as well. Our political leaders must stop demagoguery before the world repeat what happened when Adolf Hitler manifested evil in its most horrific form.

Richard Holbrooke, former U.S. Ambassador-designate to the United Nations, could not explain the resurrection of Hitler any better as the most influential figure of the century, he said, "Adolf Hitler-would be awful to see his face on Time Magazine last cover of the millennium, but I must admit conclude, with the greatest sadness and reluctance, that the person who had the most profound impact on the events of the 20th century was also the century's most evil person: Adolf Hitler. The poison unleashed by Hitler and his terrible contemporary Joseph Stalin survives. Not only must we mourn at century's end, the tens of millions who died as a result of their actions but we can still see in many parts of the world from Kosovo to Rwanda; murderous echoes of Hitler's theories and policies, promoted through methods of mass communication and propaganda invented by Joseph Goebbels. The essence of Hitlerism-racism, ethnic hatred, extreme nationalism, state organized murders is still alive, still causing millions of deaths. Freedom is the century's most powerful idea, but the struggle is far from over."

Adolf Hitler was an Antichrist spawned by the belief in demagoguery in its most destructive display of evil the world ever witnessed. If this is an indication of what's to come in the world's future then we as Christians must expose Satan before it is too late. Today we have an individual in the highest office in the land that has characteristics of a demagogue. The irony here is that Christian Evangelicals selected him as their choice to lead the world. Christians and our leaders cannot afford to continue to ignore the leader of the free world characteristics. The biblical scriptures describe the Antichrist as the "Lawless One." Doesn't this definition describe the characteristic of the leader of the free world?

What happened to the integrity of our institutions here in America? It was stated by some of our public officials that a cancer has infested our government. Everything he touches turns to corruption. It doesn't matter if its people or institutions corruption becomes the law of the land in this new world order at the hands of a dictator.

The credibility of America is at stake. How do NATO and our allies perceive America at this crucial time in world history? Corruption by our leaders helps to lessen the credibility of American standards in the eyes of other democracies.

As a veteran this is not the America I served in the military for. I am quite sure the soldiers who died in past wars would not be proud of the way our country has moved away from the teachings of God. The warning signs are all around us. The making of a dictatorship is on the horizon. The making of an autocrat is knocking on our door. Fascism is rearing its ugly head. A demagogue was in the White House. A biblical prophecy is being fulfilled.

CHAPTER 11

THE KINGDOM OF GOD IS COMING

The Holy Bible teaches us that a literal new government is coming that will consume all present governments. Yes, that includes America and the British Empire. The gospel of Jesus Christ tells us in Mark 1:14-15, "Now after that John was put in prison, Jesus came into Galilee, preaching the Gospel of the Kingdom of God, The time is fulfilled, and the Kingdom of God is at hand: repent ye and believe the gospel." Jesus Christ is the King who will rule over all governments and initiate his new kingdom that will last forever.

When will this happen? God has ordained a certain time period for this miracle to take place. It is written in the Holy Scriptures when we see the resurrection of the European Union or the last Roman Empire, this will be the deciding moment that will institute the return of Jesus Christ to earth. This has already happened in the last 25 years with our present day European Union in which the British Empire is trying to break away. These events are alerting us that the return of Jesus Christ is imminent.

For the past two thousand years the church has been the instrument God uses to prepare Christians to be utilized in his

Kingdom. When the Kingdom of God arrive here on earth Christians who have been trained to teach the Gospel of Christ will play an important role in transitioning from today's government to the Kingdom of God.

The Christian Church must remind parishioners that the coming Kingdom of God must continue to be preached throughout the religious order. This gospel by Jesus Christ must not be forgotten or omitted from daily teachings. This particular gospel is so important to today's theology that the patriarch Paul announced a curse would be place on those who preach any other foreign belief. Galatians 1:8-9 "But though we, or an angel from heaven; preach any other gospel unto you than that which we have preached unto you, let him be accursed." "As we said before , so say I now again; If any man preach any other gospel unto you that ye have received; let him be accursed."

When will this Kingdom of God comes? The biblical scriptures warned us that the coming of Jesus Christ will be like a thief in the night. During the time of Noah people were busy going about their lives unaware that their fate was sealed. The Pharisees asked Jesus when will the Kingdom of God appear. Luke 17:20-36 "And when he was demanded of the Pharisees; when the kingdom of God should come he answered them and said, The Kingdom of God cometh not with observation." Many people of the world today will not be observing the scriptures if it is not being taught by our ministers and priest. People who do not believe in Jesus will miss the opportunity to be saved because they pay more attention to their fake God's like the love of money, sex, and corruption.

Ministers with different beliefs will proclaim that the Kingdom of God is within you. Some will say that the kingdom of God is in the sciences. Still others will say it's just in the mind. The biblical scriptures captures these sentiments in this written text. Luke 17:21-23. "Neither shall they say; Lo here! Or, lo there! For, behold, the Kingdom of God is within you. And he said unto the disciples , the days will come, when ye shall desire to see one of the days of the son of man, and ye shall not see it." "And they shall say to you. See here; see there; go not after them, nor follow them."

Just like the days of Noah today people are following the same path that brought the wrath of God upon them. Today people are partying and drinking and marrying whom ever they choose and ignoring God's laws. Luke 17:26-30 "And as it was in the days of Noel, so shall it be in the days of the Son of man." "They did eat, they drank, they married wives, they were given in marriage until the day they entered into the ark, and the flood came, and destroyed them all." "Even thus, shall it be in the day, when the Son of man is revealed."

When the world begins to accept homosexuality as part of the norm especially in marriage you will no that the time of the Kingdom of God is near. Romans 1:26-27 "For this cause God gave them up unto vile affections, for even their women did change the natural use of into that which is against nature." "And likewise also the men, leaving the natural use of the women, burned in their lust one toward another; men with men, leaving the natural use of the women, burned in their lust one toward another......"

These are the reason that Sodom and Gomorah was destroyed as well as the Flood coming and destroying the world during Noah's time. The people at that time ignored the word of God even until the day of judgment. They must have heard the preaching of Noah warning them that God disliked the way they were behaving. If Churches of today do not teach the Kingdom of God is coming how will they be ready. People will continue to have a deaf ear to ministers and those who follow the teaching of Christ.

The Gospel of the Kingdom of God must be taught to people in order for them to be saved. It is very important to the gospel of Jesus other wise Christ would not have sent out seventy men, the apostles, and his disciples to spread this message throughout the world. The Christian Church's mission is to prepare ministers and followers of Christ to teach in the new Kingdom of God that this world desperately needs.

King Nebuchadnezzar's Dream

Today some of the prominent theologians believe that the Kingdom of God is the Christian Church. If we ask the average person on the street they will tell you that same belief. Still some people believe it's what's in a person's heart. But the biblical scripture stresses the point that there will be a real Kingdom of God governing people on earth and when it arrives it will consume all governments.

King Nebuchadnezzar was a great ruler in 605 BC to 562 BC in Babylon, who became the longest reigning king of that period. The bible tells us that he had a dream that puzzled him into madness. The dream drove him to seek help in deciphering it. He recruited the Chaldeans, magicians, sorcerers and astrologers to tell him the meaning of the dream and what it meant for him and his kingdom. They all failed in their attempt to decipher the dream which caused King Nebuchadnezzar to request for Daniel, the prophet.

Daniel's resume equipped him with the knowledge of visions and dreams which was perfect for the task at hand. Daniel 1:17 "And as for these four children, God gave them knowledge and skill in all learning and wisdom: and Daniel had understanding in all vision and dreams."

What Daniel revealed to King Nebuchadnezzar was so important it implicates what happens to our world today. The King's dream proclaim that there is a God in heaven who created the world and everything in it. Daniel revealed to the King that the God of heaven can know all secrets and can see into the future. He revealed that all governments are ruled by God.

Today the leaders of the world believe that they are controlling the nations and that they have all the answers to the many problems mankind is facing. They don't realize that the bible explains how all governments will come to an end in our time.

Daniel revealed to King Nebuchadnezzar that the whole purpose of the dream was to introduce him to almighty God and to be prepared for the Kingdom of God to come, and reveal what will happen in the later years, and our world today.

King Nebuchadnezzar's dream describe four kingdoms to come including his own. It is described in the bible this way:

> Daniel 2:31-36: "Thou, O King sawest, and behold a great image. This great image, whose brightness was excellent, stood before thee: and the form thereof was terrible. This image's head was of fine gold, his breast and his arms of silver, his belly and his thigh of brass, his legs of iron, his feet part of iron and part of clay. Thou sawest till that a stone was cut out with hands, which smote the image upon his feet that were of iron and clay, and break them to pieces. Then were the iron, the clay, the brass, the silver, and the gold, broken to pieces together, and became like the chaff of the summer threshing floors: and the wind carried them away, that no place was found for them; and the stone that smote the image became a great mountain, and filled the whole earth. This is the dream; and we will tell the interpretation there of before the king."

This is the dream that God sent to King Nebuchadnezzar, the King of Babylon of an image that describes the kingdoms that would rule the earth from Babylonian's time until the end time. With astrologers, magicians, Chaldeans, and sorcerer all trying to no avail to interpret the dream, only Daniel was ordained by God to meet the challenge.

Daniel's interpretation is as follows:

> DANIEL 2:36-43 "this is the dream; and we will tell the interpretation thereof before the king; thou o kings, for the god of heaven hath given thee a kingdom; power, and strength, and glory, and who so ever the children of men dwell, the beasts of the field fowls of the heavens hath he given into thine hand, and hath made thee ruler over them all. Thou art this head of

> gold, and after thee shall arise another kingdom inferior to thee, and another third kingdom of brass, which shall bear rule over all earth, and the fourth kingdom shall be strong as iron, for as much as iron breaketh in pieces and subdueth all things; and as iron that breaketh all these, shall it break in pieces and bruise, and whereas thou sawest the feet and toes, part of potter's clay, and part or iron, the kingdom shall be divided, but there should be in it of the strength of the iron. For as much as thou sawest the iron mixed with miry clay. And as the toes of the feet were part of iron, and part of clay, so the kingdom shall be partly strong, and partly broken. And whereas thou sawest iron mixed with miry clay, they shall mingle themselves with the seed of men; but they shall not cleave one to another, even as iron is not mixed with clay. And in the days of these kings shall the god of heaven set up a kingdom, which shall never be destroyed: And the kingdom shall not be left to other people, but it shall break in pieces and consume all these kingdoms, and it shall stand forever. For as much as thou sawest that the stone was cut out of the mountain without hands, and that it break in pieces the iron, the brass, the clay, the silver, and the gold; the great god hath made known to the king what shall come to pass hereafter: And the dream is certain, and the interpretation thereof sure."

Daniel's interpretation of King Nebuchadnezzar's dream accurately predicted the past history of the world and gives a glimpse of what will happen to the governments at the end of the world. The prophet Daniel Interpreted that Nebuchadnezzar's head of gold was the Medo-Persian period, the beast plate of silver. Alexander the Great of Greece defeated the Babylonians, its symbol was of brass. The Roman Empire its symbol of iron defeated Alexander's empire which divided into eastern and western empires. An important note to observe is that, the strength of the iron Kingdom becomes weaker as we move closer to today's time period. It is because the feet and toes of the image is mixed with iron and clay. These two materials cannot mix and hold together.

The Roman Empire did weaken and became partly broken and reformed in today's world as the United States of Europe or the European Union. The image in King Nebuchadnezzar's dream represents all the kingdoms of the world from the past to the present that will ultimately be destroyed by the return of our Lord and Savior Jesus Christ bringing with him his Kingdom of God.

Nebuchadnezzar dream was of a gigantic statue that terrified him. It had a head made of gold, its arms and breast was made of silver, its belly and thighs made of brass, its legs made of iron, and its feet made of iron and clay. In his dream he saw a stone from heaven smashing into the statue and broke into small pieces and blown away by the wind. Then miraculously the small stones reappear and becomes a great mountain that spread over the whole world.

Daniel informed the King that the head made of gold was him and after his kingdom would be another kingdom, and another kingdom of brass will follow. The prophet Daniel explained to the King that these images were actually governments that would appear ending in a government of God that would rule the earth forever.

We must pay attention to the time element presented by the prophet Daniel that brings attention to our day. When we see the reforming of the Roman Empire "shall the God of Heaven set up a kingdom, which shall never be destroyed...but it shall break in pieces and consume all these kingdoms, and it shall stand for ever."

Christ is King

Jesus Christ is returning as King of Kings and to remove Satan from the throne. His Kingdom will consume all nations and put an end to all governments. As world trouble spin out of control with the advent of nuclear weapons that threatens the existence of all mankind, God will intervene other wise all humans will be destroyed. Matthew 24:22.

Jesus Christ is coming as King of Kings and Lord of Lords. Revelation 19:16 "And he hath on his vesture and on his thigh a name written, KING OF KINGS, AND LORD OF LORDS." He is coming as ruler of all people on earth. He is coming as divine God ruler of the whole universe. He is coming to judge the nations with a "rod of iron". Revelation 19:15; 12-5. He is coming to establish his government that will reign forever.

When Jesus Christ returns to judge the nations it will be done to uplift his holy name and demonstrate his sovereignty. God is beckoning the nations to be still for a moment. Listen quietly and obey his commandments. The continued ignorance of God's laws will bring judgment to all the nations. Listen to the words of the prophet Isaiah. "Jehovah has indignation against all the nations; and rage against all their army. He must devote them to destruction; he must give them to the slaughter. And their slain ones will be thrown out; and as their carcasses; their stink will ascend; and the mountain must melt because of their blood." (Isaiah 34:2-3)

The prophet Isaiah has given us a grim portrait of our world in the near future due to the disobedience of mankind. Today is the time to repent of your sins and come to know Christ while there is still time. "Your fate is in your hand; either you choose a life in eternity or death." (Isaiah 55:6)

When Jesus Christ returns to earth he will not be welcome with open arms at first. The biblical scriptures tells us that the ministers of Satan will convince our leaders that Jesus is the Antichrist. Even the Christian Church will be convinced. (11 Corinthians 11:13-15) "For such are false apostles; deceitful workers, transforming themselves into the apostles of Christ." "And no marvel; for Satan himself is transformed into an angel of light." "Therefore it is no great thing if his ministers also be transformed as the ministers of righteousness; whose end shall be according to their works."

A day is coming like no other. This particular day is called "The Tribulation Period." It will be the day when Jesus Christ intervenes into this world. By the time this dramatic event happens the world will be involved in WWIII. On this day a massive army will try to fight Jesus Christ and his armies descending on the fields of Armageddon.

Not only will the governments be judged on that day, people who has not called upon the Lord in our lifetime will partake in the wrath of God. Jesus has given us time to search the scriptures for ourselves and read about God's wisdom. Do not take it for granted that the Bible is just another book like any other. It does not cost you anything to be a little curious and study the word of God. Stop for a moment from your daily routine and ponder the thought. It may save your life.

On the day of our Lord and Savior Jesus Christ's return to earth the sun, moon and stars will not shine. It will be a day when the whole universe rolls back to reveal its secrets. "For the stars of the heavens and their constellations of kesil will not flash forth their light; the sun will actually grow dark at its going forth; and the moon itself will not cause its light to shine." (Isaiah 13:10)

As Christians awaits Jesus Christ's second coming many people still want believe in him. Although many Christians have never seen Jesus we believe in the teachings of God's word. By faith we believe in his second coming because the bible tells us so. "And as it is apppointed for men to die once, but after this the judgment; So Christ was offered once to bear the sins of many; and unto them that look for him shall he appear the second time without sin unto salvation." Hebrew 9:27-28.

As the disciples watched in astonishment as Jesus ascended to heaven, two angels suddenly appeared and said to them, "men of Galilee," they said, why do you stand gazing up into heaven? This same Jesus, who was taken from you into heaven, will so come in like manner as you saw him go into heaven." (Acts 1:11)

Today there will be many nations who do not believe in Christ even after his gospel has been preached throughout the world. They will be in defiance that the Kingdom of God is coming and that there won't be any judgment. Even when Jesus Christ return and hands out his judgment people will curse him. Revelation 16:9 "And men were scorched with great heat, and they blasphemed the name of God who has power over these plagues; and they did not repent and give him glory."

People who thrive on hatred will have their moment with the Lord. When people are divided by someone's superiority complex, you are bringing judgment upon yourself. When the sinner continue to commit sin and the corrupt politicians continue their thirst for power at the expense of others your judgment is coming. Listen to the words of God, Isaiah 17:7-8 "In that day earthling man will look up to his maker; and his own eyes will gaze at the Holy One of Israel himself. And he will not look to the altars, the work of his hands; and at what his fingers have made he will not gaze, either at the sacred poles or at the incense stands."

While the world is engaged in WWIII Jesus Christ will return in dramatic glory. As the feuding nations battle each other with devastating weapons their eyes will suddenly be fixed on the arrival of Jesus Christ in the air and landing on the Mount of Olives, the same place he departed from over two thousand years age.

> "For as the lightning comes from the east and flashes to the west, so also will the coming of the Son of Man be....Immediately after the tribulation of those days the sun will be darkened; and the moon will not give its light; the stars will fall from heaven, and the powers of the heavens will be shaken. Then the sign of the Son of Man will appear in heaven, and then all the tribes of the earth will mourn, and they will see the Son of Man coming on the clouds of heaven with power and great glory." (Mathew 24:27).

The nations of the world will not submit to the second coming of Jesus Christ so easily. While they battle each other in Jerusalem they will turn their attention to the forces of Christ landing in the war zone. To the nations they will be convinced that Christ is an alien invasion coming from outer space and will attempt to fight Jesus upon his return. The bible gives us a vivid account of what takes place in this war of the worlds.

> "Then the Lord will go forth and fight against those nations. As he fights in the day of battle. And in that day his feet will stand in the Mount of Olives, which faces Jerusalem on the east. And the Mount of Olives shall be split in two, from east to west, making a very large valley; half of the mountain shall move toward the north and half of it toward the south." (Zechariah 14:3-4).

The warring nations will be no match against the awesome power of our Lord and Savior Jesus Christ. The bible describes the battle with gruesome visualization of soldiers dying on the battlefield.

The whole Middle East will become a field of invading armies. That day will be the greatest hour in the history of the world. The war of Armageddon will be the greatest battle mankind will ever witness. The battlefield will become a river of blood. Armored tanks and airplanes and all weapons of war will be consumed in fire. The eyes of soldiers will rot and their flesh will literally melt where they are standing. Zechariah 14:12 "And this shall be the plague wherewith the Lord will smite all the people that have fought against Jerusalem; Their flesh shall consume away while they stand upon their feet, and their eyes shall consume away in their holes, and their tongue shall consume away in their mouth."

Every eye on earth will see Jesus returning from the heavens. With him will be his angels who will help set up his new kingdom. Satan will be bound for a thousand years and will no longer be capable of deceiving mankind with his invisible rule. Revelation 20:1-3 "And I saw an angel come down from heaven, having the key of the bottomless pit and a great chain in his hand. And he laid hold on the dragon, that old serpent, which is the Devil, and Satan, and bound him a thousand years, and cast him into the bottomless pit, and shut him up, and set a seal upon him, that he should deceive the nations no more, till the thousand years should be fulfilled; and after that he must be loosen for a little season."

The human nature of mankind will be changed due to the correct teachings of Jesus on how to live a more prosperous way of life that brings good health and good will to all mankind. Helping in this endeavor will be the Church who will administer God's new kingdom from the headquarters of New Jerusalem.

It is interesting to note here as Jesus returns to this earth the Christian church in which the biblical scriptures call the "Mystery, Babylon the great" will attempt to make war with the armies of Jesus. This final resurrection of the Roman Empire will be a union of church and state that will be against the returning King of Kings. The late Pastor Herbert Armstrong explains why the Christian Church will be against Christ return as it is outlined in the biblical scriptures, Revelation 17 confirms this, "She (the church) rules over "many waters" which are described in verse 15 as different nations speaking different languages. She posed as the Church of God-which scriptures says (Eph. 5:23); Rev.19:7; Matt. 25:1-10; etc.) is the affianced "bride" of Christ, to be spiritually MARRIED to him at his second coming."

When Christ return to earth his kingdom will rule over all nations. All present governments will be under the control of God's kingdom that will create a new vision for mankind. A world that have complete utopia where the eyes of man could only dream of. Can you imagine a world where there is peace among mankind? A world where there is no more gun violence. A world where the blind is made to see and a paraplegic can walk again. A world where hatred is no longer a necessary tool to use against your fellow man. A world where every man is your brother. A world where disease is eradicated. A world where Jesus Christ is King of Kings and the world is at peace for a thousand years.

The following scriptures outline the reason I am so excited about the return of our Lord and savior Jesus Christ. Isaiah 33:21-24. And the inhabitant shall not say I am sick: the people that dwell there in shall be forgiven their iniquity." I am looking forward to this amazing time when Christ reveal to the world his awesome power. In Isaiah 35:3-6 further describe this coming world of miracles, "Strengthen ye the week hands, and confirm the feeble knees. Say to them that are of a fearful heart, Be strong, fear not: behold, your God will come with vengeance, even God with a recompense; he will come and save you. Then the eyes of the blind shall be opened, and the ears of the deaf shall be unstopped. Then shall the lame man leap as an hart, and the tongue of the dumb sing."

Good health is what we all desire. It is worth more than any amount of money. In this world we live in your bad health is an opportunity for health care services to take advantage of people by charging them outrages amounts of money. From senior citizens to young adults it doesn't matter how old you are, health care systems has become like vultures preying on the vulnerable. But God has the remedy if we obey his commandments and repent of our sins. The scriptures tells us what God will do for us, "For I will restore health unto thee, and I will heal thee of thy wounds….Jeremiah 30:17.

After 6 thousand years of mankind being cut off from God he will finally see a reunion with his maker. God's law will transform this world by spreading salvation to every man, woman and child. Every eye shall see God's kingdom and will go there to learn of his ways as it is outline in scripture, Isaiah 2:2-4 and in Micah 4:1-3. "And it shall come to pass in the last days, that the mountain of the Lord's house shall be established in the top of the mountains, and shall be exalted above the hills; and all nations shall flow unto it. And may people shall go and say, Come ye, and let us go up to the mountain of the Lord, to the house of the God of Jacob, and he will teach us of his ways, and we shall walk in his paths; for out of Zion shall go forth the law, and the word of the Lord from Jerusalem. And he shall judge among the nations, and shall rebuke many people; and they shall beat their swords into plowshares, and their spears into pruning hooks; nation shall not lift up sword against nation, neither shall they learn war any more."

What an amazing scripture that foretells our future world under the leadership of God Almighty. Can you imagine a world where even wild animals obey well here is the scriptures that proclaim this, Isaiah 11:6-9. "The wolf also shall dwell with the lamb, and the leopard shall lie down with the kid; and the calf and the young lion and the fatling together; and a little child shall lead them. And the cow and the bear shall feed; their young ones shall lie down together; and the lion shall eat straw like the ox. And the sucking child shall play on the hole of the asp, and the weaned child shall put his hand on the cockatrice den. They shell not hurt nor destroy in all my mountain: for the earth shall be full of the knowledge of the Lord, as the waters cover the sea."

Even all religious holidays will be changed by the New kingdom to come. Holidays such as Christmas and Easter are pagan days celebrated by millions of people around the world. Most christian churches observe these pagan days with the belief that Jesus uphold these days as acceptable. In fact God hates those pagan holidays because he ordained certain festivals to be celebrated by those who obey his commandments.

The Christian church must return to the holy days God decreed from the beginning. God ordained seven annual festivals and holy days that must be celebrated as explained by the late Pastor Herbert Armstrong, he said, "Seven annual festivals were given to Old Testament Israel and were ordained forever. Their true meaning had long remained a hidden mystery. They pictured God plan of redemption-the divine plan by which God is reproducing himself. The Passover pictures the death of Christ in payment for the penalty of human sin repented of. The seven days of the Festival on Unleavened Bread picture the Church coming out of sin, even as Israel came out of Egypt. The day of Pentecost, originally called the Feast of First Fruits, pictures the Church as the first to begotten and born as children of God during the Church age. The Feast of Trumpets pictures the Second Coming of Christ to take over earth's throne and to rule all nations. The Day of Atonement pictures the putting away of Satan. The Feast of Tabernacles pictures the thousand year reign under the rule of Christ and the born children of God. The Final Great Day pictures a day of judgement."

The Festivals God ordained for mankind to obey must be put in practice or punishment awaits those who follow all the pagan religions and holidays. It is imperative that the Christian Church return to the holy days God decreed. If this commandment is not obeyed God will send plagues that will infect the world as it is outlined in Zechariah 14:17-19. "And it shall be, that whoso will not come up of all the families of the earth unto Jerusalem to worship the King, the lord of host, even upon them shall be no rain. And if the family of Egypt go not up, and come not, that have no rain; there should be the plague, wherewith the Lord will smite the brethren that come not up to keep the feast of tabernacles. This shall be the punishment of Egypt, and the punishment of all nations that come not up to keep the feast of tabernacles."

We have been so accustom to celebrating Christmas and Easter throughout the years that it would be hard to change. The magic of it seems so exciting but is that the right thing to do? If it is not pleasing to God then why do we continue to dishonor him by celebrating these pagan holidays? Maybe because we continue to dishonor him is the reason our world is in big trouble. Racial tension is on the rise. Gun violence has become the norm. Even a plague has infected our world. This is why we must return to God's commandments and begin to see the real blessing he has in store for us.

CHAPTER 12

TODAY'S TESTAMENT

INCIDENCES OF GOD IN THE MODERN WORLD

In the year 2019 God appeared to a man name Randolph and gave him a gift of life. This gift will be the new symbol of Christianity. It will be used for the purpose of setting a new course for the believers of Christ. This gift of life will advance Christianity to a greater awareness and restore the credibility of the Church and also prepare the way for the second coming of our Lord and Savior Jesus Christ.

From this day forward the symbol of Christianity shall be a pentagon shape with a cross in the center that represents any man or women who can achieve the highest form of divinity in man. In other words we should pattern our lives in the image of Christ. In any circumstance in our daily lives we should ask ourselves what would Jesus do? A Christian mind must be linked to the mind of God. He can no longer do the things as before. He must be converted in the spirit of God. The Apostle Paul said, "Let this mind be in you, which was also in Christ Jesus." (Phil. 2:5).

What is a Christian? A Christian must grow in the knowledge of God. He must feed his character from the spiritual waters of Jesus Christ. The pentagon shape and cross made from the hands of God is a gift that I must share with fellow Christians as an inspiration to achieve the highest form of Godly character.
The following picture is the gift God gave to all humanity for a new beginning in Christianity:

The Christian Church must get its house ready for the return of its creator Jesus Christ. He is coming for the Church that upheld his holy name throughout the ages. The Church must prepare itself like its being prepared for a wedding. For Christ is returning for his bride. Have your ministers, priests, bishops, and deacons light the candles that illuminate the halls of righteousness. Have your ministers, bishops, priests, and deacons confessed their sins. Make sure the Christian Church building is seen as a holy place for worship and not for show. The Christian Church must return to its original name, The Church of God. The Christian Church must participate in every day affairs. The Christian Church members cannot hide behind its building. It must become an instrument that sits on the board of litigation. The Christian Church must return to worship on the Sabbath day. It must respect the holy days that was decreed by God. Have celebrations on the day of Pentecost. Shoes must be taken off your feet before entering God's house. Where you stand will be holy ground.

The return of Jesus Christ to this earth is related to the Messenger in prophecy. If the Messenger's message is not received by the Church, Jesus Christ will not return. Therefore, this book had to be written and this prophecy had to be fulfilled. "Behold, I will send my messenger, and he shall prepare the way before me; and the Lord, whom ye seek, shall suddenly come to his temple, even the messenger of the covenant, whom ye delight in; behold, he shall come, saith the Lord of hosts" (Malachi 3:1-2). The temple of God is the Christian Church shining bright so the whole world can see. The Church must be restored to the way it was intended to be by its founder and head of the Church our Lord and Savior Jesus Christ.

A Christian Pledge

When Satan tips the balancing scale of justice towards evil, a Christian is the hand that levels the playing field.

When hope is lost, a Christian will find light at the end of the tunnel.

When politicians have lost their sense of direction, whether to go left or right, a Christian will show you the way.

When someone is hungry, a Christian will feed a multitude.

When there is no hope, a Christian will show you a miracle.

When a loved one is in the hospital in sickness and pain, a Christian will pray with you.

When someone dear to you has died and you are left in sorrow, a Christian will be with you and dry your tears.

When someone is homeless, a Christian will give you shelter.

When a Christian finds himself hopeless and in despair, he will rely on the word of God.

Ghost, Incidence of God in the Modern World

This true story is about on the job romance and how God works in mysterious ways. Bruno believed he was the most handsome guy in the world because the ladies would do anything just to be with him. He had no problem finding victims that would succumb to his charm. You see, Bruno was considered to be a rolling stone and playboy who only wanted to go to bed with as many women as he possibly can and place another notch on his list of conquest. To him bedding women was a sport that only he could win.

Sarah was a young 18 year old who had dreams of becoming a doctor one day as she landed her first job at the same company Bruno worked. For the first few months at the company there was no attempt by Bruno to seduce Sarah but as time went on his prowling became noticeable by her. They went on their first romantic date that quickly became an intense relationship that blossomed into making love on numerous occasions. The love affair would have continued until Sarah gave him the shocking news that she was pregnant. Upon learning the news that Sarah was pregnant other co-workers came forward and informed Sarah that Bruno wasn't the right man for her because he had fathered numerous children with women there at work and in the city. Bruno took the news harshly and warned Sarah that he did not want anymore children. But he assured her that he would take care of her and the baby. Sarah was happy to hear that he wouldn't abandon her at this crucial time in her life.

After a month had passed Bruno and Sarah stayed late working overtime until about 10 p.m. when the building was empty of all employees except the security guards who were down on the first floor and they were on the 16th floor. As Bruno and Sarah was approaching one of three elevators Sarah notice that Bruno looked a little nervous and ask him what was wrong as they approached the elevator that was inoperable then suddenly the doors opened and Bruno pushed Sarah into the abandon elevator shaft. She felled 16 floors to her death.

Bruno returned to work the next day as if nothing happened and proceeded to work as he normally does. After 6 months had passed there was no sign of Sarah, only newspaper articles of the missing Sarah. Then enter another employee who's name was Janie who was the same age as Sarah who got her first job at the same company. Many months past but Bruno was on the prowl again surveying his next victim.

Janie came from a Christian home where her parents trained her to take God with her where ever she goes. After a few months on the job Bruno made his move toward Janie and convinced her to go to the movies with him. With a blink of an eye she felled head over heels for Bruno and before you know it they were in love. After 6 months of a blissful romance Janie gave Bruno the happy news, she was pregnant. As you can imagine Bruno took the news hard and was furious but assured Janie that he would take care of her and the baby. Of course Janie was happy to hear him say that he would take care of her and the baby.

After working late one night Bruno and Janie approached the same elevator of the horrible crime Bruno committed months before and now he was planning to do the same thing to Janie. As he methodically maneuvered Janie to the empty shaft Bruno began to pull Janie as she was hesitant and became resistant. As soon as Bruno began to shove Janie down the empty elevator shaft to her doom a dark figure came out of the shaft; it was the ghost of Sarah who pulled Bruno into the empty elevator as he cried out, "it can't be you! I killed you," and he fell 16 floors to his death.

The ghost of Sarah told Janie not to be scared anymore and raise your baby with loving care because God loves you, then she disappeared.

There are many incidence of God in our daily lives that need to be told. Ministers in the Christian faith has done a superb job in bringing the word of God to eager listeners but the message becomes boring when people know the story and know what you are going to say next. My best friend who is a devoted Christian told me the other day that she fell a sleep in church because she new what the pastor would say. She became tired of the same story being told the same way Sunday after Sunday.

The Christian Church should pay more attention to people testimony because you will find that God didn't only work in ancient times he is working in our daily lives every single day. Just listen to the people in the congregation and you will find that their story is just like or similar to the stories in the bible but told in a different way.

Take for example the story of Job who loved and obeyed God's commandments and hated evil. He was a man of great wealth who endured many trials and hardship and prevailed because of the belief in God.

Today we can find men like Job who withstood many hardships and continued to believe in an unseen God. A man by the name of Bob Thornton's story can be compared to the life of Job because of his preservation when God took away his wealth. He lost everything he owned. Mr. Thornton is a man of God who has an undying love for our Lord and Savior Jesus Christ. He is what all Christians should strive to be like. His devotion for Christ was tested when on a sunny day his life changed forever.

Mr. Thornton millionaire status drew the wrong kind of people to his business. One day after leaving for work gunmen entered his home and tied up his wife and three children and held them for ransom. The gunmen demanded 20 millions dollars for the life of his family. He paid the ransom money but the gunmen wanted more. They raped and killed his family and got away with all his money. Devastated and filled with grief Mr. Thornton had to endure the pain and agony of an unbearable lost. How could any man recover from something like this? This scenario also brings attention to that age old question, "Why do bad things happen to good people?" All Christians and even people without faith ask this same question. The bible gives us the answer when we suffer devastating lost. As a Christian we must remember to call out to God regardless of the plight you find yourself in. God is willing and able to hear your plea.

Mr. Thornton remained a loyal servant of the Lord regardless of his ordeal and prayed to the Lord for compassion and mercy and did not blame the Lord for his great loss. Mr. Thornton remembered the scripture that says, "Shall we accept good from God, and not trouble."? (Job 2-10)

As time went by Mr. Thornton continued to pray to God and was able to cope and live with the circumstances that changed his life forever. In time God restored his wealth and a new family with five children and a wealth of happiness.

Incidence of God in the Modern World, The Laying of Hands

The biblical scriptures describe The Apostle Peter laying his hand on a sick person and that person was healed. The bible describes it this way, "Silver and gold have I none; but such as I have give I thee; In the name of Jesus Christ of Nazareth rise up and walk. And he took him by the right hand, and lifted him up; and immediately his feet and ankle bones received strength. And he leaping up stood, and walked, and entered with them into the temple, walking, and leaping, and praising God. And all the people saw him walking and praising God" (Acts 3:6-9). There have been many ministers and soothsayers, snake charmers, magicians, and charlatans who claimed that they could heal people with just a touch of their hands. There were many churches in the United States who demonstrated that their minister had the power to make people walk again, or make the blind see again. Churches were filled with people with the hope that they too could be healed by the deceiving minister. Most if not all ministers had a hoax going on that people could not perceive. It was all smoke and mirror and fire and brimstone. This scenario does not rule out the possibility of healing by ministers and priest who prayed for the sick and some miraculously were healed.

In our world miracles do happen. It happens on a daily basis but go undetected by scientist and government officials. A child was diagnosed by doctors of a rare disease that would have ended her life in a short span of time but a miracle happened and the rare disease disappeared. Puzzled by the child's sudden recovery doctors searched for an explanation and concluded that it was a miracle sent by God.

A boy and his friends were playing on a frozen pond and the ice broke sinking one of the boys who descended quickly to the bottom of the lake. It takes only 5 minutes for a brain underwater to be destroyed and be considered as brain dead but this boy stayed in the water for 30 minutes then the rescuers pulled him ashore. While in the hospital he told his parents and the doctors and nurses that while under water he saw a man reached out his hand towards him with a bright light surrounding him touching his head and then disappeared. The boy miraculous recovered with no brain damage.

A fiery car crash as a result of a train reaction that involved multiple cars with many casualties on a rainy slick highway prove to us that miracles still happen and God is still in control. In this particular car one of the victims said a man pulled her out of the car before the car caught fire then disappeared. The paramedics and ambulances were not on the scene at that moment and she later tried to locate the person but was unsuccessful. She described the accident this way, she remembered as she was driving a man appeared in her car window before the accident warning her to pull over, the next thing she remembered was her sitting in the grass on the side of the road while up ahead she could see a pillar of smoke and fire and mangled cars.

Who were those strange figures that saved them from certain death? Were they angels sent by God to intervene in their lives at that precise moment? Many people describe their near death experience associated with a tunnel and a bright light with Jesus inside of it assuring them that they could return to their life as it was and that their time on earth is not completed. Many people have reported the same phenomena which make it hard to be discredited as hallucinations or a dream.

It is hard to explain why God saves some and allow others to perish. The bible explains that we must trust in the Lord's wisdom and his purpose and plan. We must remember that God's mind is superior to man and he does not think like we do. God says, "For my thoughts are not your thoughts, neither are your ways my ways.....For as the heavens are higher than the earth, so are my ways higher than your ways and my thoughts than your thoughts." (Isaiah 55:8-9).

An Act of God, Incidence of God in the Modern World

After I served in the government for 35 years I retired in 2006 and moved to another state due to the economical blessing there. My family and I stayed in a hotel until we found the house that we thought was our dream home. The house we found was brand new and nobody ever lived in it. We paid the down payment and was about to close the deal. At that moment my wife and I was very happy because living in a hotel for two weeks was boring and expensive. But after we returned to the hotel a strange feeling came over my wife and I. It was something about that particular house that disturbed both of us.

That night after we settled in the hotel my wife and I began to discuss our sudden displeasure with the new house and couldn't explain why. We stayed up until 3 o'clock in the morning trying to figure out how we could get out of the contract and get our deposit back and start all over again searching for a home to live in. While we were contemplating on how to get out of the agreement there was a terrible rain and wind storm with thunder and lightning that terrified all of us due to the power kept going on and off with the loud crackling of thunder. We hardly slept a wink as we worried throughout the night about our sudden ordeal. The only consolation was prayer that helped us to calm our fears. We placed everything in Jesus hands.

The next morning around 6 am we were awakened by a phone call from the Real Estate agent informing us that the house we chose burned to the ground from a lightning strike. The agent said, "this was an act of God." I was shocked and amazed at the news especially after hearing the agent's explanation of what happened. Friends and relatives who heard the news about the brand new house being burned to the ground expressed the same explanation that it was an act of God that intervene in our life.

I knew immediately after hearing the news from the agent that God answered our prayers and he would not abandon me when there is time of trouble. I learned long ago to put things in the hands of God and he would do the rest.

The Real Estate agent returned the deposit and we started looking for a new house all over again just like my wife and I prayed for. After a few days of searching for a home we finally found our dream home on CROSSVIEW, the home God chose for us. It is a place where miracles do happen.

Angels, Incidence of God in the Modern World

The bible describes heavenly angels sent by God to intervene in the affairs of man. In the story of Sodom and Gomorrah angels warned Lot to leave the city immediately and bring his family with him. (Genesis 19:1) "And there came thou two angels to Sodom at even; and Lot sat in the Gate of Sodom; and Lot seeing them rose up to meet them; and bowed himself with his face toward the ground." The Bible also describes Mary seeing angels in the tomb where Jesus laid. (Matthew 28:1-2) "In the end of the Sabbath, as it began to dawn toward the first day of the week, came Mary Mag'dalene and the other Mary to see the sepulcher. And, behold, there was a great earthquake: for the angel of the Lord descended from heaven, and came and rolled back the stone from the door, and sat upon it." The angel told the women that he knew that they came to seek Jesus but told them that Jesus is not there, he had risen.

In the modern world God not only use his angels of heaven to do his will he also use people to bring about a certain type of miracle.

Mother Teresa who became a champion for the poor is an example of how God uses people to do his will. In the bible it depicts angels who were directed by God to intervene in the affairs of mankind to bring them to a certain reality that would enhance their well being. But in the modern world angels who are visible to mankind and are humans themselves work diligently to help people who are in need. The human aspect of angel's on earth is what I am concern with.

Humans who are not normally called angels cannot make a blind person see again or heal the sick but they have superpowers in another form. That is why I chose Mother Teresa to talk about because in spite of her frailties and weaknesses she still persevered.

Mother Teresa was born on 16, August 1910 and died 5, September 1997. Her place of birth was in Skopje part of Kosovo Vilayet of the Ottoman Empire today the capital of North Macedonia. She left her home after 18 years and settled in Ireland and India. She became a Roman Catholic Nun and missionary and was honored in the Catholic Church as Saint Teresa of Calcutta.

Mother Teresa's missionaries of charity began on 14 May 1937 when she was a teacher at the Loreto convent school on Entally, eastern Calcutta. She served there for 20 years and was designated headmaster in 1944. There she became disturbed by the poverty that plagued the city. It was known as the Bengal famine of 1943.

In 1946 Mother Teresa got her calling from God, she describes it this way, "the call within the call, I was to leave the convent and help the poor while living among them. It was an order. To fail would have been to break the faith." Her missionary work began in 1948 where she started a religious community to help the poor.

By 1950 she began the Missionary of Charity, a Roman Catholic religious congregation that had 4,500 members. Her religious group gave free service to the poorest people that included soup kitchens, orphanages, children and family counseling programs, dispensaries, HIV/AIDS. Her charities developed and branched out to form in 1997 13 member Calcutta congregation that had 4,000 sisters who managed the poor and the homeless of natural disasters. The Missionaries for Charity grew to about 450 brothers and 5,000 sisters all over the world with 600 schools in operation.

Mother Teresa received numerous awards and recognition for her devoted mission to care for the poorest of poor. She received the Nobel Peace prize in 1979 and a host of other awards throughout her life.

While Mother Teresa accomplished many goals for the plight of the poor she also had to endure Satan's continued attack on her as a child of God. She had to endure doubts of the existence of God while administering to the needy. There are numerous reports of Mother Teresa's doubts and shortcomings by critics who labeled her a hypocrite.

For over 50 years Mother Teresa struggled with her belief in God and said, "She felt no presence of God whatsoever ... in her heart or in the Eucharist." This statement is according to her postulator, Brian Kolodiejchuk. Mother Teresa is no different than any of us who has a strong belief in Jesus Christ but falls short of the glory of God. That is what separate angels from man but makes human achievement more rewarding because you have to earn it. I believe Mother Teresa believed in God and like all of us who loved the Lord sometime struggle with Satan the father of doubt.

According to Mother's Teresa postulator, Brian Kolodiejehuk, she felt like Jesus Christ who gave the same sentiment of doubt when Jesus said when he was crucified, "My God, my God, Why have you forsaken me?"(Mark 15:34). While Jesus was hanging on the cross he experienced human emotions like any man would and so did Mother Teresa.

In spite of all the struggles and doubt Mother Teresa became an inspiration to us all who love our Lord and Savior

Jesus Christ and showed us how to continue to fight for the poor and the weak and to strive for justice and equality.

Mother Teresa is our human angel who fought the good fight and like Martin Luther King, and Gandhi who fought for justice and equality are human angels sent by God to give humanity a boost in the right direction. It is peculiar that the angels in the Bible all have human appearance.

What about the unsung heroes or other human angels who contribute to the needs of the poor and destitute? There are millions of soup kitchens and charities open up around the world by loving and caring people who is inspired by the teaching of Jesus Christ that goes unnoticed. These people are not looking for an award they just do the will of God. They are the first responders when there is an earthquake, tsunami, or tornado. What inspire a person to open up an orphanage or give shelter to the homeless? It is the inspiration of God who uses people to do his will. They are the people who work tirelessly to help others. When their time has ended here on earth they would have earned their wings. They are the true angels of the world.

Angels of a Different Color, Incidence of God in the Modern World

Who was Martin Luther King, Jr.? Was he an angel sent by God? Mr. King said, "Do not judge a man by the color of his skin but by the content of his character." These words were not spoken by just any average man. This man knew God and kept his faith close to his heart. To understand who Martin Luther King was we must examine one of the most important figures from the bible that had qualities of a human and not an angel from heaven. This man was just like Martin. His name is Moses.

Moses was a great man of faith who allowed God to use him to do his will. The bible tells us that this prophet accomplished great things with the guidance of Jehovah.

Although he accomplished miracles performed by God he was just a human being like you and I. Moses experienced the same things you and I deal with on a daily basis. He could not have accomplished those trials of life without faith. His faith in God equipped him with the armor to conquer any adversity.

The Reverend Doctor Martin Luther King, Jr., who was a descendant of slaves like Moses, was a Christian minister who became a leader in the Civil Rights Movement in 1955 and was assassinated in 1968. Mr. King who had a strong belief in Jesus Christ was inspired by the life of Mahatma Gandhi who advocated non-violence to bring about change. Mr. King became a champion for justice and equality for the black community and hero for all people who yearn for freedom. His accomplishments include the famous March on Washington in 1963 where he delivered his famous speech called "I Have a Dream" that drew millions of people to the Nations Capitol.

Mr. King was awarded the "Nobel Peace Prize in October, 1964 for combating racial inequality and helped organize the Selma to Montgomery marches. He became an advocate for the poor and was against all wars. Just before his death he was planning an occupation of Washington, D.C. named the Poor People's Campaign. He was later assassinated on April 4 in Memphis, Tennessee.

Both Moses and Martin had an assignment from God that required great loyalty. In spite of the dangers that lurked before them they endured many challenges that without their faith in God would have caused them to go down in defeat. But they both trusted God. They must have read this passage from the bible, "I will by no means leave you nor by any means forsake you." Hebrews 13:5.

Oskar Schindler, Friend of the Jews, Incidence of God in the Modern World

The prophet Moses saved thousands of Israelites from the hands of Pharaoh and his army as they charged against them to slaughter and kill every one including women and children. With their backs to the ocean with no where to go they knew certain death was imminent but God almighty at the command of Moses opened up the Red Sea to allow the Israelites an escape route saving thousands of lives. God didn't only worked miracles two thousand years ago he displayed his awesome power in the modern world when he saved 1,200 Jews during the holocaust. By using a member of the Nazi Party, only God could have impressed on this man's heart to save the life of these people when soldiers of his on party was sending most of them to the gas chambers. How can a member of the Nazi Party become a righteous man and savior of the Jews?

This story also reminds me of the Patriarch Paul who persecuted Christians and slaughtered many at the direction of the Romans after the crucifixion of Jesus Christ. One day, on the road to kill more believers, Paul was interrupted by the appearance of Jesus who blinded him and impressed upon his heart to become an advocate for Christ. It is amazing to see how God turns even the enemy into a champion for his cause and inspire them to do his will.

Oskar Schindler was a German industrialist and a member of the Nazi Party who saved 1,200 Jews during the holocaust by allowing them to work in his ammunitions and enamelware factories in Poland and the Protectorate of Bohemia and Moravia. By using bribery and gifts of luxury items as a way to appease the Nazi officials he saved many Jewish workers from certain death in the concentration camps. While many Jews were sent to the gas chambers Mr. Schindler protected his Jewish workers from harm. What made Schindler show compassion for these people when his fellow comrades became monsters?

Mr. Schindler grew up in Svitavy, Moravia. Where he joined the military intelligence service of Nazi, Germany, in 1936 and joined the Nazi party in 1939. He collected information on railways and troop movements for the German government. Schindler preferred hiring Jewish workers over others because they were considered cheap labor. When ever his factory workers were threatened with deportation, he claimed exemption for them. He saved women and children as well as people with disabilities were necessary to work in his factories.

In 1941 the Nazi began moving Jews out of the ghetto and into concentration camps and certain death in the gas chambers. Even before the Jewish community was moved they were gun down on the streets by the Nazi as they exterminated everyone in the city. Schindler upon hearing the news of the massacre kept his workers at the factory overnight which saved their lives. This horrific event compelled Schindler to get out of the Nazi party and save as many Jews as he possibly could.

In 1943 Nazi officials tried to move Schindler's factory to Plascow concentration camp but Schindler convinced the Nazi's with flattery and bribery from moving but convince the Nazi to allow him to build a subcamp at Emalia to allow his workers plus 450 other Jews to work and live there. While staying there they were well fed, and were permitted to worship freely.

In the spirit of Moses this man Oskar Schindler saved many lives and sacrificed his wealth for the lives of others. Schindler had the opportunity to live a luxurious life among his Nazi peers but instead he chose to live his life saving the lives of Jews. The prophet Moses believed the same thing as it is outlined in Hebrews 11:25. "Choosing rather to suffer affliction with the people of God, than to enjoy the pleasures of sin, for a season." Schindler died on 9, October 1974 and is buried in Jerusalem on Mount Zion. No other Nazi Party member was honored this way. On Schindler's grave his inscription reads in Hebrew, "Righteous among the Nations", the German inscription reads, "The unforgettable Lifesaver of 1200 Persecuted Jews."

A Female Slave Called "Moses," Incidence of God in the Modern World

The story of the prophet Moses was duplicated in the life of others many times in the history of the world as I already outlined in this chapter. Although the story of Harriet Tubman did not have the impact to the world as the prophet Moses from the bible, this American icon could be apart of the "Me Too movement" in the early development of America. Harriet Tubman was a very religious woman who kept Jesus Christ close to her heart. She was definitely a women God used as a vessel to do his will. The title of "Moses" is not given to a person without merit. The people of her time must have seen that she was no average person but a woman of destiny and gave her the prophet's name "Moses."

Harriet Tubman was born into slavery in 1822 and had to endure whipping and beatings by her many slave owners. Her life story began in Dorchester County, Maryland where an irate slave owner threw a heavy object intended for another slave hit her instead that caused a brain injury that plagued her throughout her life. She complained of experiencing dizziness and hallucination, strange dreams, and visions of God. That event caused her to become a devoted believer in Jesus Christ that motivated her to lead slaves to freedom.

Tubman only traveled by night after she escaped the whip of her slave owner only to return and rescued her family member one group at a time bringing them to freedom. She continued to return to the place of slavery and guided many other slaves to freedom. When the Fugitive Slave Act of 1850 was passed, Tubman continued to gather other runaway slaves and guided them into Canada.

By using a network called the Underground Railroad she managed to bring many slaves to freedom. This Underground Railroad was well established with free and enslaved blacks and white abolitionist. The Religious Society of Friends or Quakers were also apart of this system.

For over 11 years, Tubman smuggled slaves out of bondage from slave owners that took 13 attempts. She was so successful in freeing slaves they named her "Moses" in reference to the prophet in the Book of Exodus who led the Hebrews to freedom. Tubman's strong belief in God became her best ally when attempting dangerous missions of rounding up potential runaways. She trusted in God to keep her safe and to complete the mission.

In January 1863, President Lincoln issued the Emancipation Proclamation in an attempt to liberate all black people from slavery. This event became the catalyst for Tubman to join the Union Army.

During the Civil War Harriet Tubman worked for the Union Army as a nurse and cooking meals for the soldiers. Her duties also include becoming a spy and armed scout. She was the first woman to liberate 700 slaves in the raid at Combahee Ferry. The newspaper heralded Tubman as an example of a patriot. She described the battle scene this way, "And then we saw the lightning, and that was the guns, and then we heard the thunder, and that was the big gun, and then we heard the rain falling, and that was the drops of blood falling, and when we came to get the crops, it was dead men that we reaped."

In spite of Harriet Tubman patriotism she did not receive a salary or pension which left her in poverty. Finally in 1890 the Dependant and Disability Pension Act rewarded Tubman with a pension. As family members and friends gathered around her death bed in 1913, she said her final words, "I go to prepare a place for you." Those same words were spoken by Jesus Christ.

If Harriet Tubman was alive today she would certainly be apart of the "Me Too Movement" that has become a champion for woman who do not have a voice in today's society. In her time Tubman joined the Suffragist movement that advocated for woman to vote. She became the voice of those who were purposely silenced from men who stood in the way of change.

Pope John Paul II Meets The "Man of Sin," Today's Testament In The Modern World

Pope John Paul II became head of the Catholic Church in 1978 after Pope John Paul I died who only served 33 days in office. Pope Paul helped to end communism which was one of his greatest achievements which led to the liberation of his home town Poland and eventually the rest of Europe. He served as Pope longer than any other Pope in modern history after Pope Pius IX. He was also the most seen and widely travel Pope in modern history visiting 129 countries.

This Pope furthered the teachings of the Catholic Church by upholding the belief that there should be a right to life, artificial contraception, and the ordination of women. He believed in the dignity and equality of women and a strong family bond for the survival of humanity. He was against Apartheid in South Africa and called for economic sanctions against its government. He gave a powerful speech condemning apartheid at the International Court of Justice in 1985. He said, "No system of apartheid or separate development will ever be accepted as a model for the relations between peoples or races."

When Pope Paul II went on a pilgrimage to Haiti he brought with him his strong opinion reminding ruler Jean-Claude that, " yours is a beautiful country, rich in human resources, but Christians cannot be unaware of the injustice, the excessive inequality, the degradation of the equality of life, the misery, the hunger, the fear suffered by the majority of the people." The Pope's visit reminded the people that Haiti and to other countries where the rich get richer and the poor get poorer due to the corrupt leadership to,"Lift up your heads, be conscious of your dignity of men created in God's image."

Throughout this book I've stressed the point that today's Christian Church must take an active role outside of the Church when dealing with important issues that effect humanity. Although in my opinion the Church must stay out of political situations that move an opinion from the right or to the left, still it must have a strong voice and a seat at the table.

It is amazing to see that Pope John Paul II shared the same sentiment as I have when describing the plight of the Church and how it should step out of the box and take a visible role in current affairs. He said, "Politics has a fundamental ethical dimension because it is first and foremost a service to man. The Church can and must remind men-and in particular those who govern-of their ethical duties for the good of the whole of society. The Church cannot be isolated inside its temples just as men's consciences cannot be isolated from God."

Although the Pope believed that politics is a service to man the Church has an even greater service to man because it is the instrument that brings people to seek salvation in the house of God. Society is in trouble today because the Church of God has been omitted from participating in the political arena, but politics is where biblical prophecy is unfolding and mankind need the Church to point him in the right direction.

An Atheist Shakes Hands With a Pope

In 1989 Pope John Paul II met with the Soviet Union leader Mikhail Gorbachev at the Vatican where this visit became the momentum that launched a spiritual inspiration that help bring down the Iron Curtain. Gorbachev is able to remain in the center of politics while keeping both hands in the fire. He assures the left and the right including spirituality that he is the maestro of all now that he had met with the Pope who gratefully gives him a Papal blessing for perestroika. A Russian leader who is atheist comes to visit a Pope is truly a miracle. This is the moment the "Man of Sin" arrives in the world.

Mikhail Gorbachev was responsible for bringing down the Berlin Wall and the fall of communism in the old Soviet Union which later collapsed but he had help from Pope John Paul II who gave Gorbachev the blessing to have a peaceful revolution that resulted in the fall of communism without firing a shot.

Pope John Paul II had many accomplishment and was loved and adored by millions of Christians around the world. He died 2 April 2005 and his "canonisation commenced one month after his death with the traditional five-year waiting period waved. On 19 December 2009, he was beatified on 1 May 2011 after the congregation causes of Saints attributed one miracle to his intercession, the healing of a French nun called Marie Simon Pierre from Parkinson disease."

American Evangelist Pastor Billy Graham, Today's Testament in the Modern World

Pastor Billy Graham was the most influential Christian Evangelist in the modern world. He was born on November 7, 1918 and died February 21, 2018. As I was growing up I watched and listen to his many sermons on television which inspired me to study the biblical scriptures. As a young boy I loved to read about comic book characters but Pastor Graham became a unique superhero who guided me to the one superhero who is more powerful than all of them, his name is Jesus Christ.

Pastor Graham was born to deliver the gospel just like Jesus created him to do, and no one did it better than him. Pastor Graham lived up to this prophecy and became one of the most well known leader in the modern world. Matthew 24:14 "And this gospel of the kingdom shall be preached in all the world for a witness unto all nations." He held out door and in door sermons that was broadcast on radio and television all over the world. His listeners numbered 210 million people in a 185 countries and in 1996 his television broadcast reached a reported 2.5 billion people worldwide. Due to his crusades, he preached the gospel to more people in person in the history of Christianity according to his website.

As Pastor Graham gained in popularity, he became a spiritual adviser for many U.S. presidents that include Harry S. Truman, Dwight D. Eisenhower, Lyndon B. Johnson, Richard Nixon and Barack Obama.

In 1953 at a rally in Chattanooga, Tennessee, Pastor Graham made it known to the public that segregation was not the appropriate way to bring people to God. He did not like the placement of people with whites only on one side and people of color designated to a specific section. He told his followers if they did not tear down the barriers they could go on without him. He said to a white audience, "we have been proud and thought we were better than any other race, any other people. Ladies and gentlemen, we are going to stumble into hell because of our pride."

Pastor Graham supported integration and became a good friend of Martin Luther King Jr. whom he met during the boycott in Montgomery in 1955. In 1960 King and Pastor Graham attended the Tenth Baptist World Congress of the Baptist World Alliance. King told a Canadian television audience that Pastor Graham had a "strong stance against segregation."

Pastor Graham had a strong view why he was against segregation because that is not the world God had designed. He once told a Ku Klux Klan member that, "there is no scriptural basis for segregation." He went on to say, "The ground at the foot of the cross is level, and it touches my heart when I see whites standing shoulder to shoulder with blacks at the cross."

The names of people whom I've identified in this chapter has uplifted the name of Jesus Christ in the modern world. There are millions of other pastors around the world who has done the same. Some have worked tirelessly with devotion against impossible condition. God's work is not complete. In fact we are just getting started.

Herbert W. Armstrong

This book could not have been written without the inspiration of pastor general of the World Wide Church of God. He died in 1986 and was loved and respected by governments and dignitaries all over the world. Although I personally did not get to meet him in person but he ministered to me from the grave. He left a treasure of books pertaining to the Kingdom of God and the Love for our Lord and Savior Jesus Christ. His Plain Truth Magazine in which he was editor in chief was distributed all over the world and enlightened people with the purpose and plan of God and how we should be preparing ourselves for the second coming of Jesus Christ.

While writing this book late at night in the quietness of my room a peculiar thing happened. While I was in deep thought, concentrating on what to write next, a repetitious knock on the wall of the room was heard. I wondered to myself how could that be when I was the only person in the room so I continued writing and then suddenly it happened again. This time I turned my head in the direction toward the wall and said to myself this can't be happening because the other side of the wall is the outside and my house is two stories high. As soon as I began typing the next sentence, a knock of four repetitious sounds, like someone is knocking on the door happened again. This time it startled me, so I jumped up staring at the wall in horror. I ran to the next room to alert my wife that something is in the room with me. They were all there in the room with me. All the spirits of the people I was writing about.

When Jehovah Witnesses knock on your door do you run for cover? Or do you allow them to come in and give you the word of God?

Before Jesus Christ ascended to heaven he assured his disciples he would send the COMFORTER to be with them. The Comforter or Holy Ghost is the Spirit of God who comes to those who believe and to help them complete a certain goal.

Heavenly Father, our world is in turmoil and in grave danger at this hour. Please father God help us to uplift your CHURCH that it will continue to be a beacon of hope for the world. You said that you would come and smite this world if a certain message was not received by the CHURCH. Please heavenly father give our world another chance to redeem ourselves.

The count down has begun, the Tribulation Period is at hand. At the writing of the book, over half a million people have been lost to COVID-19. Only you heavenly father can stop this pain and suffering. Let it be your will not mine father God in healing this land. Every word in the scriptures must be fulfilled. Please father God let "thy will be done, on earth as it is in heaven." Matthew 6:9-13. In Jesus' name, Amen.

"There are only two ways to live your life,
One is as though nothing is a miracle. The
other is as though everything is a miracle."
Albert Einstein

EPILOGUE

Hell

Is Hell a real place or just a figment of someone's imagination? The Holy Scriptures tells us that there is a place created for the purpose to hold sinners who do not believe in God. Personally I've always felt that Hell is right here on earth because of all the evil things mankind perpetrate on another human being. What if it is true that earth is actually the place called Hell and if it is then our ministers should teach the word of God from the perspective that we humans are born into sin therefore if we want to go to heaven we must repent of our sins and work our way out of EARTH.

We must first examine the Holy Scriptures that identifies where Hell is located. People will be shocked to learn that earth is the place called Hell and some of them won't even care. Before the beginning of time God created angels who administered his commands throughout the universe. Most of the angels were obedient to God until Satan rebelled against the creator and was banished from heaven. Where God sent him is the topic of this discussion. He banished him to earth, Matthew 25:41 says, he banished him, "into everlasting fire, prepared for the devil and his angels."

The Holy Scriptures tells us that Satan is the God of this earth. But we are assured by the Holy Scriptures that Satan's reign will be shortened by the second coming of our lord and savior Jesus Christ as King of all Kings.

It is no wonder that everything evil under the sun is done by man on this earth. Murder and mayhem is an every day occurrence with reckless abandonment. Corruption and greed by politicians who seem to get away from law enforcement who look the other way. Our civic leaders can't seem to come to an agreement on the violent use of guns. Most importantly the blatant ignorance of the teachings of Jesus Christ by government officials who rather uphold the snares of Satan.

What if earth remain this way because we have made a choice to not obey the teaching of Jesus? What if earth is slowly slipping into the abyss where lost souls are being tormented day and night at this very hour? Yes, there is a place called Hell, and it is right here inside the earth.

After Jesus died on the cross His soul descended inside the earth to a place called Hell where He stayed for three days and three knights. Matthew 12:40 states, "for as Jonah was three days and three nights in the whales body; so shall the Son of man be three days and three nights in the heart of the earth." Therefore, Hell is inside the earth where sinners go after they die. The Bible makes it clear to all who are not sure where Hell is. In Ephesians 4:9 speaking of Jesus, "Now that he ascended, what is it but that he also descended first into the "Lower Parts of The Earth."

Jesus Christ warned us that Hell is a place of FIRE and TORMENT. Today scientist has discovered that inside the earth core the temperature is 12,000 degree Fahrenheit. How can anything that is alive withstand such heat. Jesus Christ tells us that Hell is an "everlasting fire" in Matthew 18:8.

Hell is a place where if a person finds himself there, fire will torment him day and night. His whole body will be consume in flames and he will live through it feeling the pain and agony. His thirst will not be quenched and he will be wailing and gnashing of teeth. Hell is a place where a person's WORM will never die. This person will be tormented forever. Mark 9:43,44,45,46,48.

For those who still do not believe in Jesus Christ today's scientist has discovered a Worm that lives deep down inside the earth that can withstand tremendous hot temperatures. Scientist appropriately named him the DEVIL WORM. This fascinating article states, "When scientist discovered a worm deep in an aquifer nearly one mile underground, they hailed it as the discovery of the deepest-living animal ever found. Now American University researches, reporting in Nature Communications, have sequence the genome of the unique animal, referred to as the "Devil Worm" for its ability to survive in harsh, subsurface conditions. The Devil Worm's genome provides clues to how an organism adapts to lethal environmental conditions." This article explains how the devil worm can withstand intense heat and is able to live deep down in the crust of the earth. Scientist named the heat loving species Halicephalobus mephisto, which means, "he who loves not the light."

Over two thousand years ago Jesus Christ warned us about a WORM that can survive tremendous amount of heat that rages forever. Why did God used a worm as an analogy of someone being tormented in Hell? It is because our human body after death turns into WORMS and according to what we do here on this earth determines where we will end up. Your WORM after death will continue to live and survive the tremendous heat and flames as scientist has proven with the discovery of the devil worm. Your Worm harbors your soul and contain everything about you. Matter of fact it is you. That is why Jesus Christ warned us about going to Hell. Mark 9:43 states, "And if thy hand offend thee, cut it off: it is better for thee to enter into life maimed, than having two hands to go into HELL, INTO THE FIRE THAT NEVER SHALL BE QUENCHED; WHERE THEIR WORM DIETH NOT, AND THE FIRE IS NOT QUENCED." Jesus Christ gives us a strong warning to do what is necessary in life to not end up in Hell. He said in Mark 8:36 "For what shall it profit a man, if he shall gain the whole world, and lose his own soul"?

As we go about our daily lives there are millions of people being tormented in Hell. They are in an eternal flame of fire that will never burn out. The most frightening thing about this eternal fire is that a person who end up there will be alive and able to feel pain. In Luke 16:24 it states as a man cries out,

"And he cried and said, Father Abraham, have mercy on me, and send Lazarus, that he may dip the tip of his finger in water, and cool my tongue; for I am tormented in this FLAME." In Matthew 25:41 Jesus says; "And shall cast them into a furnace of fire; there shall be wailing and gnashing of teeth." People who has not yet come to know Jesus or refuse him shall pay a harsh penalty. In Revelation 20:15 says, "And whosoever was not found written in the book of life was cast into the LAKE OF FIRE."

If you want to be saved from this Hell of fire you must repent of your sin and believe in Jesus Christ. We are presently living in the book of Revelation and time is running out. God is a God of love. He loves us so much he sent his only son. "For God so love the world, that he gave his only begotten Son, that whosoever believes in Him should not perish, but have everlasting life." John 3:16.

Guns

You know we are in Hell when you see a one year old, a 8 year old, a 9 year old, a 11 year old, a 12 year old, a 13 year old and a 15 year old all die from gun violence in a span of one week and the Church remained silent. It is no wonder why Satan feels he is winning and is about to be crown as King of earth. This is truly Satan's world as the biblical scriptures foretold.

I chose the title of this book "Why the Church is killing Christ a second time" to get religious leaders to pay attention to world events because it could be biblical related. As the world is about to go over the edge into the bottomless pit, the church must take an active role in world affairs. Now is the time for the church to be an activist to fight to get guns out of the hands of people. In order for this nation to survive the cunning of Satan, the church must fight to disarm the public.

When innocent children are being caught in the crossfire its time for the church to wake up and give solid solutions to stop gun violence. Why can't the church or religious leaders make a suggestion that our nation should adopt gun policies in the image of countries that forbid citizens from owning a gun. As anyone can see our civic leaders and government officials do not have the will power to do the right thing. Sometimes it takes a higher power to convince our leaders that they must listen to their moral compass and do something for the good of humanity and be on the right side of history.

It is heart breaking to see our fellowmen children being gun down by senseless and unspeakable violence. These senseless killings will never stop until the church get involve and take a stand. I believe the brightest minds in the world is in our Church leaders who just need some guidance and a little push and they will change the world. Its time for the Church to make a loud noise. It is no time to be SILENT.

In the spirit of the late Congressman and civil rights leader John Lewis who said, "If you see something that's wrong or not right, you have the moral obligation to say something, do something." This statement describes the way the Church should behave in today's evil world. It is time for our religious leaders to "say something, and do something", instead of falling asleep in the Church. Let's step out of the Church and role up our sleeves and do something.

BIBLIOGRAPHY

"A pair of nuclear powered Russia AHawk submarines…" Excerpt from the Washington Times dated Aug. 5, 2009. https://www.nytimes.com/2009/08/05/world/05patrol.html?

"A suited Mr. Gorbachev with…" Cartoon Bank, https://www.cartoonbank.com/product

"Certain it is that the saint's early life…" St. Francis of Assisi - Detailed Biography, https://www.franciscanfriarstor.com/stfrancis/stf

"Constantine's Vision" https://christianhistoryinstitute.org/study/module/constantine/

"Demagoguery" https://www.hurriyetdailynews.com/opinion/semih-idiz/the-rise-of-populist-demagoguery--106120

"Francis father, Pietro Bernardone…" The Early Years, https://www.franciscanfriarstor.com/stfrancis/stf

"Gorbachev, tear down this wall;" Cartoon Bank, https://www.cartoonbank.com/product

"Harriet Tubman" https://en.wikipedia.org/wiki/Harriet_Tubman

"He saw a vast hall hung..." "These, said a voice..." St. Francis of Assisi - A Detailed Biography, https://www.franciscanfriarstor.com/stfrancis/stf

"Hypocrisy" https://en.wikipedia.org/wiki/Hypocrisy

"In fact, Gorbachev's mandate for the future." http://www.rense.com/general12/gobie.htm

"In October 1917 we parted with the old world..." http://www.rense.com/general12/gobie.htm

"Keep an Eye on Gorbachev" from article by Anne Theroux https://www.rense.com/general12/gobie/htm

"Man is the worst beast in the field" *unknown*

"Martin Luther King Jr." https://en.wikipedia.org/wiki/Martin_Luther_King_Jr.

"Mikhail Gorbachev has accused the U.S.," https://www.telegraph.co.uk/news/worldnews/europe/russia/19332233Gorbachev

"Moses" https://en.wikipedia.org/wiki/Moses

"Mother Teresa" https://en.wikipedia.org/wiki/Mother_Teresa

"Mr. Gorbachev, tear down these walls..." ABC News

"My hope is that this charter will be a kind of Ten Commandments," "The environment crisis is the cornerstone for the New World Order," https://www.rense.com/general12/gobie/htm

"Oskar Schindler" https://en.wikipedia.org/wiki/Oskar_Schindler

"Over the last few days some media…"
https://en.wikipedia.org/wiki/Mikhail_Gorbachev

"Sanhedrin Trial of Jesus"
https://en.wikipedia.org/wiki/Sanhedrin_trial_of_Jesus

"Simon Magus" https://en.wikipedia.org/wiki/Simon_Magus

"St. Francis is for me, the alter Christus…"
https://en.wikipedia.org/wiki/Mikhail_Gorbachev

"The Coming of the Lawless One." Scripture taken from King James Version Bible. 2 Thessalonians 2:9-12.

"The Day the Earth Stood Still." Film taken from 20th Century Fox, produced by Julian Blaustein, directed by Robert Wise.

"The Free Masons are another secret society…" "From Free Masonry…" "Other organizations believed…" https://en.wikipedia.org/wiki/New_World_Order_(conspiracy_theory)

"The latest events in the Caucasus," ITAR-TASS

"The State of the World Forum" takes place sponsored by the Gorbachev Foundation… cyberpatriot@hotmail.com

"Tuskegee Syphilis Study"
https://www.cdc.gov/tuskegee/timeline.htm

"United States Space Force"
https://www.spaceforce.mil/About-Us/SPD-4

"We are told that hard-liners in the Soviet Union…"
cyberpatriot@hotmail.com

"When about twenty, Francis went out…" Perugia and Spoleto, St. Francis of Assisi, https://www.franciscanfriarstor.com/stfrancis/stf

A second Parliament of World Religion is held in Chicago, cyberpatriot@hotmail.com

ABC News reported, "Trump has been criticized by public health experts…"

American Bible Society New York, (The Holy Bible, King James Version 1611)

American University. "Researchers sequence genome of the 'devil worm'." ScienceDaily. July 13, 2020. www.sciencedaily.com/releases/2019/11/191121075419.htm

Andrei Sinyavssky said, "The many countries crushed into some semblance," courtesy of Time Magazine, Man of the Decade, January 1, 1990 Edition

Andrzej Wujdu said, "Polish society, often badly assessed," courtesy of Time Magazine, Man of the Decade, January 1, 1990 Edition

Anti means "to take the place of" or "instead of," Webster Dictionary

Armstrong, Herbert. "explains why the Christian Church …"

Arpad Goncz said, "I am proud that the historical changes…" courtesy of Time Magazine, Man of the Decade, January 1, 1990 Edition

Awake Magazine, article by Carl A. Raschke, ("It is no wonder drugs, heavy metal music influence young minds," 1994)

Awake Magazine, article on the Master Criminal, ("Transnational crime effects everybody," 1994)

Awake Magazine, mass killings were documented, (Yugoslavia Auschwitz and the Vatican, 1994)

Berardelli, Jeff. "Massive Sahara desert dust plume" June 26, 2020. https://www.cbsnews.com/news/saharan-dust-gorilla-cloud-today-united-states/

Boyer, Paul, article from Washington Post Magazine (Apocalypse Now 1997)

Brokaw, Tom, reported on NBC News ("Milosovic would not stop the mass killings of Muslims until he heard from Mikhail Gorbachev," 1992)

Brokaw, Tom, reported UFO's landed in Moscow, (NBC News, 1989)

CFR member and Trilateralist Henry Kissinger write… cyberpatriot@hotmail.com

Charles, Gibson interviewed Mikhail Gorbachev in 1996 on ABC Television, Gibson; "It is an interesting paradox," Gorbachev; "Well, let's recall another example," https://www.spiritoftruth.org/anti.html

Cheetham, Erika, The Final Prophecies of Nostradamus (Perigee Books, 1989)

Cheetham, Erika, The Further Prophecies of Nostradamus: 1985 and Beyond (Perigee Books, 1985)

Cicero, 42 B.C., "A nation can survive its fools…"

CNN reported "if those people wore a simple thing as a mask…"

Cohen, John. "A WHO-led mission…" July 15, 2020. https://www.sciencemag.org/news/2020/07/who-led-mission-may-investigate-pandemic-s-origin-here-are-key-questions-ask

Collins, Dr. Francis. "Genes, Blood Type Tied to Risk of Severe COVID-19" July 12, 2020. https://directorsblog.nih.gov/2020/06/18/genes-blood-type-tied-to-covid-19-risk-of-severe-disease/

cyberpatriot@hotmail.com, Jeremiah Novak's article "The Trilateral Connection appears in the 'Atlantic Monthly'" "For the first time…"

cyberpatriot@hotmail.com, The History of the New World Order, "What is at stake is more than one small country, it is a big idea- a new world order,"

David Underbars, Former U.S. Ambassador to Romania, tells… cyberpatriot@hotmail.com "The History of the New World"

Dunbar, Paul Laurence, "We Wear The Mask" https://www.poetryfoundation.org/poems/44203/we-wear-the-mask

Edvin Sugarev said, "until now silence has been the only…" courtesy of Time Magazine, Man of the Decade, January 1, 1990 Edition

Einstein, Albert. "There are only two ways to live your life, One is as though nothing is a miracle. The other is as though everything is a miracle."

Excerpt from “Armageddon Script” by Peter LeMesurier, St. Martin's Press, New York, N.Y., p. 252

Excerpt from “Chariots of the Gods” by Erich Von Daniken, G.P. Putnam/Berkley Edition, 1977

Excerpt from “The Conspiracy” and “The Coup de tat”, https://en.wikipedia.org/wiki/soviet_coup_attempt_of_1991

Excerpt from a Detailed Biography from Catholic Encyclopedia Online… St. Francis Receives the Stigmata… “During this retreat the sufferings…” “The saint’s right side is described… ” https://www.franciscanfriarstor.com/stfrancis/stf

Excerpt from Bob Woodward’s book, Rage. “In total, 10 Republican senators who voted to acquit said in statements and interviews Trump’s actions were wrong…” “political survival decision.”

Excerpt from Bob Woodward’s book, Rage. “Senator Lamar Alexander said, ‘When elected officials inappropriately interfere…’”

Excerpt from Bob Woodward’s book, Rage. “Senator Mitt Romney said, ‘Corrupting an election to keep oneself in office…’”

Excerpt from Gary Kah's book, The New World Religion, “Among those at the forefront of this movement…”

Excerpt from Reuters World Service, December 8, 1996, Sunday, BC Cycle, “Gorbachev is frank, though hardly contrite,” Gorbachev’s response, “How do you explain Judas?”

Fawcett, Lawrence and Greenwood, Barry J., Clear Intent, (A Spectrum Book, 1984)

Field Enterprises Educational Corporation, (World Book of Encyclopedia, 1963)

General Brent Scowcroft, from a taped radio broadcast on the eve of the Persian Gulf War, "Gentleman, comrades, do not be concerned…" https://www.rense.com/general12/gobie/htm

George Bush states, "back into the world order" cyberpatriot@hotmail.com, "The History of the New World Order"

Gerson, Michael. "the conscious use of a mask…"

GESENIUS (1786-1842) Dean Stanley, History of the Eastern Church, out-of-print. See also Dan Styles, "Keeping Perspective When We Differ," https://www.tidings.org/editorials/editor200005.htm

Ghost Wars, by Steve Coll "The battle lasted for about a week,"

Gorbachev Foundation, "U.S. could start New Cold War," https://www.gorby.ru/en/rubrs.asp?art

Gorbachev says, "NATO growth aimed at isolating Russia," Gorbachev Foundation, https://www.gorby.ru/en/rubrs.asp?art

Gorbachev says, "revolutionary actions should be a last resort." https://www.NOLA.com

Gorbachev says, "We need a new paradigm…" http://www.rense.com/general12/gobie.htm

Gorbachev stated, "At our meeting in Geneva…" https://www.uforc.com/database/UFOs-Changed-History_George-Filer_020908.htm

Gorbachev's Address to UN, "world progress is only possible." cyberpatriot@hotmail.com

Graham, Billy. https://en.wikipedia.org/wiki/Billy_Graham

Hockstader, Lee, article from Washington Post (I will fight to the bitter end, 1996)

Hockstader, Lee, article from Washington Post (Two Beast Sent By The Devil, 1996)

Hockstader, Lee, article from Washington Post (History is a capricious lady, 1996)

Ibid. 513-514 "our rockets have bypassed the moon."

In "The Keys of this Blood" Pope John Paul II, as quoted by Malachi Martin (New York: Simon and Schuster 1990)

In an address to Congress entitled "Toward a New World Order," George Bush says; cyberpatriot@hotmail.com

In his book, "The Keys of this Blood," by Catholic priest Malachi Martin says, "By the end of this decade…"

In his State of the Union Address in 1991 George Bush says, "what is at stake…" cyberpatriot@hotmail.com "The History of the New World Order"

In religion, the term "false prophet…" https://en.wikipedia.org/wiki/False_prophet

In U.N. address, President Bush speaks of the… cyberpatriot@hotmail.com

J. B. Handlesman, Cartoon Bank; https://www.cartoonbank.com/product

Jephraim P. Gundzik, "The Ties that Bind China, Russia and Iran," Asia Times Online, June 4, 2005, https://www.atimes.com/atimes/china/GF04DO7.html

Johnson, Paul, (History of the Modern World from 1917 to the 80's)

King, Martin Luther, taken from speech ("Free at Last and Let Freedom Ring," 1963)

Kissinger, Henry, article from Washington Post ("Most importantly Dr. Kissinger fears that NATO-RUSSIAN Permanent Joint Council will let Russia intrude in NATO's own decision making." 1997)

LeMesurier, Peter; Nostradamus: The Next 50 Years (Berkley Books, 1994)

Levi, Bernard. "Madness in the Age of the Virus." "leader of the free world…"

Lewis, John. "If you see something that's wrong…"

Margaret Thatcher reminded us, "President Reagan won the Cold War…" https://www.uforc.com/database/UFOs-Changed-History_George-Filer_020908.htm

Michael Cummings, First published by Sunday Express on 14 Feb. 1998; https://www.cartoonbank.com/product

Mikhail Gorbachev returns to Russian politics, by Adrian Blomfield in Moscow, Published 7:20 p.m. BST, September 29, 2008, https://telegraph.co.uk/news/worldnews/europe/russia/3104623/Mikhail-Gorbachev-returns-to-Russian

Mikhail Gorbachev stated, "The phenomenon of UFOs does exist," "UFOs changed communist world history," https://www.uforc.com/database/UFOs-Changed-History_George-Filer_020908.htm

Moscow Center on Paranormal research, "Zinaida Gavrilova had gone for a walk…" https://www.uforc.com/database/UFOs-Changed-History_George-Filer_020908.htm

Nelan, Bruce W., The Mandate to Heaven, (Time Magazine, 1990)

Newsweek Magazine, Levy Steven, (Man vs. Machine, Deep Blue, 1997)

Norman Cousins says, "World government is coming"

PBS Television, Frost, David, (Interview with Mikhail Gorbachev, 1996)

Plain Truth Magazine, excerpt from Ronald Reagan speech, (They preach the supremacy of the state, 1989)

Pope Francis. "do not let us fall into temptation." "I am the one who falls…"

Pope John Paul II. https://en.wikipedia.org/wiki/Pope_John_Paul_II

Quotes from Gorbachev, "I think that we can find ground…" Taken from AFP quoted, Gorbachev as saying, https://www.phayul.com/news/article.aspx?id=204168&+=1&c=1

Quotes from Mikhail Gorbachev's book, (The Search for a New Beginning: Developing a New Civilization) "Democracy means moral value…"

Quotes from Mikhail Gorbachev's book, (The Search for a New Beginning: Developing a New Civilization) “Whereas I understand those who are mindful…”

Redfield, Robert. “That the mask can give better protection than a vaccine.”

Relman, Eliza. “Trump shares tweet that argues face masks represent 'silence, slavery, and social death'” Business Insider. May 28, 2020. https://www.businessinsider.com/trump-shares-tweet-that-says-masks-represent-slavery-and-social-death-2020-5

Ronald Reagan stated, “God has a plan for everything.” https://www.uforc.com/database/UFOs-Changed-History_George-Filer_020908.htm

Ronald Reagan stated, “I couldn't help but - when you stop to think…” https://www.uforc.com/database/UFOs-Changed-History_George-Filer_020908.htm

Ronald Reagan stated, “I was in a plane last week, I looked out the window…” https://www.uforc.com/database/UFOs-Changed-History_George-Filer_020908.htm

Russian Orthodox Patriarch Alexei II told the Russian media, “In Italy Gorbachev spoke in emotional terms…” https://en.wikipedia.org/wiki/Mikhail_Gorbachev

Shakespeare, “The tongue is sharper than the sword…”

Smith, Houston, The Religious of Man, (HarperCollins Book, 1986)

Taken from “Soviet disinformation chief: A master at using words as Cold War weapons.” New York Tribune, July 27, 1987; “We have no right ever to forget that…”

Taken from The Pledge of Allegiance. "One nation under God, indivisible with liberty and justice for all."

Teen Magazine, article on Satanism ("Instead of commanding members to suppress their natural feelings," 1994)

The "Twilight of Sovereignty" by former Citicorp chairman Walter Wriston, cyberpatriot@hotmail.com

The Washington Post Magazine, Talbott, Strobe, ("What has been created in Russia is not democracy and free markets in the western sense," 1996)

The Washington Post, article by Rick Atkinson, (Pope Speech in Berlin, 1996)

The Washington Post, Harris, John F., (The Enlightenment of Freedom, 1999)

The Washington Post, Harris, John F., (The Wars in the Balkans by Madeleine K. Albright, 1999)

The Washington Times, ("Mishaps put Russian Missiles in Combat Mode," 1997)

The Washington Times, ("Political power flows from a barrel of a gun," 1999)

The Washington Times, excerpt from an article ("Despite Arms Control," 1997 by Bill Gertz

Thorndike and Barnhart Dictionary

Time Magazine publishes "The Birth of the Global Nation" by Strobe Talbott, cyberpatriot@hotmail.com

Time Magazine, (Man of the Decade photographs courtesy of Time Magazine, 1990)

Time Magazine, article on Yitzhak Rabin, ("If you ask me what is the obstacle to the current peace process," 1997)

Time Magazine, excerpt from article by Lance Morrow, ("Natural Evil, or Man Made," 1997)

Time Magazine, May 25, 1992, "A chat with the Gorbachev's," p.51 "An alternative between capitalism and communism is in the offing."

Time Magazine, taken from article (Man of the Century by Richard Holbrooke, U.S. Ambassador, 1999)

Time-Life Books, (Mysteries of the Unknown, The UFO Phenomenon, 1987)

Trueheart, Charles, excerpt from Washington Post (Massacre in Algerian, 1998)

Václav Havel, "In everyone there is some longing," courtesy of Time Magazine, Man of the Decade, January 1, 1990 Edition

Vernon J. McGee, Through the Bible, Vol. 3 (Nashville, TN: Thomas Nelson Publishers, 1982) "we have deposed the czars of the earth"

Wartofsky, Alona, The Washington Post, (Marilyn Manson, 1997)

Watchtower Magazine, the cross and swastika, ("During WWII hundreds of thousands of Serbs and Croats were massacred in the name of Religion," 1997)

Wen, Dr. Leana. "Our entire response has been hampered by mixed messaging…"

White House Chaplin. "A spirit of darkness…" https://www.cnn.com/2019/07/18/politics/house-chaplain-demons/index.html

Witherspoon, John. "If your cause is just, you may look with confidence…"

Wolf Biermann said, "I must weep for joy," courtesy of Time Magazine, Man of the Decade, January 1, 1990 Edition

Woodward, Bob. "you just breathe…" Excerpt taken from tape recording as reported by CNN and the book "Rage."

Wuer Kaixi said, "The pressure against the system is building," courtesy of Time Magazine, Man of the Decade, January 1, 1990 Edition

www.ingramcontent.com/pod-product-compliance
Lightning Source LLC
Chambersburg PA
CBHW071305110426
42743CB00042B/1183
9780578779201